STUCK
IMPROVING

RACE AND EDUCATION

SERIES

Series edited by H. Richard Milner IV

STUCK IMPROVING

Racial Equity and School Leadership

DECOTEAU J. IRBY

HARVARD EDUCATION PRESS
CAMBRIDGE, MASSACHUSETTS

Paperback ISBN 978-1-68253-657-5
Library Edition ISBN 978-1-68253-658-2

Library of Congress Cataloging-in-Publication data is on file.

Published by Harvard Education Press,
an imprint of the Harvard Education Publishing Group

Harvard Education Press
8 Story Street
Cambridge, MA 02138

Cover Design: Ciano Design
Cover Photo: Sandipkumar Patel/DigitalVision Vectors via Getty Images

The typefaces used in this book are Museo Slab, Myriad Pro, and Scala

CONTENTS

SERIES FOREWORD

by H. Richard Milner IV
Race and Education Series Editor

School improvement is tough. School reform and transformation can be even more difficult as educators work collectively and collaboratively to better meet the needs of young people across different sociopolitical contexts. Decoteau Irby's book, *Stuck Improving*, advances the Race and Education Series of the Harvard Education Press in important ways—centering a discussion about racial awareness and justice in a suburban school. What does it mean for educators to study themselves, interrogate policies, and reimagine practices with an increasingly diverse student population in a suburban school? As educators work overtime to understand and construct equitable policies and practices, how do they interpret relatively small gains among those who struggle most? How do school leaders build morale, coconstruct organizational expectations, and pivot toward equity when the data sources suggest that Black and Brown students, for instance, are not faring as well as expected? These questions are pondered throughout this book as educators find themselves stuck improving in the midst of complex structural and systemic challenges.

Irby introduces readers to what he calls *school capacity for racial equity improvement* as an analytic tool to make sense of and describe the leadership journey, struggles, and commitments of leaders committed to maintaining equity—even as they feel "stuck" improving. But this book is about much more than leadership. It is a book for every educator, from pre-Kindergarten to higher education, who has experienced and understands what it means to be committed to equity and to practice transformation but still not see the kinds of outcomes expected, needed, or deserved among students of color. These students of color, particularly Black and Brown students, tend to be most grossly underserved in and through the educational system. Irby amplifies the humanity of these young people and situates them in the context of suburbia, an understudied place and space among Black and Brown communities.

Stuck Improving describes the racial equity resources, inquiry-based leadership practices, and professional learning culture that capture a school's will and capacity to get better. Educators from different contexts will relate to the stories in this book—rural, urban, as well as the focused context, suburban. Irby explains that leaders in suburban schools must realize if they are going to meet the learning needs of their Black and Brown students, they must understand what it means to be stuck improving. As these educators (and young people) were stuck improving, what did the school actually do to improve? What did their attempts to get better look like? Why did they make the decisions they made to improve their environment? How did those putting in the work of transformation and improvement feel in the midst of their efforts? How did the educators determine what needed to change over time? Who decided what needed to change? How did the educators make those changes? And perhaps more than anything, why did these educators decide to stay in the fight for equity—even as they felt stuck in the challenges and complexities inherent in and through reform, transformation, and improvement work?

Thus, Irby skillfully, astutely, and compellingly crafts a book about leadership, practices, and organizational culture and change during a time when we need such a book the most. The book addresses issues of conflict and confrontation. It centers the roles of identity and reconstruction. The book addresses the cognitive as well as the affective as readers are introduced to educators' feelings of inadequacy, incompetency, anxiety, and frustration. Concurrently, readers are shepherded through feelings of hope and possibility as educators make sense of and describe their interrelated practices and experiences.

But the book is about more than these aforementioned issues. The book is also about the role, importance, and centrality of resolve—that is, determination. Indeed, this book is an educative tool that helps educators build their professional repertoire. It is also an inspirational text that showcases educators who refuse to quit and who refuse to give up on the young people they are committed to teach and lead. A must read in race and equity studies, *Stuck Improving* is the book that we surely need.

INTRODUCTION

S chool leaders are under immense pressure to enhance the educational opportunities and outcomes of Black, Latinx, and Native American students. Close the achievement gap. Reduce discipline disparities. Pay back the educational debt. Create equitable learning opportunities. Graduate students who are college and career ready. Foster a sense of belonging. Develop teacher cultural competency and empathy. Embrace diversity. Talk about race. Rewrite the curriculum to be more racially representative. Lead for social justice. Teach for equity. Dismantle racist structures. Understand systemic racism. I could go on. The problem is this: most White educators can't quite do, either individually or collectively, the things or achieve the outcomes that the current wave of racial equity reforms call for them to do because their racial knowledge and capacities to enact racial equity improvements are insufficient. They don't have all that it takes to improve their schools. Yet, the need remains urgent.

Stuck Improving is for educators who want to stop the violence of school-based racism; transform schools into racially equitable and affirming places for Black, Latinx, and racially marginalized students; and improve students' educational experiences and outcomes. The phrase *stuck improving* emerged over the course of a multiyear research partnership with a school I call Central Waters High School (CWHS) as I tried to reconcile administrators, teachers, staff, and students' struggles to make their predominantly White school community intellectually, socio-emotionally, and culturally affirm its increasing Black and

Brown student population. Stuck improving references the intersection of multiple phenomena. It is the experienced dilemma of making progress and not making progress in the pursuit of racial equity. It is the conscious discovery that racial equity is not a tidy concept. It is the conscientious pursuit of racial equity as an unending learning opportunity to improve oneself through challenging the violent conventions of white supremacy.

Throughout *Stuck Improving*, I help readers understand the complex process of building school capacity for racial equity improvement. I focus on what improving means in a white supremacist society where we're damned if we don't try and damned if we do. I surface invisiblized structural problems, behaviors, and thinking that are baked into US schools, such as meritocracy, exclusionary discipline, retributive punishment, and the pervasive disbelief that Black students possess valuable knowledge that can contribute to school improvement. In addition, I acknowledge the emergent racial consciousness that compels people to yearn for and pursue a racial equity vision that is ever expanding and therefore always just out of reach. I portray stories where people find themselves questing to achieve racial equity only to realize that racism by definition ensures that racial equity is elusive. I show people giving up. I give specific attention to how dilemmas, and in particular CWHS's capacity to work within and through dilemmas, evidenced an ever-expanding capacity to enact increasingly progressive racial equity reforms. If educators are serious about creating racially equitable schools, they have to understand what it means for their schools to have the organizational capacity for racial equity change.

I want to convey to readers two things. First, most White educators' racial knowledge and their schools' capacities are insufficient and thus not able to enact racial equity change. Students are not empowered to participate and cocreate the design of their school's academic and social opportunities. Teachers refuse to break their scripts to become colearners with students. Administrators fear parental backlash. Teachers resist content that affirms Black and Brown people, refuse to partner with community members who are racially and ethnically dissimilar (if they even know them), and are fearful of delivering content to students on topics that make them feel vulnerable. This does not have to be the case. Second, a critical part of racial equity work is developing the capacity to enact change through doing the complex and context-specific, devastating, cathartic, and uncertain work of pursuing racial equity. To do this, educators must understand the rich organizational racial resources that are present in their schools and learn how to cultivate and leverage these resources for the purposes of improvement.

A CAPACITY-FOCUSED PERSPECTIVE ON RACIAL EQUITY REFORM

School capacity refers to an interactive collection of organizational resources that support schoolwide reform, teacher change, and ultimately the improvement of student learning. In education and organizational studies, it is widely accepted that if an organization lacks the capacity to reform or improve in an identified area, even the best-laid efforts at improvement in that area are doomed to fail. The agreement that organizational capacity is important for school improvement has resulted in an increased focus on organizational leadership practices that indirectly impact student experiences and learning outcomes. Some of these practices include cultivating a school culture of data-driven instructional improvement, establishing effective teacher collaboration and learning routines, and cultivating organizational trust and collegiality.

Although leadership for data use, teacher learning, and collegial trust do not directly affect student experiences and learning outcomes (i.e., lagging indicators), the presence and strength of each are reliable leading indicators of what types of improvements one might plausibly expect to be accomplished in a given school. Data use, teacher learning, and collegial trust are organizational resources that correlate to teacher job satisfaction and performance. One is likely to find higher teacher job satisfaction and performance where the resources are well established and strategically leveraged. Notably, these leading indicators correlate with student experiences and learning outcomes. When they are combined with other organizational resources, such as a shared vision, well-crafted policies, distributed leadership, effective and reciprocal communication, well-defined goals, a culture of collaborative inquiry, and sufficient time and structure to cultivate adult learning, one can reasonably expect to see a high performing school.

School leaders are attuned to the need to leverage resources (e.g., data) and build teacher capacities to improve schools (e.g., to use data for learning). However, school leaders give inadequate attention to cultivating specific organizational resources that are essential to building a capacity for racial equity improvement. *School capacity for racial equity improvement* is the interactive collection of organizational resources that support schoolwide racial equity reforms, teacher racial consciousness development, and improvement of learning experiences and outcomes for students of color. *Stuck Improving* focuses on this school capacity aspect of school-based racial equity work. CWHS leveraged and cultivated five resources as they attempted, with mixed success, to enact their school's racial equity improvement reforms, which include

- Black and Brown People's Influential Presence
- Curated White Racial Discomfort
- Courageously Confrontational Communication Culture
- Collective Awareness of Racial Emotions and Beliefs
- Race-Conscious Inquiry Cycles (Leadership)

Administrators, teachers, and educators more broadly need to understand these organizational racial resources because if they do not, they risk misunderstanding the complexity of trying to achieve racial equity change. In many districts throughout the United States, White people and predominantly White organizations are responsible for enacting equity reforms that they are insufficiently prepared to undertake. When given a task that seems nearly impossible, the easy option is to not try or, after trying, to quit. This tendency is pronounced among White people whose *professional charge* is to provide Black and Brown students with improved educational opportunities but who, beyond their professional life, have low stakes in ensuring Black and Brown children succeed in life. So if school communities don't get the outcomes they wanted, expected, or are told they must achieve, they give up. Before giving up, they feel stuck.

In the pursuit of racial equity, educators will face conventional problems of improvement and change management. They will also face the pervasive racism and white supremacy that shape all aspects of schooling in the US from school curricula to notions of appropriate behavior to beliefs about what constitutes success and failure. Crucially, the very White people who themselves are socialized by and benefit from racist institutions must actively dismantle the very system they are convinced benefits them. Schools like CWHS, its leaders and educators, cannot successfully implement racial equity reforms without building their schools' organizational capacity for racial equity improvement. White supremacy and racism insist on reasserting themselves into any antiracist actions or antiracist thinking that challenges its presence. So even when a school makes an improvement, a new, often more complex instance of racism will present itself. Similar to what we know about the relationship between organizational capacity and improvement generally, when schools fail to identify, cultivate, and leverage racial equity resources, even their best-laid efforts at equitable improvement are bound to fail. The presence and use of racial equity resources (or lack thereof) are reliable leading indicators of what types of improvements leaders, teachers, and staff could plausibly expect to accomplish in their school.

My simple point is this: racial equity improvement is vastly more complex than most school improvement research suggests. It requires more than developing an understanding of racism or preparing individuals to become antiracist. It requires creating organizational conditions which make racism visible and challenges white supremacy so that it becomes difficult for racist structures, policies, thinking, and behaviors to remain intact. *Stuck Improving* analyzes a racial equity reform process through presenting what CWHS tried, what trying looked and felt like, how their efforts evolved over time, and how what they learned in the process strengthened their resolve to continue their efforts. In the process of unpacking the collaborative racial learning and improvement processes that came to define our collective work, I pinpoint the organizational racial resources and constituent guiding principles that improve the educational experiences and outcomes of Black, Brown, linguistically, and opportunity marginalized student populations.

Research Setting

Thirty years ago, Central Waters was an almost exclusively White rural middle America town with about 7,500 residents. It was a tight-knit community where people knew one another, their children knew one another, and the ties between home and school blended seamlessly. In the past twenty years, the town grew into a sprawling suburb. It is a twenty-minute (forty-five with traffic) commute to Halsey, a mid-sized US city that is the state's political and educational center. Central Waters' appeal stems from its hometown feel, its strong economy, housing stock, and close proximity to Halsey, home to the world-class Halsey University, and the highly educated workforce the university attracts. In 2000, a powerhouse software development company located its global corporate headquarters in Central Waters, adding to its attractiveness by bringing with it some 15,000 jobs. The software company's relocation catalyzed a rapid period of economic growth, a housing boom, and influx of racially, socioeconomically, and ethnically diverse workers who were attracted to a multitude of skilled and unskilled jobs that followed the relocation. At the time, the demanded number of employees exceeded the number of Central Waters residents.

Today, Central Waters is regarded as a region that is composed of numerous towns that comprise what is now called Central Waters *Region*. The wide swaths of relatively flat developable land that surrounded the once-upon-a-time farming town offered affordable land for developers and are now dotted with residential developments, apartment complexes, and big-box retail, shopping, hotel, and entertainment districts that infill the miles of land that once distinguished the region's hodgepodge of small towns. Three- to four-lane highways, complete with medians, turning lanes, and traffic signals replaced the two- and four-way stop signs that previously dotted the Central Waters Region, creating a seamless interconnection between Halsey, Central Waters, and the multiple outlying areas that comprise its region. The simplest way to conceive of Central Waters is that it is now an extension of Halsey and a central town in its own right, mostly because its district serves the surrounding region. In the midst of the growth, Central Waters' Main Street and the original grocery store that served the town remain like relics of times past. Along Main Street, a five-minute walk from the grocery store, sits Central Waters High School.

Central Waters High School is a resource-rich school that used to serve students who lived in the immediate vicinity of the school and whose parents also attended the school. As the Central Waters population increased and absorbed the region's school-aged children into the district, its schools' racial and ethnic diversification ballooned in comparison to years past. When I initiated the research that informed this book, Central Waters staff of nearly 200 adults served a racially diversifying student body of almost 1,600 students who come to school from vastly different geographic settings, ranging from Central Waters proper, regional towns, to Halsey. The school boasts a predominantly White but eclectic student body of White suburban students; White rural students; Black urban and suburban students; Latinx urban, suburban, and rural students; and Asian rural students, and so on. Immigrant and English language learners comprise a substantial portion of newcomers to the school. As for Black students, many of their families relocated to the region pulled by employment prospects and seeking a better quality of life that large cities throughout the region failed to offer Black families and children. The sprawling physical distance between the numerous students Central Waters served meant that students who went to school with one another literally lived separate home lives. The Central Waters administrative, teaching, and staff population remained virtually all White.

I first met Central Waters Regional School District's director of student services Suzanne at a state leadership conference in the summer of 2013. She and her colleague Ethan, an associate principal at the district's only high school, invited me to lead a professional development session about rethinking discipline approaches. Central Waters High School students brought with them a vast range of cultural experiences—Central Waters proper and region, students who lived on the southernmost edge of Halsey, and students who lived in unincorporated regions that are encapsulated within the region's sprawl. Yet despite an enviably diverse student body, a diverse regional economy, resource-rich district, and close proximity to a major university, Central Waters consistently failed to adequately serve its growing Black and Brown student population. Central

Waters High School's inability to leverage its wellspring of local resources makes the school more similar for Black and Brown students than different to its neighboring city Halsey, and numerous other suburban districts and schools throughout its state and indeed the United States.[1]

In the 2011–12 academic year, the state's Department of Education mandated the district reduce disparities and improve all outcomes for Black and Brown students as part of a consent decree intended to correct racially disparate mistreatment of its Black and Latinx students. The consent decree scrutinized the districts' discriminatory practices and outcomes, which included racial discipline disparities, overplacement of Black students in special education, underrepresentation in college-track and advanced courses, and continued failure to graduate students who were college and career ready. I later learned that my workshop was one part of the school's effort, spawned by the consent decree, to address the numerous educational disparities that district schools produced. When we agreed to collaborate for the research project, several improvement efforts were newly underway to respond to the consent decree. These included partnering with an organization to racially integrate Advanced Placement courses and partnering with state technical assistance providers to implement Positive Behavior Interventions and Supports.

Research Partnership

In the fall of 2013, I formed what was initially a highly collaborative research partnership with CWHS to support their efforts to improve the school's culture and climate. The stated purpose of the larger study was to engage school administrators, teachers, and staff in a participatory design-based research project that would build the capacity of the school to improve educators' approaches to managing student discipline and ultimately improve schoolwide culture and climate. Over time, the project expanded to include a strong emphasis on developing the school community's capacity for racial learning. From the 2013–14 academic year to the 2015–16 academic year, I led a team of university-based research collaborators through a process of iterative development and implementation of racial-equity–focused professional learning opportunities. Over the three years, we used explicit modeling and gradual release of responsibility approaches to build the capacity of CWHS educators to take on the work of improvement planning and implementation.

By the 2016–17 academic year, I worked exclusively with the administrative team and formal school leaders to strengthen their capacity to lead their own equity change efforts. Throughout, I collected data to capture the school's conditions, outcomes, collaboration, and colearning. By the 2017–18 academic year, I completely withdrew from formal participation in the field. My research assistant and I continued nonparticipatory data collection, in the form of retrospective interviews, occasional school site visits, and progress monitoring of the school's efforts and outcomes, which I continued until December 2019.

Audience(s)

I wrote this book primarily for school-based educators of all races who work in school settings that employ White administrators, teachers, and staff members to serve disproportionally high Black and Brown student populations. My goal in writing this book is to push school-based educators to think differently and deeply about how to improve their *practices* and thinking in ways that will establish better organizational and learning conditions for Black and Brown children, who are and remain the population I am centrally committed to supporting. When I started this project, Central Waters High School employed only two Black people in a school of nearly two hundred employees. Therefore, much of what I cover in the book examines and analyzes White people's efforts to improve themselves, the school, and the educational opportunities and outcomes of Black, Latinx, and Native American students. In that regard, *Stuck Improving* is highly useful for White people to learn about what it means to be White while working in a school where racial equity is a priority. It is also highly relevant to Black and Brown educators who, like I am, are frustrated, angered, and jaded by White educators' continued failure of Black and Brown students.

For Black and Brown educators, the book offers insights into what our (Black and Brown people's) work with, loving critique of, and support for White educators might look like. The book positions us in the rightful place of possessing experiential racial knowledge that is invaluable and sorely needed. If the increasing number of Black and Brown students are to stand a chance in schools that operate under the conventional norms of racism and white supremacy, White people have a lot of work to do. And for better or worse, Black and Brown people are bound up in and central to that work. If White educators can't quite do what is demanded of them (as study after study suggests), I believe educational researchers of all races can support racial equity change by producing relevant, accessible, and illuminating scholarship that compels White educators to improve their *practice* and thinking in ways that benefit Black and Brown students and that ultimately benefit themselves.

While I did not write this book with academics in the forefront of my mind, I do believe race scholars, educational researchers, anthropologists, and sociologists of education who are interested in antiracism, racial equity, and school improvement will find this book useful for both its methodological and conceptual contributions. I illuminate aspects that may appeal more directly to academic researchers, educational researchers, and race scholars through the use of chapter endnotes, methodological notes, and appendices.

BOOK ORGANIZATION AND CHAPTER OVERVIEWS

The book is organized into six chapters that each differently advance the book's three central arguments: schools must cultivate organizational racial resources to increase their capacity to enact equity change, racism reasserts and reveals itself anew, and making the effort be equitable and learning in the process is the primary way to increase the capacity for improvement. Each chapter explores a single organizational racial resource that reinforces the resources explored in other chapters. For example, the cultivation of Black and Brown Influential Presence contributes to the cultivation of Collective Awareness of Racial Emotions and Beliefs. Race-Conscious Inquiry bolsters a Courageously Confrontational School Culture and so forth.

Chapter 1, "Black and Brown People's Influential Presence," analyzes the emergence of Voices Rising, a social justice course that CWHS offered beginning in the 2018–19 academic year. I demonstrate how the emergence of Voices Rising results from CWHS cultivation of Black and Brown influential presence.

Chapter 2, "Curated White Racial Discomfort," demonstrates that discomfort, distress, guilt, confusion, and cognitive dissonance and related experiences are critically important, indeed foundational, for White educators to experience if we expect them to change their racialized ways of knowing.

Chapter 3, "Courageously Confrontational School Culture," conveys the ubiquitous presence of racial violence at CWHS and explores how CWHS leaders and teachers developed a racial critique of their aversion to conflict, enabling them to shift toward a communication and problem-solving practice I call courageous confrontation.

Chapter 4, "Collective Awareness of Racial Emotions and Beliefs," presents a series of self-talk exchanges and episodes that demonstrate how CWHS increased its collective awareness of racial emotions and beliefs. It demonstrates that making private thoughts and beliefs public in the form of self-talk is critical for learning and equity improvement.

Chapter 5, "Race-Conscious Inquiry Cycles (Leadership)," offers an overview of the iterative practice of initiating *race-conscious inquiry cycles* that partially fostered CWHS's capacity to improve. I show the process we used to continually broaden the range of racial perspectives and representations that enabled the CWHS community to *see* problems in race-visible ways that allowed them to envision new possibilities for how to address them.

I conclude *Stuck Improving* with an exploration of how the increased capacities created new possibilities for CWHS.

This book reflects my attempt to convey how, in a white supremacist society, racial equity is perpetually within view and just out of arms' reach. I wrote this book to be quiet, contemplative, and sobering. I intend for each chapter to evoke distinct emotions that relay the quiet day-to-day intensity that comes with thinking about and doing racial equity work in schools. I present no major triggering events or racial episodes that riled the school community. I do not report racial shouting matches or protests. Rather, I amplify the complexities and contradictions of trying equity work, bringing the organizationwide practice of inquiry-driven racial equity leadership to the forefront of leadership and school improvement practice. Be clear. This book is about fighting against the myriad manifestations of racism and white supremacy in schools. So it is filled with instances of mundane racial violence—the sense of frustration, anger, loss, and hurt that white supremacy demands be ever present. I also show acts of courage and kindness, reconciliation, joy, and solidarity that white supremacy can never fully stamp out. I want readers to end this book knowing that working to make schools more racially equitable is very hard. And that it is worthwhile. To become stuck improving is to fight against the violence of racism. I do my best to make racism and white supremacy visible and to show how they might be continually challenged so educators can see how to do better. If educators use this book to make trouble for themselves, their schools, and local school communities, and in the process of doing so get stuck improving, I will consider my time and efforts as meaningful.

1

BLACK AND BROWN
PEOPLE'S INFLUENTIAL PRESENCE

B lack and Brown people possess distinct knowledge that stems from experiences of white supremacy and racism as well as the generational resilience that stems from the effort to live as free as possible from racial subjugation. Black and Brown students, families, and educators who carry forward this expansive experiential knowledge are present in schools throughout the United States and bring with them a wellspring of understanding and practices—perspectives, ideas, ways of being and doing, and verve—that should rightfully enrich their schools. Indeed, we know that Black and Brown people profoundly influence and enrich the intellectual, cultural, economic, and social fabric of the United States. But Black and Brown people's experiential knowledge and cultural practices often have little influence on the school-based decision-making and structures that shape their day-to-day school experiences.

Black and Brown people's influential presence refers to the combined physical presence and deep integration of experiential knowledge and cultural practices into the fabric of the organization. Black and Brown people's influential presence is evidenced when Black and Brown people's multiple experiential knowledge, priorities, and ways of being reshape power structures in the school organization. Influential presence contains elements of representation; however, Black and Brown people can be present, represented, and yet remain minimally influential—what I call merely present (or mere presence). US schools are a case in point. Black and Brown students are a majority of the public school population. Their representation continues to increase. Yet if Black and Brown people have minimal influence over the varied forms of power that dictate their educational access, opportunities, experiences, or outcomes, they will be subjugated to mere presence.

In most schools, White people possess influential presence even where they are numerically underrepresented or not at all present. They control and influence power in decision-making and structural resources such as what is taught, how it is taught, the bell schedule, and the program of professional learning, to name a few. Simply put, White presence is by default influential. Therefore, whiteness is a well-established feature of day-to-day life in a school organization. Its counterpart is usually Black and Brown mere presence. Black and Brown students attending school experience White people doing school "to them" as opposed to "with them." As Black and Brown representation and mere presence increase, White people become more intentional in their exercise of influence over what "schooling" looks like and feels like. Indeed, increasing Black and Brown presence often results in more entrenched White efforts at reifying White influential presence. White educators focus their energy and concerns on controlling Black and Brown students' movements and behaviors rather than with educing and expanding students' knowledge of self and experiences, or cultivating intellectual curiosity.

When Black and Brown people are present but not adequately recognized, they are less powerful than they rightfully should be. When Black and Brown people are not operating in their full rights, no one—White people included—is able to fully benefit from the well of racial resources that Black and Brown people have to offer. Recognizing, elevating, and deeply integrating experiential knowledge and cultural practices into the fabric of an organization are thus essential practices that build the capacity of the organization to enact racial equity change. Establishing and growing Black and Brown influential presence are as foundational for racial learning and equity-focused school improvement as integrating science and math knowledge into the fabric of a school that adopts science, technology, engineering, and math (STEM) as its curricular model. It is not possible for a school to improve the way it serves Black and Brown students, or enhance the educational experiences of White students, without growing Black and Brown people's influential presence to integrate racial knowledge into all areas of decision-making, teaching, and learning in a school community.

In this chapter I convey how cultivating Black and Brown influential presence increased the capacity of Central Waters High School (CWHS) to become a more equitable school by telling the story of Voices Rising—a social justice course that CWHS offered beginning in the 2018–19 academic year. Voices Rising represents a window into CWHS's past years, a turning point in its journey, and signpost for where it has the potential to go. In the first part of the chapter, I help readers understand the racially oppressive and alienating CWHS I encountered in the first year of our partnership. I center Black and Brown people's voices, stories, and experiences and amplify the racial knowledge and cultural practices of Ms. Moore, the school's sole Black administrator, and others who were present and agential but minimally influential. I then jump forward a few years to show the priorities and interventions—include Black and Brown students' voices, experiences, and considerations in decision-making; increase the numerical representation of Black and Brown adults who are routinely present in the school; and create structures that allow students to cultivate racial affinities—that expanded Black and Brown people's influential presence in all areas of school life.

Throughout, I analyze the multiple *meanings* of working to establish Black and Brown influential presence. I make it plain that a seemingly simple task like "hiring and retaining Black and Brown" people is not as simple as it seems. I point out dilemmas that emerged when Black and Brown people are inadvertently positioned to educate White people, students are positioned to educate teachers, and so forth. Ultimately, I argue that there is evidence of progress in these dilemmas and challenges and that as Black and Brown people's influential presence increases so too will Black and Brown students' intellectual curiosity, desire to learn, and skills to improve the school for their own self-benefit. In the process, these very same resources optimize organizational conditions for White teachers, leaders, and students to engage in the racial learning that is essential for racial equity change.

A MESSAGE TO NON-BLACK MEMBERS OF THE CENTRAL WATERS COMMUNITY

When I logged into my email, the subject line "N-Word Lesson Plan—Invitation to View" stuck out. It was a message from Elizabeth, the principal of CWHS. I worked with her closely for four years to improve their school's racial culture and climate. I was almost two years removed from on-site data collection. So her message was a surprise. I clicked the email to find her brief note: "The lesson plan was collaboratively designed by students and teachers in our new social justice course. This is a big step for us. Teachers and staff already completed the lesson. Students are up next. I thought you'd like to see that we're still moving along." I opened the link and started to read the lesson plan that students developed as one of the course assignments:

> **Learning Objective:** Students and teachers will be able to reflect on their own understanding of the N word and build empathy for why Non-Black members of the Central Waters community should not be saying it [the N-word] under any circumstances and that it is a word that we would like all students and staff to refrain from using in the academic setting for our inclusive community.

> **Why this Lesson:** We don't have to show you any charts or numbers to explain why we are doing this lesson because we have bandaged the emotional scars of our students and our colleagues sustained while navigating their own identities around the N word and its use. The lived experiences of people in our school community is enough to make this a relevant conversation.

"Non-Black!" I quickly scanned the lesson plan. By the time I finished, a second email had arrived: "N-Word Video created by Central Waters Students." I clicked the link and was directed to an online video. Forty minutes! That evening, as I taught my class, I was antsy to get home. Students making bold statements about what non-Black people should and should not be doing? "Yoooooo!" This was different. Six years earlier, the CWHS message to "non-White people" was: "You don't belong here." But now, it seemed that the very students who years earlier were subjected to being called niggers and taunted as having "dirty blood" were more than merely present.

"LET'S JUST ERASE IT"—THAT'S THE KIND OF ENERGY IN THIS BUILDING

The word *nigger* floated around Central Waters quite a bit. It wasn't new. But the fact it was being addressed was. In the 2013–14 academic year when I first started the research project, a White student hacked into the email account of a Black first-year student named Jamal to notify him in writing that he was a nigger. "This just happened last week," Jamal explained. He suspected the same White student who was bullying him, Steven Manor, was the culprit. Jamal immediately shared the email with Ms. Moore. He trusted she would take action. Ms. Moore emailed Jason, the associate principal in charge of freshmen: "Someone hacked into Jamal Bryant's email and wrote him a racist message—called him a nigger. Jamal thinks it was Steven Manor. You may or may not know that Steven has been bullying Jamal. I'd appreciate if you follow up." Jason never did. Miss Moore expressed her frustration:

> Can you believe that Jamal came to me almost in tears because he almost got into a fight with this kid Steven? Jason never followed up. If a student is called a nigger, that's something you need to follow up on. Jamal's mother came up to the school on Monday and told me that no one called her. These are the kinds of things that happen in this school.
>
> I met with a group of students the other day who wanted to march around the district with signs and all of that. I think that there's a lot going on right underneath the surface right now with students feeling that they aren't being treated fairly; teachers, I think, really trying to find a way to build relationships with students who they're not accustomed to building relationships with. That's a lot of the conversation that's going on right now. The climate is a little tense.

Ms. Moore was an administrator at the school for two years. When she was hired, she was the second person of color to have a leadership role in Central Waters. She was responsible for all things "culturally responsive and all things related to equity." At the onset she was up for that challenge. She soon changed her mind. While leading the school's equity team, she came to grips with the depth of racism at CWHS. Even with help of a handful of highly committed teacher leaders, the challenges were much more than she could overcome. The following week Ms. Moore shared her frustration during an interview:

> People write the "N" word on the bathroom stalls. The hate is literally right on the surface for us to see. I see nobody [adults] trying to find out who's doing it or to stop it. If I even inquire about it, it's just, "Let's just erase it." That's the kind of energy in this building. I often wonder . . . how is this affecting these kids on a day-to-day basis, to be in this kind of environment?

The Day-to-Day of Racism

My research team and I spent the 2013–14 academic year gathering multiple forms of data that we later used to help CWHS "see" how students and staff experienced the environment on a day-to-day basis. We conducted interviews and observations as a major part of our data collection. As we expected, racial identity and racism shaped students' and staff's experiences. Supporting students of color required intentioned effort, careful calculation, a strategic weighing of the pros and cons and risks that supporting White students did not. There was no way around it: CWHS was a nurturing and supporting place for White students. Adults afforded grace to the students who looked like them and who shared their beliefs and ways of being. White students had ample opportunities to succeed (and to fail and rebound). That so many adults showed up and empathized mattered. But these experiences were largely invisible and ignored, like *nigger* in the email. When someone—anyone—pointed them out, the modus operandi was to erase racial problems, like *nigger* off the bathroom stall. Kevin was one of a handful of Black students who was very vocal about his and other Black students' experiences of racism. One day, Kevin stormed into Ms. Moore's office.

> **Kevin:** Ms. Moore, Ms. Moore, this is crazy. I just want you to know what just happened. She just closed the line in my face after she served the students who was in front of me.
>
> **Ms. Moore:** Slow down. Calm down and explain to me what happened.
>
> **Kevin:** I was in line standing behind two students. Two White boys. So I'm standing in line to get some soup and salad. The lunch lady serves them. When I get up there, she closed the line! Right in front of my face like nobody else was there. I couldn't get my soup.
>
> **Ms. Moore:** Let's go figure this out.
>
> **Kevin (as they walked him back to the cafeteria):** And if I say something, I get in trouble. I'm mad, Ms. Moore.
>
> **Ms. Moore (speaking to the cafeteria worker):** Excuse me, I need to understand why you did not serve this young man when you served two students who were right in front of him.
>
> **Cafeteria Worker:** I thought he was going to want a whole meal.
>
> **Ms. Moore:** Even if he wanted a whole meal, what's wrong with that? Why would you close the line right in his face?
>
> **Cafeteria Worker (looks at Kevin):** I can give you some soup.
>
> **Kevin:** I don't want any soup now. I just want you to know that I know what you did.
>
> **Ms. Moore:** Are you sure you don't want to eat?
>
> **Kevin:** I'm *not hungry anymore.*

Although Black students were more expressive in pointing out their experiences of mistreatment to people who treated them unfairly, they were not the only ones who yearned for support. Leemai and other Asian students at CWHS were less apt to openly confront racism head on. Perhaps they could not name it. Perhaps they did not want to cause problems. In a school community where Black and White racial conflict took center stage, Asian students were present but invisiblized. Teachers who wanted to support Leemai and other students as they were transitioned into Advanced Placement (AP) courses were fearful of speaking on be-half of students. Leemai recounted her experience:

> One day, they called me to the front office. I was there for more than the full class period because the bell rang. They basically changed my schedule. They told me I was not going to be in ESL classes. But I like my classes and I feel I'm doing just fine. I wasn't really given a choice. They did ask me how I felt about taking Advanced Placement. If I wanted to change classes. But I just said okay because I felt pressured. They were like, "You can do it." They told me that my life would be better, like "You'll get a good job and make good money." I guess I could have said no.

Meanwhile, Latinx students endured the environment by sticking to themselves. They found a sense of belongingness on the hall serving ESL students. White students dubbed it "Little Mexico." Within this marginalized school subcommunity, Latinx students self-described as having "dirty blood." Ellen, a veteran ESL teacher, cringed at the term. The internalization of xenophobia and racism amongst Latinx students ran deep: "Their experiences in Central Waters makes them think it is okay to describe themselves as having dirty blood." She explained that there was "a lot of really kind of intense stuff" that forced her to learn about racism just by virtue of spending so much time with her students.

> I had a mural project that my kids took very seriously. They did this in-credible mural that addressed some gang stuff because these conflicts were really pressing issues. When they finished, we planned to unveil it and invited the entire administrative team and student services staff. Sheila, the only person of color, came. And so did some of the social workers. The administration didn't even respond.
>
> I naively had told the kids, "Oh, everyone's coming to see it. Yada, yada, yada." When three people showed up, they were really hurt. They had a bad day that day. *They acted up.*
>
> This was about three, four years ago. I still have a grudge about nobody showing up for them. Repeatedly. I remember just the learning

curve for me talking with students about racism, which was really the only way to explain the stuff that was happening.

People didn't show up for Latinx students. The mundane racism of not showing up chipped away at Ellen's belief in the school as she witnessed its daily impact on her students' sense of dignity. She held a grudge about the mural project. She held a grudge about how CWHS masterfully supported White students, who seemed almost impervious to any fault. She blamed the administrative team. And for good reason. They showed up for White students, for whom the environment worked, as should be expected in an organization that is overwhelmingly shaped by White influential presence. Teachers hinted at it to us, mentioning in passing how "White girls can get away with stuff our Black students can't." But no one elaborated until we asked Ms. Moore outright, who explained to us that Sarah, Jenny, Becky, Susan, and a group of their friends coordinated a cheating scandal that caused a stir for the entire school:

We had a huge cheating scandal at this school this year actually. All the students involved were White students. One of the students took a picture of a test and sent it to all of her friends. One of the parents found out about it and wrote a letter to the principal and the superintendent. The kids sat around the table in the principal's office. The administrators were all there along with the eight to ten students involved. I clearly thought the girls would be in trouble, but what happened next just shocked me.

Ms. Moore recounted the conversation:

Becky: We didn't cheat. We just wanted to pass the test.
Sarah: The class is really hard and the whole class was confused. Nobody in the entire class gets it because she doesn't really teach us the right way.
Jenny: If we understood what the teacher was saying, we wouldn't have had to figure out how to pass. We just did not understand the teacher. We're really sorry that people think we cheated.
Administrator: What can she [the teacher] do to help you better understand the material?

After recounting the brief conversation, Ms. Moore reflected:

> These kids' defenses were the class is really hard and it was the teacher's fault. So what happened next? The teacher who the girls stole the test from was directed to hold study sessions for the girls. That test they all cheated on was thrown out. They retook the test. That was it. End of story.

One teacher explained, "If there were other (not White) students who had cheated, I could think of how different that outcome would have been. Kids get suspended over a lot less than that." White adults play an essential role in shaping student experiences for the better and for the worse. In focus groups, students opened up to us about how teachers treated students differently:

Juliette (White female): There's two kids in one of my classes—one Black, one White—that usually screw around doing stuff that kind of disrupts class. I feel like my teacher punishes the guy that's Black more than the guy that's White and I don't know why. But I don't think that's fair.

Moderator: And they do the same things?

Juliette: Yes.

Jacob (Black male): Teachers do that to me too.

Moderator: Say more.

Jacob: When our friends, who be White, we talk and goof around or whatever. It's me and one of my friends. But she [the teacher] would hear something and be like, "Jacob! What are you doing!" And I'm like, "It wasn't even me this time."

I'll just look at her thinking "The thing that you just did is disrespectful to me, but you want me to give you so much respect." I don't understand that.

Don't get me wrong, sometimes I do mess around. I won't deny that. But it's more than just me, though. It's me, it's another kid . . . I don't know if I say names or not.

Moderator: We'll scratch them out if you do.

Jacob: [speaking to peers] You know who I'm talking about. It's me, Turner, Luke, Sebastian, we're always messing around. If she doesn't see Turner with her own eyes, she assumes that it's me or Luke. We are both Black. She's always coming at us and we're always like, "We didn't even do nothing."

So we just get mad at her. We have the right to be mad. But she doesn't get that [we have that right]. She is going off her instinct even if she's not looking. That's just one thing.

Jasper (White male): It's weird. I'm on the opposite side. I'll sit in the front row in my classes and have my phone out and have my headphones put in the entire class session. One guy next to me pulls out his phone just to text a little. He gets yelled at, and I'm still there. I can go entire class periods without any teacher noticing my behavior. And it's not really fair at all.

Moderator: Do you have teachers that are fair? If so, what are they doing different than those teachers who might be picking out students?

Jacob: They talk to us. They get to know who we are as a person, what our characteristics are, what makes us mad, what makes us happy, before they try to point the finger and make conclusions. They start with getting to know us before they try to teach us.

Juliette: Yes, they don't just look at you and then label you after the first few days and then treat you that way for the rest of the class . . . they get to know you first.

Jasper: My English and my history class, they're interesting because my history teacher, she's a really happy lady. She's really nice.

Jacob: I love her, she's cool.

Jasper: It's a class of mostly Latino and African American people, and we're all treated really well by her. We love her. She's a great person. My literature teacher is a harder teacher. Not so loving. But she got to know us pretty well and she knew who would be causing issues. Race or not, she always checked before she called someone out.

Then we got this substitute when she left because she had a child. He's really trying to get to know us all. He's a nice guy, but he can't really enforce the behavior part. So our literature class has become less of a learning place, at least lately.

The students who agreed to talk with us understood that race profoundly shaped teachers' and administrators' responses to their behaviors. White students claimed "I don't know why" while explaining why. Although they did not name it, they knew that something unfair and related to students' racial identities was at play. Students did not shy away from the ways their actions and behaviors contributed to the school's racial disparities. White students explained the ways their behaviors, even when problematic, would not likely lead to punishment. For students of color, it was the opposite. They were overrepresented. This disparate treatment cumulated over decades. The increasing presence of students of color made discipline disparities all the more prominent.[1]

Numbers-Centered Equity Reform

Before we came to CWHS, the school's efforts to address the racial disparities were well underway. The change strategies the school chose were to implement Positive Behavior Interventions and Supports (PBIS) and to increase the racial diversity of Advanced Placement courses.[2] Although the interventions were well founded, numerous teachers expressed discomfort with the discipline and academic reforms. One person explained, "Staff and students are feeling very overwhelmed right now as it relates to a lot of the discussions around equitable classroom practices. We're having discussions around AP and getting more students of color in AP classes." Likewise, many teachers felt that students who were designated to take AP classes were not prepared for the rigor. They described the chosen strategies as ill informed, forced from the top down, and out of touch. Adults talked often about how the school's culture and approach to equity reform efforts impacted students:

> **Teacher A:** I think that's the culture here: to force equity on people. For example, on scholarship committee, administration and site council just says, "You will have equity within scholarship this year. You will do this. You will."
>
> **Teacher B:** It's a district thing too. "You will remove Black kids out of special education so our numbers are good." Even if they need it.

Teacher C: I think the goal is great. I believe the representation should be better. But you read the site council minutes and they're just trying to meet a quota. They're not actually concerned about the kids that are going into these [Advanced Placement] classes.

Teacher A: Obviously, there are huge disparities across the board. Special education, suspension rates. Everything. But how will we get to 100 percent equality by next year? Does that mean, okay, now we're not going to suspend students of color without addressing the huge, huge, complex underlying issues?

Teacher C: Why do you think there's not as many kids in detention? They've got to get them out of detention. The State Department of Instruction said the number of detentions was far too high. So, we're on their "watch" list. So they just don't do detention anymore.

Teacher D: When that stuff happens, and this is my first year here, so whatever, but students pick up on that, and I think it's very belittling for a district to have these goals and these ideas and think that kids are so stupid they're not going to pick up on that.

We're going to just hire people of color? We going to get rid of the staff that you have a relationship with, but fill it with a person of color and then you're going to feel better because you are a person of color? For the kids, that is very insulting. So when things like that are done, or taking the one African American administrator you have and have that person read something for Black History Month and then that's all you do for the entire month, like kids pick up on that.

It's very disappointing that we are assuming that students are so ignorant that they're just going to buy into this crap. We don't have good intentions and heartfelt intentions behind it. So, I think that's just—it's just very belittling to our students.

Ms. Jenkins, Leemai's advisor and teacher, was livid: "All of these adults planned her whole life out. Her career and her salary, the whole thing. In one hour. Leemai had no relationship with any of them. All because they want her in AP. To make the district numbers look good." Ms. Jenkins was a strong advocate for students who were not native English speakers. She was outspoken. When we conducted focus groups to surface organizational problems, Ms. Jenkins spoke at length about the hurt that students experienced, including her anger about how Leemai was treated. Other White teachers weighed in too:

> **Ms. Jenkins:** There's this organization the district hired to create equity within AP classes across race and income. The message is that "we need more students of color in AP courses and you're going to do it," and that's where it's left. The organization has a formula. They run some numbers and then just put the kids into the AP classes. Leemai was in ESL classes her entire life. She was thriving academically. But she came up in the formula as someone who should be in Advanced Placement. So there it is.
>
> She cried for two days after that meeting. She asked me if they knew how much being in ESL helped her learning. I was honest with her. I said, "No, they don't know because they've never been in any of your classes." To make a leap from ESL to Advanced Placement without really any kind of support or any community or whatever is ridiculous.
>
> **Teacher B:** It's a district thing. The message is "You will remove Black kids out of special education so our numbers are good. Even if they need it. This will happen." That's the culture.
>
> **Teacher A:** Same thing on scholarship committee. Administration and site council just saying, "You will have equity within scholarship this year. You will."
>
> **Ms. Jenkins:** It's about making the numbers look good.

As the first year of the project wound down, we absorbed the energy. We were learning the good and the bad. Our initial work of information gathering was done. But our work was just getting started. CWHS was on the "watch list." The priority was getting off the list and out of hot water with the Department of Education. *Nigger* graffiti on the bathroom stalls? Just erase it. Erase Kevin's hunger and Leemai's learning experience. Erase the hurt in "Little Mexico." Erase Becky and Sarah's lies and deception. Erase "they get to know us first." That was the kind of energy in *this* building.

The Violence of Erasure

Moving numbers doesn't stop erasure. It doesn't address the "soft" mundane racism that wounds and harms but that is impossible to fully account. Although some teachers and students recognized the kind of energy in the building, most did not and could not name it. Since they couldn't name it, it didn't exist. So anger, hurt, fear, and withdrawal festered. The emotional and relational disconnect between students of color, teachers, and administrators was deep. Adults' and, in particular, White adults' voices, perspectives, and prerogatives drowned out Black and Brown adults' and students' critical voices, perspectives, and insights. Black educators like Ms. Moore and White educators like Ms. Jenkins possessed higher capacities to believe and believe in Black and Brown students, parents, and community stakeholders as having much to contribute to educational decision-making at CWHS. And this is what students at CWHS needed—adults to believe them and believe in them. More importantly, students needed adults to treat them as though they believed them and believed in them.

Most White teachers are socialized to not believe and believe in Black and Brown students. White supremacy demands that if a person (or group of people) is not White, that person or group is dishonest, inaccurate, and untruthful. In a context of white supremacy, being Black is to be either perpetually dishonest or at best to lack the capacity to be right. Alternately, to be White is to be right, honest, accurate, and truthful. Black and Brown students come to school knowing that White people do not believe them or believe in them. So it was not surprising at all when Janae, Tameka, Treyvon, and Yasmeen took their concerns about what was happening in their social studies class to Ms. Moore:

> **Yasmeen:** We are telling you this because we think it's messed up. And we don't know what to do. So we started discussing race in America in class. One of the activities, the teacher put the race and gender on a post-it board. Then we [students] had to come up and write initial reactions to that particular race, to that particular gender and race, whatever.

Treyvon: So I'm sitting there looking at the African American male chart and the White kids just filled it up negative stereotypes. Nothing positive at all. So we looking at each other, like what is happening? Is the teacher going to say something? What is she gonna do, right.

Yasmeen: Then the teacher put us in groups of five or six to discuss the charts. In our group, this White boy said, "I am so glad I am not Black."

Janae: Like, that's his opinion but he said that in our face and nobody said anything. Like was he saying that because people said negative things about Black people? Or maybe like he thinks Black is bad? I don't know.

Treyvon: We just want to you to know. 'Cause if we say something, you know we'll be in trouble. They won't listen to us.

The unit on race continued. After several more lessons where the teacher failed to address blatant racism that they experienced, Yasmeen, Janae, Treyvon, and Tameka asked Ms. Moore to talk to the teacher about what was happening. They felt so uncomfortable moving forward that they couldn't remain silent and sit through another class. Ms. Moore never doubted what the students told her. She believed them. So she immediately agreed and began to think about what to do. First, she invited the students to have a conversation. Second, she asked a White male administrator and the teacher to join the conversation to listen to students' experiences:

Yasmeen: We are really stressed out about the race topic. It's not that African Americans at this school don't want to talk about race. It's that you let the White students say ignorant stuff right in our face. Black people are not the negative stereotypes. Teachers don't even say anything.

There should have been a discussion around what that meant versus just leaving that there.

Janae: When we say something in response, White students say we are overly sensitive. Or they say reverse racism. We are not the teacher, so we don't want to argue with them. But it's not right we have to sit there. And it's not just your class.

Treyvon, Tameka, Yasmeen (crosstalk): Right! It's all over. Teachers just sit there.

Yasmeen, Janae, Treyvon, and Tameka determined to not merely be present but to be influentially present. They proactively sought help. They determined to "stick with the class" despite their experiences of racism and the anxiety it caused. They took the courageous step to point out the wrong and in doing so advocated for not only themselves but also for their teacher. They believed in their White teacher, that she could get better. Without belief in their teacher's capacity to change, taking the time to share is futile. The students realized two things. First, they were being denied the opportunity to learn. Second, everyone, even a White teacher who stood idly while White students filled a chalkboard with harmful racial stereotypes about Black people, should have the opportunity to learn. Students created the learning opportunity for their teacher by speaking up. They talked directly to the teacher about their feelings. They gave her advice about how she could handle the lesson the next time she taught it. The social studies teacher reflected on their conversation:

> We ended up having a meeting. Administrators and all four students. They talked to me a little about the activity. How they think it should have gone. I was surprised, but I got what they were saying. They thought I wasn't brave enough, I guess, to even help. Or that maybe I didn't care. What impacted me most was that they end up feeling like they have to have the responsibility of correcting their peers, which is not fair to them.

Ironically, the teacher did not notice or appreciate that the students took on the responsibility to correct her. Four Black students and one Black adult bore the burden of creating a learning opportunity for one White teacher. With no affinity spaces or program of professional development for White people to take on racial learning, these sorts of incidents were handled on individualized case-by-case bases. Under such an ad hoc individualized model, it's not feasible for Black and Brown people to educate White people. In part, the school's low capacity to ensure White teachers receive feedback stems from the fact that there are not enough colleagues or students to offer enough feedback. Second, asking Black and Brown people to do this work is a dilemma. If Black and Brown people do not advocate and teach, White educators learn less. They also would not have access to the rich experiential knowledge that Black and Brown people have to offer. Whose responsibility is it to help White teachers improve their practice? Black and Brown people can play a role. But how much is too much? Especially when there is only one Ms. Moore to go around.

Black and Brown students experienced racism in classrooms throughout the school. White students outnumbered Black students by a large margin. In a class of thirty students, if there were four students, as was the case in the social studies class, administrators acknowledge that four "is a lot, honestly. That's probably the most." Many students we talked to expressed never having been in a class with more than one or two African Americans or "minorities." The exception was English language learners and special education students whose classes disproportionally contained Black and Brown students.[3] In other words, CWHS racially segregated students via academic tracking. This was an issue that the Advanced Placement integration and special education de-identification reforms aimed but ultimately failed to address. But integrating students of color into classes with White teachers did little to address the underlying problem of white disbelief in Black and Brown students' capabilities.

Integrating students into AP classes is one thing. Ensuring White teachers believe and believe in Black and Brown students is a learned practice. The way adults "counseled" Leemai into Advanced Placement courses is a case in point. She could have been treated as a person who was capable of actively participating in decisions about her future, which is how Ms. Jenkins wanted her to be treated. In a context of white disbelief, Leemai's and Ms. Jenkins's responses could easily be interpreted as low aspirations. Or as Leemai and Ms. Jenkins not wanting Leemai to have access to AP-level academic learning. Or as a broader belief that

"they want self-segregation." And so on, until the number of explanations spiraled into the abyss of white disbelief in Black and Brown people's voices, perspectives, and prerogatives.

The few people who did have the insight of student stories as their
source of evidence—the Moores, Ellens, and Jenkinses—were damned
if they acted and damned if they didn't. So they resigned themselves to
mere presence at worst and minimal influential presence at best. Would
it have mattered if Ms. Jenkins spoke up for Leemai? Perhaps. But she
chose not to do so as she had many times before. Ms. Moore did speak up.
Her racial practice was rendered invisible and underappreciated. And it
came with a cost. She leveraged her positional authority as administrator to influence the school. In the process, she drew on racial ways of
knowing, being, and doing. She was calculated. She took precautions
to ensure the teacher would not feel attacked. Having a White administrator colleague in on the conversation might reduce that likelihood.
The presence of a White administrator also legitimated what four Black
students and an adult were saying. Ms. Moore understood these racial
dynamics. But Ms. Moore was one person. And fed-up White teachers
changed the trajectory of her work so much so that she decided to leave.

Erasing Ms. Moore

Given what we learned, the work ahead of us seemed overwhelming—
dare I say, doomed to fail. Ms. Jenkins felt helpless. Ms. Moore had
enough. Her courageous confrontations to support and affirm Black
students earned her teacher and staff complaints. White teachers' accusations against Ms. Moore were the exact same ones they used against
Sheila, CWHS's first Black female associate principal who Ms. Moore
replaced. She was "only there for the Black kids. She could only relate
to the Black kids." Sheila left in the 2011–12 academic year after working at CWHS for four years. The turning point for Sheila was when fifteen teachers went to district and school administrators to express their
concern that she favored Black kids. Soon after, administrators directed
Sheila to "move around a little bit and work with the full student population." The message was clear: "Don't be so Black student-focused." How
could she not? Black students sought out adults they felt would listen and

believe them, understand their problems, and ultimately help them in times of need, which was often. Like Ms. Sheila before, Black students leaned heavily on one administrator because she was the only Black adult in a building. Of nearly two hundred adults in the building, two were Black. Only one had even a modicum of influence. That was Ms. Moore. How could Ms. Moore not focus on Black students? On her way out, she offered us some parting words:

> From the district level, you have people who are well intentioned and really want to make a difference. But I know for a fact that at the district level equity is not a district goal. It's just not. The goal is that things are adequately documented; that efforts have been made, not that things improve. What matters at the end of the day is how we treat these kids. This is high school so kids are still coming into themselves [developmentally]. And I just can't imagine attending this high school and this being my experience before I go off into the world. That would be hard.
>
> The good thing is that with your research group a lot of good things are going to happen anyway, in spite of. Even if the intention is to just document effort, I know that you all are here for a reason. Some of the staff here can come along. But there is a large part of the staff that is tired of having the conversation around equity because they feel like it's all talk. Even folks who really care are starting to question is anything really changing or are they just talking again? Are we going to change anything at the end of the day?
>
> Sometimes good things come from where people didn't see it coming. I feel like this research project could be that. I'm very hopeful.

GOOD THINGS ARE GOING TO HAPPEN ANYWAY, IN SPITE OF . . .

In the 2013–14 academic year, our research team undertook an extensive information-gathering process that racialized CWHS's problems. It was what made Ms. Moore hopeful. We conducted surveys, focus groups, and interviews that placed race and racism front and center. We went beyond the numbers. We focused on experience: the disparate treatment, everyday racism, the racist structures, the white supremacist ideologies, and the erasure. Ms. Moore left at the end of the 2013–14 academic year, two months before CWHS held its first summer *data retreat* in 2014. She skirted the 2014–15 academic year of racial reckoning in which CWHS experienced a substantial amount of conflict, plus teacher and staff turnover (see chapter 2). It was not a good year, especially for administrators. During that year, the school felt chaotic. It was difficult to see that anything close to good was happening and naïve to assume that anything would. But as the 2014–15 year wound down, we started coplanning a summer retreat with administrators and a small group of teacher leaders who weathered the year of racial reckoning with a determination to improve the school. Good things started to happen.

As the year of racial reckoning neared an end, administrators, teacher ambassadors, and our research team coplanned the relationship retreat to accomplish three objectives: foster a culture of honest direct communication within the school community, strengthen the sense of belonging for students of color, and improve the climate and discipline in the school community. The relationship retreat happened as it did because the core group—administrators and teacher leaders and staff who formed a relationship ambassador team—undertook the self-work to reconceptualize behavioral problems, disparate engagement, and large variances in academic performance as consequences of deep-rooted racial inequities. Who better than Black and Brown students should partner to address these issues?

During the 2014–15 summer relationship retreat, we invited Black and Brown students into the colearning and equity improvement processes. This was a pivotal moment because it was the first time CWHS offered a structure for White teachers to collaborate with Black and Brown people over an extended period of time that openly acknowledged that the school had a serious problem with race and racism. The retreat disrupted the conventional white practice of not believing by holding a space where multiple Black and Brown people echoed similar experiential knowledge such that White people had to accept Black and Brown people's ideas as true and right. The time spent partially reshaped the organization into one that better affirmed Black and Brown students' presence by offering White people opportunities for racial learning. It also gave students an opportunity to experience the power of contributing ideas, being heard, and shaping school policy and practice.

Over two intensive days, administrators, teachers, and students worked in a range of configurations (students only, administrators only, and representational groupings) to develop commitment statements, plans for honoring the commitments, and strategies for communicating the commitments to members of the school community who did not attend the retreat. As the retreat wound down, teachers, students, and administrators shared their collective commitments with the full group. A group of adults and a single student shared the results of their conversations about the schoolwide problem of tardiness and on-time arrival to class.

> As adults in the building, we are committed to helping every student get to class on time because I am dedicated to maximizing student engagement and time in class. We will honor our commitments by being present in the hallway during passing time, smiling and acknowledge each student, and encouraging students to be on time. We will start class on time with an engaging activity. We will clearly communicate expectations and importance of timeliness.

> As students, we are individually committed to getting ourselves and encouraging our peers to get to class on time. Doing so is important because I value my education as it empowers my voice and leadership within this school. I will start with myself by doing the following: Be aware of the time, arrive to class on time, encourage my peers, and remind my friends of the benefits of arriving on time.

Within their student-teacher-administrative groups, students expressed the need to develop separate statements from adults: "It doesn't make sense for us to develop a commitment with teachers because we're not teachers. We can develop our own." They recognized their sphere of influence, what they could do and not do, as well as what they didn't want the responsibility to do. The students were so conscientious that they found it difficult to develop commitments for students that did not attend: "We can't make our friends go to class. I don't want to try to make anybody do anything. I can model and encourage, that's it," one student explained. As we rotated and observed, we noticed that students talked more about what *I* can do. Adults talked more about what *we* can do. As teachers and students worked in teams, their final commitments, enactment plans, and progress monitoring complemented one another.

Teams talked, critiqued, explained, and refined their thinking to develop the commitment statements. In the process, they learned. One by one, each group hung chart paper with the results of the collective learning around the room. After each round of presentation, Kane, a member of our university research team, invited people to "use markers and sticky notes on your table to offer feedback to each group." Teachers and students painted the white chart papers that we hung next to each group's commitment statements with fluorescent pink, green, yellow, orange, and blue sticky notes.

In time, Kane's directions were not needed. Participants expanded the feedback routine. People drew arrows to connect ideas and drew stars and smiley faces on the parts they appreciated most or wanted to revisit. They drew question marks on areas they had questions about. Through the use of the routine, participants began forming shared understanding and vision. It grew harder to distinguish who drew what line or wrote what note to offer feedback on the policy and practice changes. Students were influencing the White adults who had so much power over their educational experience. The retreat offered possibilities. People left the school hurt and frustrated. Those who stayed experienced strained relationships. All of this, however, created new possibilities that increased CWHS capacity for improvement. Despite the administrative, teacher, and staff turnover that placed tremendous strain on the cultural fabric of the school, good things were happening.

About a month after the summer relationship retreat ended, I sat in the fifth row of the school auditorium. It was the first day of reporting for the 2015–16 academic year. As usual, I turned on my recorder to capture audio of the whole school meeting. Against a backdrop of intermittent claps and welcoming praise, new teachers and staff members introduced themselves:

> My name is Florence. You can call me Flo. I'm actually French, and my first language is French, but I'll be teaching Spanish here. I will be striving every day to instill the curiosity to learn about other places in this world to my students, so thank you for having me.

> Good morning. My name is Ben Hand. I am coming from Greater Central Region School District, ten years at the high school there. I will be the school-parent community liaison here at CWHS.

> I'm Laura. I am the addition to the student services school counselor. I am from this state. I have been in education for twenty years. I come from a school district, public school on a Native American reservation where 95 percent of students are Native American.

The twenty-plus new teachers who introduced themselves attended the 2015 summer relationship retreat as their first two days on the job. Administrators and ambassadors planned to ensure new teachers would have a professional development experience grounded in Black and Brown people's influential presence. Elizabeth required their participation as part of their induction process and hired people based on their availability to report to the retreat as the first days on the job. The enthusiastic new teachers did not realize that what they experienced at the retreat was not a CWHS norm. They stood in the front of the auditorium introducing themselves to their new colleagues, many of whom did not and would not share their enthusiasm. One new teacher, David, proclaimed during his introduction that "the support at the school was through the roof." For many, David's proclamation rang hollow. The disconnect existed because David attended the retreat, which was a microcosm of what is possible when Black and Brown influential presence is leveraged for the purposes of racial equity improvement. Still it was but a moment in time. In fact, CWHS did not provide support that was "through the roof" for everyone. This remained true for students and adults alike. But just as adults gained a sense of possibilities from the collaboration, so too did students. It changed their outlook on what they could and should be doing. The shared experience catalyzed the continued cultivation of Black and Brown influential presence. With strategy and intention, CWHS created the organizational conditions for Black and Brown people's experiential knowledge and cultural practices to rise to a level of influence that increased the school's capacity for racial equity improvement.

ERASING ERASURE: PEOPLE DIDN'T SEE IT COMING

When I opened Elizabeth's email, it recalled for me the time I encouraged Nnenna to keep going and to hold onto her commitment to antiracism despite the lack of support she found in her school. Nnenna participated in the research project during her first year at CWHS. Born in country in East Africa, her family immigrated to Central Waters when she was in elementary school. She was fascinated with the Black experience in the United States and was intrigued to have the opportunity to explore this experience as a peripheral part of her schooling experience. But joining in occasional research activities did not satisfy her questions. So she asked me to share survey data from our project for her to complete a project for her sociology class. I immediately shared whatever data she needed. She used the data and conducted her own interviews to produce a final class project called "Race and Racism and CHWS." When she finished the project, she thought administrators and teachers would appreciate her efforts. After all, teachers and administrators said they were committed to equity. That was the message since her first year. She'd been in retreats and professional learning opportunities where racial equity guided the conversations, analysis, and planning.

When Nnenna attempted to share her findings with the school, she was denied the opportunity to showcase them beyond her class. Instead of sharing the series of educational videos with the school, as she hoped, she shared her project only with her teacher and with me. It was insightful. It was truthful. It revealed CWHS racial problems from a student perspective. Adults suppressed it. I never mentioned Nnenna's disappointment to her teachers or any administrators. Years after I encouraged Nnenna to take on a project about racism in the school and naively cheered her on, her peers and their teachers carried forward her efforts. In the 2018–19 academic year, students enrolled in the Social Justice Leadership class completed their class project by collaboratively designing and leading teacher and student learning about the N word:

> Make sure you have six pieces of chart paper, markers, pens, pencils. You will be working in groups. We'll ask you to record your reactions. My co-facilitator is passing around copies of a handout that you will use to record your individual responses to the video we will watch.
>
> We are going to begin with a Chalk Talk. A Chalk Talk promotes discussion and awareness of issues and perspectives—silently. It is an excellent way to ensure that all voices are heard. Why silence? Silence is one of the most powerful and underused tools in the classroom! It creates space for thought and sends students the message that we trust them as thoughtful learners who need time to reflect.
>
> Everyone is responsible for writing, reading other people's comments, and responding; there should be no talking; and no one should sit down until the time period is over. Opinions must be freely expressed and honored, and no personal attacks are allowed. Now we're going to post the Chalk Talk guiding questions (see figure 1.1).
>
> As you review the questions record your responses on your chart paper. Take ten minutes. . . . As you wrap up your writing, we invite

FIGURE 1.1   N-word lesson chalk talk prompts

Think about and share the places or circumstances when you have seen or heard the N word—books, music, graffiti, films, comedy shows, conversations.		Do you feel comfortable reading a social media post out loud to a friend with the N word in it? What about in literature for classes? Do you read the word aloud?
Why do you think non-Black people continue using the N word?	Do you ever think that the use of the N word is appropriate? Why or why not?	
	In your role at the CWHS, what is the appropriate response in the case that a non-Black member of the community uses the word?	What is your immediate reaction when you read or hear the N word? Where do you think that reaction comes from?

you to take the next five minutes to go on a Gallery Walk. As you walk around to view the ideas in the gallery, carefully read the questions and comments posted around the room. Feel free to add comments, ask questions, and respond to other groups' posters. . . .

Thank you, now that you are back in your original groups, review your poster and comments to search for patterns and themes (or "notice and wonder"). Take about five minutes. . . . Next each group will report out patterns and themes, round-robin style, until all noticing, wonderings, and questions are shared. Who would like to go first?

What was the experience like of "talking" silently?

The relationship retreat was now in the classroom. I appreciated Nnenna's class project anew. I thought about Yasmeen, Janae, Treyvon, and Tameka's teaching from years past and how the school's capacity to support them differed. I imagined Leemai working silently in her Advanced Placement courses. I pictured that mural filled with Brown faces and Spanish language slogans. As unjust and damaging as they were, the efforts were not in vain after all. If only they attended *this* CWHS, there would have been more adults who would acknowledge their struggles, anxieties, and dreams. More teachers to have their back, believe them, and believe in them. They would have had a place: a Black Student Union, a Latino Nation. Maybe they would have been enrolled in the Social Justice Leadership class called Voices Rising. Maybe they would have coproduced, alongside Black, Brown, and White teachers, administrators, and students, a forty-minute video that drew on research, video and archival materials, teacher and student experiences to critically explore a range of questions about the word *nigger*: its history and here and now.

Black and Brown people's ideas about school equity, justice, and opportunity influenced the formal school curriculum (e.g., course offerings, assessment methods, curricular materials), administrative structures (e.g., course scheduling, extracurricular access), administrative and teacher professional development, and teacher and student leadership structures (e.g., school improvement teams, student clubs and organizations). Concretely, students in the Social Justice Leadership class used their project to assert Black students' right to attend school that affirmed they belonged. A by-product of this assertion was the opportunity for the entire school community to learn about how racism creates a hostile environment.

PRINCIPLES FOR CULTIVATING BLACK AND BROWN INFLUENTIAL PRESENCE

Four factors that cultivate Black and Brown influential presence are summarized in table 1.1. Hire Black and Brown people. Create structures that assert Black and Brown experiential knowledge, values, and cultural practices into decision-making. Create and support racial affinity spaces for students. Welcome Black and Brown learning partners who are not directly affected by the policies, practices, and decision-making that shape the day-to-day life of the school.

TABLE 1.1   Cultivating Black and Brown influential presence

CRITICAL PRINCIPLE	ENACTING THE PRINCIPLE	RACIAL LEARNING BENEFITS
Increased racial representation is critical	Hire and retain Black and Brown administrators, teachers, and staff.	Students benefit from listeners and supporters who share their racial experience.
Black and Brown unaffected learning partners are critical	Establish Black, Brown, and White professional and working relationships on principles of reciprocity and mutual benefit rather than need, charity, or aid.	Students benefit when White teachers have colleagues to learn with who possess racial knowledge, wisdom, and understanding and whom they cannot control, silence, or compel into compliance.
Black and Brown perspectives in all decision-making is critical	Inform decisions with physical presence, quantitative and qualitative data, articles and books that offer perspectives that challenge dominant racial perspectives.	Students benefit from decisions that are considered with their experiences in mind.
Affinity spaces for students and staff are critical	Create and support race-based affinity spaces, such as clubs, extracurricular activities, and schoolwide events.	Students benefit from having opportunities to be in relationship with people who share their racial experiences and knowledge.

People Who Influence

The first principle of cultivating Black and Brown influential presence is to increase the number of Black and Brown people who are in the school and who possess experiential knowledge, cultural practices, and belief-orientations that many White people do not possess. Two groups of Black and Brown adults are particularly important: school-based employees and learning partners who are "relatively unaffected" by the school's culture of racism. Hiring Black and Brown employees is a critical step in increasing Black and Brown influential presence for two reasons. First, Black and Brown adults possess a distinct capacity to notice and name racism in its various manifestations. Second, Black and Brown adults are more likely to take action to address the problems they see. But not always. Early in the research project, Ms. Moore directed members of my research team to "see" the racism at CWHS for ourselves:

> Go down to the commons area where the students eat lunch. There are two cameras in the commons area. One camera is over the table where the majority of the African American students sit. The other camera is over the table where most of the Latino students sit. There are no cameras on the side of the commons where the White students sit. The students haven't said anything about it. I don't think they noticed.
>
> But *I noticed right away.* I was hoping it was just because of some wiring. *But I know deep down what is happening.* It's interesting. From my perspective as an adult in the building, it's those nonverbal cues sometimes that make me uncomfortable. As a new person in the district, I'm having to find a way to address some of those things.

It is essential to increase the number of Black and Brown adults in school because they noticed right away and know what's happening. Many Black and Brown people learn to notice and thus know racism from an early age. Kevin is a case in point. He is a teenager who immediately noticed the cafeteria worker mistreated him. It was because he is Black. He knew it. He couldn't "prove it." Still, he wanted the worker to know he knew what she did. When Kevin reported the incident to Ms. Moore, he did so because he knew a Black woman would know his experience was true. She never questioned his claim. They shared experiential knowledge that showed up as a capacity to notice racism. When Kevin told Ms. Moore that the cafeteria worker mistreated him, her experiential knowledge showed up as a capacity to believe Kevin. Ms. Moore and Kevin's relational interactions defaulted to and started from a place of belief that stemmed from shared racial understandings, knowledge, and cultural practice. Ms. Moore did not interrogate him.

Had he shared the exact experience with a White adult, it is very possible the scenario would have played out differently. He likely would have had to "prove" himself. White people default to rejecting Black and Brown perspectives, narratives, and ways of knowing. Their relational interactions default to disbelief that show up as questions: How did you know? What did *you* do? Are you sure she meant it like that? Did you see her give the two White boys lunch? Their disbelief also shows up as outright disregard, accusations of overreactions, and defense of White people's actions. "Kevin . . . but she's a good person. I don't see her doing that on purpose. I don't think she meant it that way. It's been a long day" and so on and so forth. White people lack experiential knowledge and thus have lower capacities to make sense of racism. So they do as Jason did: ignore the racist writing that White people put on the wall, in emails. They erase. As White people engage in the cultural practice of erasing racial problems, and in particular ones that Black and Brown students experience, they relieve and absolve themselves of the need to do anything to fight racism. Increasing Black and Brown presence counters this tendency because Black and Brown people are more likely to notice and name racism, which are essential steps required before taking action.

At CWHS, Black and Brown employees acted more often and with greater expedience, even if with caution, to redress racial problems on behalf of students who needed their support. With a handful of exceptions, White people at CWHS had very little firsthand knowledge about what students of color (or White students for that matter) experienced, thought, wanted, or needed. Despite having lots of opinions, White people at CWHS did not speak Black and Brown students' truths. Even if they wanted to, they could not. Because they did not know them. They never asked students if they were offended when the one Black adult in the school read a poem during Black history month. The few people who did have the insights of student stories as their source of evidence—the Moores, Ellens, and Jenkinses—were damned if they acted and damned if they didn't. The difference was their actions. Ms. Moore and Sheila before her acted courageously to navigate and advocate. They were punished and eventually pushed out for doing so. White teachers, on the other hand, preserved themselves through being quiet, harboring resentment, but ultimately doing little other than consoling students. Ms. Jenkins, despite her clear understanding that racism diminished the schooling experience of Latinx students, chose to not courageously confront it. She consoled students, which is indeed a demonstration of care but an individualized and thus insufficient form of enacting racial equity and justice. Consoling students does not by itself do anything to reshape the organizational conditions that make consoling necessary.

Having more Black and Brown adults in multiple positions not only benefits White administrators, faculty, staff, and students but also creates conditions that increase the likelihood that Black and Brown colleagues will proliferate antiracist practices and thinking. Having high numbers of faculty of color fosters community, buffers them from racial retribution, and reduces the potential for racial tokenism and racial taxation. These protective factors improve retention. As the number of Black and Brown adults grew, CWHS's capacity to see racism expanded. Black and Brown adults influenced their White colleagues, making everyone more forthright in pointing out racism, making it difficult to claim race-neutrality and to erase Black and Brown experiences as so often happened. But having more Black and Brown employees is not enough either. Black and Brown people must hold positional authority. Otherwise, people will be relegated to vulnerable positions, especially if their numbers are relatively low. In other words, one can increase presence, but not influence. As Ms. Moore explained early on:

A lot of the White adults at CHWS are not used to interacting with [Black and Brown] adults who are not in need, who come to the table to be respected as an equal, as a professional. That isn't something that has happened here on a regular basis. That is something that White people are not being exposed to. So as long as you're [Black or Brown] not trying to be a leader and you just do your day-to-day activities, everything is perfectly fine. That's a lot of our problem. The lack of exposure.

When there is not a high number of Black and Brown employees, Black and Brown adults must also include those who don't "need" anything from White people or the school. I call these Black and Brown people who are present but relatively unaffected by the conventional power structures and influences that reify racism within the school. Black and Brown people who are relatively unaffected are less subject to control or manipulation. They show up on terms of mutual benefit and purpose. At CWHS, our research team initially served this function. As Branden, a Black male CWHS counselor who joined the school during the fourth year of the project, expressed:

> In my experience, people of color who get in front of White people get a little timid. They get a little quiet around all these White people. And you didn't come with that approach. The genuine authenticity and the straightforwardness that you all—you and the people on your research team—have given to the staff where it's cutthroat and it's raw and it's real and it's like nothing people can do about it is great. You were direct with us and the team. As a man of color, I'm listening to you all and inside I'm thinking, "*Hell yeah.*"

White adults needed to experience Black people who were influential, not in need, and relatively unaffected. Our research team members did not have to cower or fear repercussions. We did not have any financial stake in the project. Our commitments were to Black and Brown students and leveraging adult and organizational learning to help CWHS improve its own school. It didn't mean we did not worry. Rather, it meant that we would personally and professionally be alright if and when the project ended, even if it was abruptly. The fact that CWHS had minimal power over us meant that we could take risks. Had we been Black and Brown district employees, our words and actions would have caused swift and harsh retribution. But expanding Black and Brown influential presence did not happen through hiring and retention alone. And our research team could not sustain it.

Structures That Foster Influential Presence

The second principle for cultivating Black and Brown influential presence is to create structures—the time, routines, and places—that amplify Black and Brown experiential knowledge and cultural practices. Early on CWHS adopted summer retreats, student organizations, and a series of protocols and routines that increased Black and Brown people's influential presence. When we started our research collaboration with CWHS, students of color participated in sports, clubs, and extracurricular activities at far lower rates than their White peers. As we facilitated an exploration of "why" the disparities existed, several explanations surfaced: CWHS held clubs and extracurricular activities before or after school. Students who relied on buses or other modes of transit they did not control participated less. Students who drove to school or had parents who dropped them off or picked them up participated more. Teachers had to be incentivized to stay before or after school. Some clubs required students to pay fees. Some early solutions were to add early and late buses. Incentivize teachers to lead clubs. Offer scholarships. It was a race-visible approach, but not race conscious.

The reforms maintained the same underlying structures that worked for the White kids they were initially designed to support. They required adults to do nothing fundamentally different. The structure demanded that students arrive early and stay late, *like White kids*. Pay the fees, *like White kids*, even if through the provision of a scholarship or fee waiver. Find a club advisor, *like White kids* do when they form their student organizations. The subtle message to students: it's on you. Take advantage of the resources and supports offered to you. If you want to participate, make the sacrifice to do so. Arrive early. Stay late. Apply for the fee waiver. These "opportunities" didn't reflect a possibility that many students' home responsibilities did not allow them to arrive early and stay late. The fee waiver itself was an additional step (barrier) to participation and potential badge of shame that reminded students of their financial need.

With racism off the table, these explanations remain insufficiently shallow and technical.

Putting race on the table clarified the problem as two-fold. On one side, White people believed that the structure worked. It was basically good. Where it was not, it could be fixed. On the other side, they believed that students who did not "take advantage of opportunities" created by the White people's fixes were perhaps unmotivated, unengaged, and possessed low aspirations. In a context of white disbelief in Black and Brown children and youth, the idea that Black and Brown people don't take advantage of opportunities leads into the abyss of white disbelief in Black and Brown people's voices, perspectives, and prerogatives. From the abyss of racist pathological thinking emerges the most pernicious, common, and racist statements that a person who is responsible for educating children and youth can make: "*They* don't care."

CWHS was designed to affirm White students' and families' voices, perspectives, and prerogatives. Developing a critique of whiteness alongside questioning racially disparate participation helped CWHS think deeply about how important the school schedule was to either reaffirming White students or making the school more racially inclusive. A member of the school's leadership team talked to us about the importance of changing the scheduling. She conveyed it as a major success in the equity reform efforts.

> One of the things that I helped do is design that schedule and then implement it. Our schedule change to block scheduling was part of our effort at inclusiveness. So now we have this access advisory thing on Mondays. Then students make choices Tuesday through Friday about either getting help from a teacher in the middle of the day or they can go to a club. I do the scheduling of that period.
>
> Since making this schedule change, we've had this huge proliferation of clubs. A lot of them do have to do with culture or, like, we have Latino Nation and we have Black Student Union and we have JustEd and we have, you know, and we also have Student Council and NHS and we have the science club. It's tons and tons of student-led stuff. It's been so cool.

I had talked with a friend who is not an educator about how hard this (equity) work could be. As White people we're trying to figure out, you know, what is it that I should be doing? She basically said, well, "I think we've got to make space . . . we gotta make space for other voices. Then we gotta get out of the way." And so one of the things that I've been really proud of is in this new schedule. I feel like we made some good space.

The student organizations and clubs that emerged in the time and spaces in the scheduling restructure became a training ground for Black and Brown students to learn about, experience, and exercise influence in ways that made their positive presence felt in the school. The school-based organizations and clubs were hubs for Black and Brown students to explore, learn to embrace, and expand their influential presence. Black Student Union. Brothers United. Central Waters Refugees Aid. Educators Rising. Gay Straight Alliance. Latino Nation. Multicultural Leadership Council. Sisters Supporting Sisters. The Asian Student Association. Students formed the Student Voice Union as an umbrella organization for all student-led groups and a site to express dissent, organize for reform and transformation, and learn.

New slogans emerged on the walls. Murals were no longer relegated to "Little Mexico." Gay Pride. Black Pride. Students used the spaces to organize, learn, and strategize. Now, if someone wrote *nigger* on the wall, it was a problem that could not simply be erased. Students in Voices Rising, their teachers, and eventually the entire school dealt with it head on. Student demand for affinity spaces made hiring adults who were eager to support student affinity groups all the more urgent.

The creation of a new schedule expanded student choice and gave students a role in deciding clubs and organizations. It shifted the school milieu toward democratic engagement between students and staff. Administrators, teachers, and students alike came to regard Black and Brown students' influential presence as a staple in professional development and decision-making circles. Within the first year of the research partnership, CWHS adopted summer retreats, student organizations, and a series of protocols and routines that increased Black and Brown people's influential presence. By the 2016–17 academic year, the school achieved a critical mass of adults who routinely sought counsel from Black and Brown students to inform school governance and decision-making. As equity practices proliferated, the school prioritized routines that ensured Black and Brown influential presence from adults and students in numerous decision-making arenas, including school improvement teams and teachers and staff hiring interview panels. In time, Black and Brown people's presence further influenced conversations about what the credit-bearing school curriculum should entail.

CONCLUSION: SUSTAINING BLACK AND BROWN PEOPLE'S INFLUENTIAL PRESENCE

Organizationwide racial learning is bolstered by the influential presence of Black and Brown people, not merely by inclusion. Black and Brown influential presence is a critical aspect of increasing the capacity for equitable school improvement. Black and Brown influential presence drove CWHS's change process. Before we started our research partnership, Black and Brown influential presence was a dormant racial resource. Going through a school where such spaces did not exist caused students racial anxiety. Countless daily incidents of mundane racial violence occurred in the school. Black and Brown students confided in a small number of adults. If anyone addressed these experiences, it was on an individualized case-by-case basis. Besides the college club, a program housed in the high school and staffed by a local nonprofit organization, there were no formal spaces where Black students gathered to have "a safe space." Racial learning was happenstance, reactionary, individualized, and privatized. If it happened at all, Ms. Moore and the students she supported made it happen. And then White people worked to erase her. After all, she was a problem.

Years later, during the 2016–17 academic year, Black and Brown influential presence proliferated in student affinity spaces and clubs; by the 2017–18 academic year, it worked its way into formal school structures. And then Black and Brown voices started rising. Racial learning proliferated. More Black and Brown voices rose. Black and Brown people's influential presence is important because it compels White educators to take steps toward creating more equitable schools. It also reveals to Black and Brown people their own inherent possibilities as evidenced in the student's statement describing the Voices Rising Social Justice course:

> Voices Rising functions not only as a new class focused on Social Justice rooted literature but also as a new platform for students of all walks of life to collaborate and have the narrative of their lived experiences, heard. Voices Rising has become a change agency that creatively fuses art, media, and literature to share the realities of silenced communities.

In a period of six years, Black and Brown people's influential presence catalyzed the school's commitment to racial equity. Non-Black people learn that Black people can teach them. People of color learn they can teach White people. Increasing Black and Brown influential presence also calls into question who benefits from its growth. Despite leveraging Black and Brown students' and people's experiences and perspectives, the school found itself fraught with racial conflicts and dilemmas. Efforts at inclusion led to occasional accusations of tokenism, which at times pitted Black school employees against Black students, parents, and community members.[4] Also because of the relatively small numeric presence of Black adults, it was often taxing for Black and Brown people to show up and actively participate in so many decision-making arenas. By conceptualizing influential presence as a dynamic capacity, we might come to analyze its growth as being less about who wins at whose expense. White people learn about race through up-close encounters that compel them to see Black and Brown people's goodness. Ultimately, White people believing and believing in Black and Brown people is good for Black and Brown students. The influential presence of Black and Brown adults, be it teachers, families, or relatively unaffected people, is also good for Black and Brown students. But as I hope to have made clear, Black and Brown people possess distinctively higher capacities to address racism. They learn to do this out of necessity and survival. This racial knowledge is a resource. White educators don't have to gain such knowledge as a matter of survival. So they are less likely to possess it. When they are asked to learn what they don't know or know less about, it leads to intense discomfort.

2

CURATED WHITE
RACIAL DISCOMFORT

*A paradigm shift starts with that uncomfortable stuff of looking at
yourself and knowing your place in a racist system and all that kind
of stuff. White people don't want to look at that. They don't have to.
Most of the time, life works for them, you know?*

—WHITE FEMALE TEACHER LEADER
(year five reflections)

Discomfort, distress, guilt, confusion, cognitive dissonance, and related experiences are critically important, indeed foundational, for
White educators to experience if we expect them to change their racialized ways of knowing. As the teacher in the opening quote conveyed,
racial discomfort occurs when people are confronted with experiences
or information that call into question the experiences, beliefs, ways of
knowing, and behaviors that define their racial socialization. For White
people, such racial experiences and encounters often arouse feelings of
vulnerability, anxiety, anger, and fear. But many White people are able to
come to terms with these emotions, especially if they come to understand
their dissonance is a central part of their racial learning. And that their
aversion to discomfort undermines their ability to grow as people. When
White people arrive at these understandings and establish an accepting
stance toward discomfort, they increase their capacity to treat people they
are not like with the dignity and respect that all people rightfully deserve.

Curated white racial discomfort refers to *racially discomforting learning experiences* that are continuous and thoughtfully planned with a purpose to transform White educators' personal and collective understandings of race and racism. Curated white racial discomfort relies on the ongoing planning and development of "dangerously safe" racial learning opportunities that contrast with conventional race-neutral change management overemphases on psychological safety. Although psychological safety is important, it is a mere part of a more meaningful whole of change. When it comes to school-based racism, White educators' psychological and emotional well-being is upheld at the expense of Black and Brown students' well-being. Thus, an essential requirement for enacting racial equity change is to ensure that White educators continually experience levels of racial discomfort that ensure their continued learning and by extension the continued betterment of learning opportunities for Black and Brown students.

The curated aspect of white racial discomfort is important because using discomfort as a learning resource requires careful attention so that it does not evolve into damaging experiences, the likes of which Black and Brown students experience too frequently. When teachers give students a challenging learning task but fail to provide adequate learning resources—a supportive learning community, appropriate scaffolding, time to process and engage in sense-making, opportunities to learn from mistakes, relevant context for why the learning task is important, and so forth—the learning challenge can easily turn into destructive learning experiences. The key to curating racial learning is to provide adequate resources to help people see the experiential learning value in what, without careful curation, would otherwise become destructive racial learning experiences that lead to unwieldy racial discomfort.

In this chapter I convey how cultivating curated white racial discomfort increased Central Waters High School's capacity to become a more equitable school. I weave through the story of corners of discomfort that begin with a facilitated activity my research team and I facilitated during the 2013–14 summer data retreat. I explain how racializing the school's problems created corners of discomfort that forced members of CWHS to choose a corner and take a principled stand. I center the voices of a group of teacher leaders who early began to see themselves and their White colleagues as *part* of a system that produced racial experiences and disparate outcomes that defined their school. This group became ambassadors that catalyzed the equity leadership work at CWHS. Throughout, many CWHS educators left the school for new jobs, dissociated from the equity efforts, organized to oust the principal, or retired. Simultaneously, many worked through the discomfort. They examined it. They learned from it. They learned with it. In doing so, they discovered that perhaps they could do better and be better for their Black and Brown students, for one another, and for their selves.

I amplify White people's varied approaches to dealing with racial discomfort as a means to substantiate it as a resource from which equity reform change becomes possible (or not). I analyze what White people at CWHS did with the white racial discomfort that emerged from learning about racism and white supremacy: they evaded it, they ignored it, they sought to understand it, and they consciously worked to leverage it. But, as I show, they never overcame it. And this posed a dilemma. Since it is a resource, overcoming discomfort is not a desirable outcome because doing so puts the resource back into a dormant state. When White people get comfortable, white supremacy resumes its normalization. White racial discomfort keeps racism and white supremacy on display, in consciousness, and thus available for continued critique and challenge. In other words, the goal is to do more than start a paradigm shift. The objective is to sustain it.

CREATING CORNERS: UNFREEZING CENTRAL WATERS

The first time we intentionally curated a space for White people to experience discomfort was the 2013–14 summer data retreat. We spent the full 2013–14 academic year collecting data that we used to plan the three-day volunteer-based professional development. The retreat convened the districts' director of student services, its newly hired equity director, Elizabeth (the building principal), returning associate principal Ethan, and three new associate principals—Donnell, Andrea, and Owk. Twenty teachers and four students also attended. The retreat offered three days of intensive study and learning about the problems and disparities we unearthed during our first year of surveys, observations, interviews, and focus groups. Our goal was two-fold. First, we wanted to cofacilitate a data analysis process that would yield areas of focus for improvement. Second, we wanted to unfreeze the organization to knock it out of its racial equilibrium—although we didn't explain it this way. We prepared data packets that reflected what we learned about student and adult culture and climate problems.

We opened the morning of the data retreat with a "taking corners" activity that laid the initial groundwork for the racial learning we planned for later. Kathy, a White female member of our research team, facilitated a collective agreements conversation and asked people to share their hopes and fears via a word splash. After Kathy finalized these standard practices of racial equity retreating, it was my turn to wade into the thorny topic we came to address: race and racism. I began: "On your papers, write down what comes to mind when you hear the word *Race. Racism. Culture.* What does it mean to be culturally responsive? Competent? Take ten minutes to respond to these questions." Five minutes elapsed, after which I invited participants to share their notes with at least two other people in the room.

In a room where the attendees were predominantly White, the responses varied widely. Sherman, a White male veteran teacher, wrote, "ignorance, privilege, selfishness." Amanda, a White woman, wrote, "Race: diversity, culture, separate, unique. Racism: segregation, bullying, power." Donnell, the newly appointed Black male associate principal, wrote: "us vs them, Black vs White, difficult conversations, the act of engaging in activities that disenfranchise or marginalizes individuals/groups/or communities based solely on the color of their skin." It was Donnell's first day on the job. It was not lost on me that he responded in a more elaborate and sophisticated manner than any other person in the room, who were mostly White people. Either he knew more, or he was willing to say more. Perhaps both. The initial activities helped us assess people's understanding and willingness to share. Quickly, we wanted to accelerate their learning. We came in committed to not spending three days, or even three hours for that matter, having people develop autobiographies to convince themselves they were White. Upbringings, past experiences, beliefs, and opinions are an important starting place for racial learning. But we took it upon ourselves to show and tell them they were White, explain how they became White and why, and convey what that becoming meant for them and people they are not like.

To start, I engaged attendees in a quick group activity to demonstrate the power of socializing experiences: "I will say a word. I ask you to repeat it. Then spell it. Then repeat it again. I will then ask a question. Answer the question." I moved them into a rhythmic call and response to condition their answers. As I expected, a room full of attentive people incorrectly answered questions they should be able to correctly answer. What do you do at a green light? "Stop!" They yelled. I did the activity multiple times and still they responded incorrectly. I conditioned their responses. They found humor in how easily I conditioned them, in a matter of forty-five seconds, to associate incorrect responses with otherwise simple questions. I explained to them that I was in a position of power to shape their responses. Even after I forewarned them about exactly what I was doing, they found it difficult to correctly answer the question.

"If I can condition you to make these associations in forty-five seconds, imagine what your lifetime of being conditioned to believe White is good and Black is bad has done to your capacity to relate with people you are not like," I rhetorically asked. We debriefed the exercise. We took a break before I lectured for one hour and thirty minutes. I started by drawing their attention to their racial conditioning and socialization exercise and what it can teach us about racism in schools.

A lot of educators say "We're going to be culturally responsive," but they haven't done the cultural and racial awareness work that will allow them to be more conscious and responsive. So we're going to talk a lot about race, culture, and the concept of racialization, racism, and white supremacy. My goal is to relate race and racialization to culture generally and school culture specifically, and the implications of teaching and learning.

I then moved into my main points. One. Race, like other aspects of culture, is socially constructed. Five hundred years ago, there were no Black people. There were no White people. Because the construct of race did not yet exist. Of course, different humans had different skin tones and phenotypes. But Europeans in their quest for global colonial domination developed the practice of identifying humans by racial categories to justify their genocide, enslavement, and exploitation of the globe. Racial categorizations are a consequence of Europeans' intention to dominate people. Race and racism were refined and solidified in the United States.[1] Racial categorizations were and remain unnatural. You are racialized to be White. You are racialized to be Asian. I am racialized to be Black. These categorizations are so well constructed and institutionally sanctioned that they now imprison us. Two. Interlocking institutions (family, schooling, labor, religions) socialize us to associate and conflate racial categorizations with certain character attributes, belief systems, values, and cultural practices. It is not natural that White is associated with cleanliness, innocence, and redemption. It is not natural that Black is associated with dirtiness, deviance, and deterioration. Three.

The cultural practices that emerge from your belief system, ways of thinking and being stem from your racial socialization. In other words, your belief system is a racial belief system. Your cultural forms are racial formations. You treat White students as though they are naturally innocent and intelligent. You treat Black students as though they are naturally deviant and unintelligent.

The fact that you're primarily concerned with achieving discipline through controlling Black students' bodies—removing them from one place, containing them in another, instituting rules that have little to do with the educative mission of schools—rather than engaging their intellect underscores my point. Your inability to name and challenge this socialization maintains the structures of white supremacy. White people behave like and believe they are superior to people who they are not phenotypically like.

I told them what I call devastating truths about racism, white supremacy, its adverse impacts on our abilities to be our best human selves. I expected people to recoil. Of course, the lecture was more nuanced than I have room to present here. I offered concrete examples to support my claims; showed brief video clips; and asked them to pause, write, and think about the content of the lecture in relation to their own lives and experiences. The content discomforted people. And so did I. This was not lost on me. I was a Black man telling White people their racial history, narrating how they came to be in relation to me. The discomfort was thick. Faces were red. Arms were folded. Brows were raised. Lips and mouths were clinched. People read each other. They looked to me in ways that reflected disbelief, embarrassment, and surprise. Over the years I became known as someone who "just says what it is." But at the time, we were only two hours into the retreat. I concluded the lecture by asking participants to consider: "What information that I presented in the lecture nagged you, bothered you, or triggered a visceral response. Whatever it was, note it. Write it down. . . . And then let's take a break."

After everyone returned from their break, we offered people a chance to debrief the lecture with an elbow partner. Deirdre, a Black woman and member of our research team, facilitated by offering instructions for the taking corners activity:

> We practiced this activity earlier this morning during our ice-breaker. I will read several statements and ask that you indicate your response by moving to the Disagree, Agree, or Undecided area of the room that represents your answer. If you agree, move to that section and so on.
>
> Once you are in your group, you will have approximately five minutes to develop a position statement, which you will then share with the entire group. Your statement cannot exceed two minutes. You are not allowed to comment or react verbally as groups share their position statements. After all groups have presented a statement, we will open the floor for conversation and debate.

If at any time during the activity, you are swayed by a position or statement, you can move to a new side of the room that represents your shifting stance. This morning, we practiced with a few fun statements. . . . "I like to take selfies. . . ." "This year our NFL team will make it to the playoffs." At this point I will read several statements that will invite you to share your beliefs and about the problems that impact the school. . . . Is everyone ready?

"We hold the same academic expectations for all students. . . ."

My lecture opened wounds. And now Deirdre, a Black woman, poured salt into them. The playful banter that filled the room earlier in the morning, and that diminished during the course of my lecture, now was fully given over to a stern seriousness. Deirdre's questions invited CWHS's past experiences, their fears of what was to come, and the grief of the loss of their school into the present moment. The activity reflected the school's historical pattern of racial equity trainings going about as "badly as it can go." Over time, we learned that in years past, the trend was "outside people coming in and training us [Central Waters' educators] on culture, most of them abject disasters that probably did more damage" than good.

"Old" Racial Equity Training Wounds

We were at our first retreat. But CWHS was *here* before. During the 2011–12 academic year, a group of teachers formed an Equity team to address many of the same concerns that students shared about their experiences of racism. The teachers, all of them White, were White allies who vigorously vocalized their support for Black and Brown students. They supported Ms. Moore. They unapologetically critiqued Elizabeth. "She knows the problems. She doesn't care. She doesn't listen at all. She doesn't even come into classrooms." They spoke up often at site council meetings in support of students. They encouraged students to do the same. And they did. "We are experiencing racism at this school and it's unfair." The site council members would sit and listen. They would not respond. Elizabeth was tired of their complaining. They're a bunch of "negative complainers." When CWHS was served with a notice of civil rights violations, it legitimated the concerns the small group of White allies had long expressed: CWHS is racist. Elizabeth is not committed. And the students deserve better.

The next year, now forced to take action, the newly formed Equity team, which included several White allies, attended School Equity Solutions' achieving racial equity and closing achievement gaps professional development for school leaders and teachers.[2] Equity team members who participated in the off-site professional development session described their experience as "powerful." They excavated and explored their racial autobiographies, learned about their unearned racial privilege, and developed a shared language for talking about race and racism. The Equity team members returned to CWHS with a transformed sense of urgency, hope for change, and some critical tools for making change happen. But their tools did not match the walls of resistance they encountered upon their return. The problem was *those* colleagues who didn't share their sense of urgency or have the tools to effect change. Leaders refused to listen and instead focused on making the numbers look good. Colleagues thought racism was acts of meanness. Many intentionally wanted to uphold the status quo. Perhaps if everyone attended the same training, people could get on the same page? The Equity team decided that all teachers and leaders would benefit from a School Equity Solutions racial learning workshop. And with the window of opportunity the consent decree offered, it made perfect sense to push for a full staff training.

The Equity team worked with administrators to schedule an on-site session. It turned out disastrous. People spoke cryptically, never quite naming their experience or what made it a disaster. One White teacher explained, "Some guy came in to do a racial equity and culture professional development session and, oh God, it was a disaster. He did the color line activity in an all-staff meeting . . . up on the auditorium stage. He didn't do it in a very sensitive manner. People were absolutely furious and complained afterward." A White teacher leader explained, "There was one professional development where the facilitator said, 'Okay, who's a person of color? And who's not?' Then the facilitator asked the people of color to all stand on the stage in the auditorium while all the White people stared at them. . . . I was like 'What is happening? This can't be what we're supposed to be doing?'" People talked to me about the line-up activity every year of the project. Although I never gained a clear sense of exactly what happened the day in question, I was clear on this: whatever happened was an epically bad racial episode that left everyone involved in dismay. It was a harmful experience that wounded their community. Here we were *back there*. Deirdre read additional statements aloud:

> We treat all students the same when it comes to discipline. . . . It is difficult to engage our racial and ethnic minority students. . . . I feel comfortable engaging in difficult conversations about race and racism.

The trepidation in the room was palpable. Folks moved into the corners that represented their positions and which ultimately forced them to explain those positions. The statements elicited varied reactions. Some stood thinking and were slow to move while others hurried into their chosen corners. At each turn, people "read" the room, exchanged glances to determine which corner was safe. Teachers who earlier in the morning collegially chatted with one another dispersed to opposing corners. There was no safe corner. Only the one they chose. While some held tightly to the idea of CWHS exceptionality, others called *the way*— the school mission and vision—a bluff:

> **White female teacher:** I'm thinking about the vision and mission statement that we spent a year writing and developing. For a student, I don't even think they understand what it means. So when you say a shared vision, I think the students have to understand it too because I think that's where a lot of these discipline issues come in. Students don't feel the relevance of why . . . whether it's the cell phone, the hat, if they're just a few minutes late. It's just because it's a rule.
>
> **White male teacher:** The problem is that a true shared vision isn't seventeen carefully word-smithed words in a handbook, but that's what we say it is, and that's what we pretend that we do.

Elizabeth stood listening as teacher after teacher pronounced things like "We pretend" and "We're not serious." Every statement cut deeper,

causing Elizabeth and Suzanne, the district's director of student services, extreme discomfort. The comments destroyed the tidy idea of *Central Waters family* that dominated the Midwest nice community. What
CWHS wanted to be, how it fashioned itself, and what it actually was
differed. The retreat suggested at every turn of a corner that CWHS was
a school community multiply divided and complex. It was divided along
lines of racial experience. While it possessed a tragically low number of
Black and Brown educators, it possessed no monolith of White people.
If CWHS was a family, it was one divided along lines of racial ideology. White people starkly disagreed with White people. Again, we asked,
"What did you experience, hear, or see today that nagged you, bothered
you, or triggered a visceral response? Whatever it was, note it." We spent
the final hour of day one introducing the carefully compiled data packets
we used to facilitate the group's day two and three systems analysis of
problems.

For the next two days of the retreat, participants spent dedicated and
repeated blocks of time exploring their school system as a metaphorical
tree, as outlined in figure 2.1. Our goal was to give retreat participants an
opportunity to make sense of the visible and invisible systemic factors
that made CWHS an institution that produced racist experiences and
outcomes. We broke teams into small groups to complete a tree. We
asked them to map the various data sources—outcomes, experiences,
practices, underlying beliefs, and social structures—onto a tree image.
We didn't ask them to develop the tree image in any particular way. The
goal was to help them "see" the constituent parts of the system that they
worked within by discussing the system. We reasoned that anyone who
cannot see the system and its interrelated parts cannot challenge it. We
used the tree framework because it provides a useful way of linking theory,
data, policy, and everyday practice. It also demonstrated the importance
of conceptualizing the interrelatedness of underlying root problems and
the ways that culture, climate, and outcomes (data trends and patterns)
reflect deep-seated beliefs and problems in the school community.

During the final retreat activity, participants combined their hypoth-
esized root causes into a systems analysis tree image we created by com-
bining six pages of flip charts into a 2-by-6-foot poster (the verbatim

FIGURE 2.1   Tree systems analysis

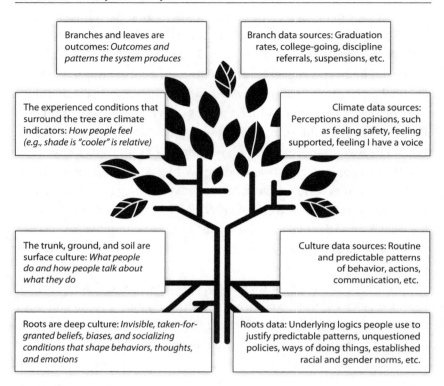

Branches and leaves are outcomes: *Outcomes and patterns the system produces*

Branch data sources: Graduation rates, college-going, discipline referrals, suspensions, etc.

The experienced conditions that surround the tree are climate indicators: *How people feel (e.g., shade is "cooler" is relative)*

Climate data sources: Perceptions and opinions, such as feeling safety, feeling supported, feeling I have a voice

The trunk, ground, and soil are surface culture: *What people do and how people talk about what they do*

Culture data sources: Routine and predictable patterns of behavior, actions, communication, etc.

Roots are deep culture: *Invisible, taken-for-granted beliefs, biases, and socializing conditions that shape behaviors, thoughts, and emotions*

Roots data: Underlying logics people use to justify predictable patterns, unquestioned policies, ways of doing things, established racial and gender norms, etc.

content that administrators, teachers, and students wrote onto the poster are presented in figure 2.2). The content was useful. But the process and experiences of creating the tree were just as important as the outcome.

When the Equity team attended the professional development, they had a powerful experience. They gained clarity on language, left with specific tools for improvement. They returned believing that their colleagues who did not attend were the problems. But they did not think of the fact perhaps they didn't learn much. They were White allies. Their learning experience merely confirmed what they already believed and clarified much of what they already knew. While the White allies were discomforted by the racism they witnessed daily at the school, and with the behaviors of their ignorant and outwardly racist colleagues, they were not discomforted in their own racial learning. They were not learning

FIGURE 2.2   Concerns surfaced through systems analysis

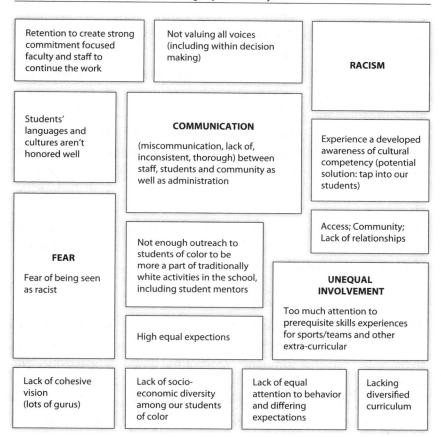

much. When people are not afforded opportunities to learn, frustration sets in. It becomes easy to see what everyone else is doing or not doing and ultimately to judge and point fingers, especially if they are not doing what you think or want them to do. The insistence that "others do as I do, think as I think, be as I am" is a cornerstone of white supremacy: you should be like me.

The difference between the data retreat and the Equity team's learning is that we curated a space that intended to radically hold differences rather than sameness—yes, even those we did not agree with. The objective to not fix each other or change each other is what caused discomfort.

This is counternormative for White people, because many White people, allies included, are hell-bent on changing people to fit into their white racial ideology, image, and ways of being. Hold Black students to the same standards that we hold White students to. If we let White students wear headphones, Latinx students should be able to do the same. Black and Brown students should be in AP like White students. And on and on into an abyss of white belief in everything White, including how to be a White antiracist ally. No matter what kind of whiteness it is, White people are socialized to deem unworthy and disposable people who cannot or will not mold themselves to their preferred way of being. But for three days, the disparate group of people showed up, unable to dispose and dismiss one another. And Elizabeth, who almost everyone described as opinionated and dismissive, had to listen. There was no meeting to run to or office door to close. We stayed together. As the 2014 data retreat ended, the sustained discomfort was just beginning.

Racial Discomfort as a Learning Resource

We spent the retreat asking White people to become uncomfortable in the work. I soon had my own turn. After the retreat, our immediate next step was to prepare a summary report of retreat learning activities and outcomes for distribution to CWHS faculty and staff. But before we could even convene our research team to begin sorting through the wealth of materials required to prepare a report, Deirdre and I found ourselves in our own respective corners, pitted opposite of Elizabeth and Suzanne. I emailed the administrative team to schedule a meeting to discuss next steps. Elizabeth replied, "We have concerns about next steps." Discomfort welled up within me. The next day, I sat in my office. Deirdre joined me for our conference call. Elizabeth's frustration pierced through the speaker phone.

> **Elizabeth:** That was not what I was expecting. The whole time I'm
> there I'm thinking, "What the ----- is happening here? What do you
> think you accomplished?" We're confused about how all of this
> is supposed to work. Where are the solutions that will help our
> students?

Suzanne: This was not a direction we were expecting from this work. We want to understand. We've had so many negative experiences. Let me use my "I" statements. I don't want this to be another line activity experience.

Elizabeth: That corners activity was a bunch of complaining. . . . We're supposed to be solving problems.

I collected myself.

Decoteau: Well . . . we didn't get to the point where we outlined goals like I expected we would. But we've repeatedly talked about this as adaptive work. The reason I . . . (cut off before finished)

Elizabeth: I feel like we didn't focus at all on the students. Our responsibility is not to the adults. What about the students? It's supposed to be student-centered.

When we designed the retreat, we conceptualized *participants' experiences* as an important text for learning. We spent the remainder of the call outlining the intent behind the retreat activities, including why we asked everyone to come in relaxed attire. We did this before the retreat. But clearly, we needed to double back and elaborate. We asked attendees to dress in regular relaxed clothes because the leadership culture we observed in our first several months was top-down, technical, and directive. Teachers feared Elizabeth and other administrators. As one teacher explained in our exit interviews: "We were always being told what to do, versus working together collaboratively to get to a certain place. The feeling in the building four years ago, five years ago, was a very negative one." As for the communication lines between the staff and administration: "It was very closed and it led to a lot of animosity." We designed a process to exploit these points of tension and make them useful for the purposes of learning. The congenial thing to do would have been to play into the Midwest nice culture and plan two full days to make people feel good, to temporarily escape from CWHS's many conflicts. We did not go into the retreat to overcome their problems. We just wanted them to notice them and acknowledge them.

We worked to show them their school's problems in as many ways as possible, including experientially. Further, we wanted administrators and teachers to learn that their positional authority shaped their practices and interactions, stifled certain voices, and smothered dissenting perspectives. Instead of giving the administrators a reading about the blind spots their positional authority causes, we instructed administrators to defer to teacher and staff voices. We asked teachers to "let students weigh in first and have the final word." To administrators, we constantly repeated, "This is a friendly reminder to allow teachers the opportunity to talk first. Give them time to exhaust their thoughts before you chime in." Given the number of students, teachers, and administrators who attended, teachers talked most over the three days. By day three, attendees reminded one another "to get students opinions first." Deferring to others is a practice. "How did it feel to practice listening to people you normally don't listen to? What did you notice about yourself when you did it? What did you notice about others?"

As Elizabeth, Suzanne, Deirdre, and I talked through the purpose of various retreat activities, we made it a point to circle back to Elizabeth's question: *What do you think you accomplished?* Administrators listened to teachers. Teachers listened to students. Students listened to teachers and administrators. Teachers listened to one another. And so on. People shared how they felt about the school's problems. Publicly. Listening causes discomfort until one develops the capacity to listen to those whom they are socialized to not listen to, such as organizational subordinates. Everyone in the retreat listened to the varied and competing perspectives that emerged from different corners. At CWHS, these were major accomplishments, even if unconventional ones. Before the retreat, people did not publicly share their views about the school. And our facilitation laid a groundwork for people to voice their concerns. Making privately held views public made them available for organizational learning.[3] The recurring themes of race, school climate, feelings of inadequate support from administrators, teachers' want for order and control, administrators' want for teachers to proactively relate to students, and the fear of racial conflict pervaded the retreat conversations. Elizabeth was devastated by what she heard.

During the call, it dawned on me that we were still retreating and learning. The retreat experience—and the discomfort of it—transcended the three days. We used our hour-long phone call to coprocess the experience. We stood in our corners. We listened to the other side. We each struggled a bit, going back and forth, creating a fuller articulation of the retreat's meanings and outcomes. We were two White women, a Black man, and a Black woman in conflict about what *we*, two Black people, had accomplished for a group of predominantly White educators. It was a power struggle that caused me to fear that a mere eight months into our work, *my* research project was in jeopardy. I publicly shared:

> I just want you to know I hear your concerns. I sense we're at an impasse of sorts about whether the way we suggest going about the work is beneficial to you or the school. If we're using an inquiry approach, I can't guarantee any particular experience or outcomes. All of us have to weigh the potential benefits of the project against the potential harms. Clearly the retreat caused you significant distress.
>
> I have an ethical obligation to remind you both that your participation is voluntary and you can withdraw yourselves and the school from the study at any point for any reason, including asking me not to return. I hope that won't be the case. I want to continue the project, but you need to know should you determine it's not worth the discomfort or risk, I understand.

We reached no resolution during the call about whether the retreat was "a success" or not. It was what it was. Its eventual effects remained to be seen. But even so, the discomforting call *meant something*. The fact that the call happened in the form it did signaled that the retreat was doing what it was supposed to do in sustaining discomfort and giving all of us an opportunity to build our capacity to fall out without cutting each other down. If the retreat had not worked, we would have not grappled trying to make sense of our individual and collective experiences. Our conversation was not the last of its kind, although as we moved forward, we were less frequently caught off guard by disagreements. It increased our capacity for later and continued conflict. At the end of the call, we all recommitted to owning the difficulty and discomfort of the work ahead. Elizabeth let us know she heard us: "No quick results. It's a process. I'm gonna have to trust the process."

The call was a pivotal moment in my relationship with two powerful influencers in the district. Our conversation underscored the very real fact that initial (and ongoing) "meetings with the boss of the school are critical." Admittedly, the conversation filled me with self-doubt. Elizabeth committed to trusting the process. But by the conversation's end, I wasn't sure I trusted the process enough to ask anyone else to. And I was glad I was a research partner and coinquirer. The stance gave me permission to be a learner throughout my time with CWHS. I imagined that I or any consultant might have been fired for the retreat. It was an important lesson. Consultants and experts had to take a knower's stance that put them in a position to fix people and solve problems. I, on the other hand, could know plenty but not be an expert. After the call, I became more intentional to remain curious, to colearn, and to take a learner's stance in a quest to seek understanding and knowledge right alongside CWHS educators who thought my influential presence might benefit. The learner's stance proved particularly important because the following academic year was fast-moving, unwieldy, and filled with twists and turns none of us anticipated.

UNWIELDY RACIAL DISCOMFORT

In the 2014–15 academic year, I witnessed White middle class people go to war against White middle class people about the future of the school. The combativeness yielded what I refer to as unwieldy white racial discomfort, that which is unplanned, unexpected, remains unprocessed, and therefore leads to destructive rather than educative ends. It is a type of discomfort that, when experienced, people prefer to remain in their corners, opt out of participation, and actively resist exploring what their discomfort offers in the way of learning and growth. In October 2014, we submitted a summary report that outlined the learning activities, systems analysis, process, and outcomes. The report presented a summary of what retreat participants theorized as a complex layered problem of school-based racism:

> Unequal access to school based opportunities is the primary problem the school must address.[4] Unequal access persists because of relational and structural inequalities.[5] Relational and structural inequalities persist because of a communication problem—the inability and unwillingness of people to talk about, listen, and honor the difficulties and discomfort that many teachers and staff have with a growing population of Black and Latino students.[6] Why are people not willing to communicate?
>
> Because increased communication would reveal and require the school to confront racism—the belief that white middle class values, norms, beliefs, and ways of being are inherently better than those of "others." Fear, denial, and defensiveness about racism have become commonplace in the school. The fear of being called a racist is pervasive. Fear leads to avoidance of addressing specific students' behaviors, talking openly and honestly with colleagues, and voicing concerns to administrators, parents, and students.
>
> Students of color and their families are also fearful of the high school because it has the reputation as a racist school in a racist district. The challenges associated with racism in society are not going to go away. There will be discomfort and conflict in the school. (*Excerpt from Data Retreat Report*)

We elaborated a concern that "the full school community has yet to engage in an honest and thoughtful conversation about the challenges and possibilities that accompanied the districts' changing racial demographics." Some received the report as a manifesto against the race-neutral colorblind way CWHS "did" school. The reactions and resistance to the release of the report, the narrative it constructed, and what it stood for were immediate and prolonged. The five members of my research team took great care to capture the precise ways that participants talked about the school's problems. Although the analysis we presented stemmed from retreat participants' exact explanations—a majority were teachers and the facilitation approach ensured their voices were prominent—opponents directed their ire toward our research team but to a much greater extent to the school's administrators.

One White teacher who attended the retreat wrote me a curt email: "Your report is not a reflection of our community. We are not racist. And I don't like that you characterized us that way." As I processed the email, I thought to myself, "Okay . . . but I have three days' worth of audio files, hand-written notes, and reflections of you and your colleagues saying that the problems the school faced were a consequence of racism, racist practices, and so on?" I didn't respond with that thought. I was not willing to take a side in a white-on-white war. I convinced myself I was a facilitator and messenger. The fight was theirs to have. So I wrote back, "Thanks for taking the time to read the report and thanks for sharing your concern."

The emails I received were miniscule compared to the backlash administrators experienced. It proved to be a year of intensive trial-by-fire learning. Teachers and parents organized a campaign to oust Elizabeth from her position as the building principal. White parents packed board meetings to yell down Elizabeth, Ethan, and whoever else they viewed as responsible for bringing CWHS "down." Teachers conducted an independent survey on teachers' satisfaction with Elizabeth's performance. Elizabeth found out about the survey after teachers delivered it and an accompanying letter to the superintendent and board stating their lack of confidence in her leadership decisions and proposed direction for the school. With a staff of nearly two hundred people, hardening factions, covert in-fighting, and the ever-looming prospect of more resignations, aspirations for a more equitable school waned. While adults figured out their corners and positions, students continued to suffer. What really, besides an intense conversation between administrators and research, did the first year's data collection and retreat accomplish?

TEACHER AMBASSADORS

Our town used to be rural and White. But it has expanded. So you have growing pains in the city as well as in this school. I wasn't there, but I heard that at the first retreat almost everyone cried. It was emotional and people who were there had healing from. As awful at it sounded, I think the whole staff should go through that sort of retreat experience because it was the folks who attended it that initiated a healing process for the entire school.

—WHITE FEMALE TEACHER (year six reflection interviews)

The CWHS teacher and staff ambassadors, as they called themselves, all attended the 2014 summer data retreat. The small group of teacher leaders self-initiated an informal leadership vanguard that busied themselves with supporting students, colleagues, and administrators. The group was composed of White allies, people generally interested in improving the workplace, and folks who took up a learning stance. The group held various levels of racial consciousness, understandings of how racism works, and as I later learned, some people who covertly cared little about racial equity. A teacher and White ally revealed to me that a teacher ambassador pulled her aside one day and said "I don't believe in white privilege" and "students of color are lazy." There was not a vetting process for being an ambassador. They did not take a pledge. We didn't have a sense of what any of them believed. But we did know that all of them shared the common experience of attending the 2014 summer data retreat.

Drawing on the curated discomfort they experienced during the retreat and the outcomes of the root cause activities, they gave their initial efforts to improving schoolwide communication. They theorized that increased and higher quality communication would reveal and require the school to confront racism. Though they never developed a formal "charge," they leveraged frank open talk and honest communication with colleagues. They expressed wanting transparency, timeliness, consistency, and openness. They voiced concerns to administrators, parents, and students. They also practiced listening to the various expressions of concern that circulated within CWHS. Their role in the school—and in particular their demonstrated willingness to continually turn toward and work through discomfort—proved essential to the school's eventual transformation. A pivotal breakthrough happened when the ambassador group studied the book *How the Way We Talk Can Change the Way We Work* by Kegan and Lahey.

Since the group left the retreat determined to increase their capacity for effective and transformational conversation, our research team busied ourselves with planning learning around organizational communication. Kathy, a member of our research team, conducted research to identify resources that might help. She recommended Kegan and Lahey's *How the Way We Talk Can Change the Way We Work*. The ambassadors and our research team dove into the text. It was a good choice. The ambassadors and even our research team (we studied the book right alongside the ambassador group) benefitted from the concrete meta-cognition tools that leveraged changing language choices a strategy to push past organizational inertia. Specifically, the ambassadors found the complaints to commitments mapping process easy to understand, simple to model and explain, and powerful to practice. It offered a common cognitive schema that guided the transformation of how people self-talked and talked with one another. It was good. Very good. But not perfect. It was race-neutral. It ignored the deeply racialized commitment that White people have for safety and comfort, even when these wants undermine justice. With these critiques in mind, the ambassadors designed their first learning opportunities for their colleagues:

> We have developed a facilitated Community Building Conversations Series. The conversations series will provide a space for staff and school leaders to engage in conversations related to school climate and discipline with a focus on developing the capacity to be more relational. Dr. Irby and his research team will co-facilitate along with ambassadors.
>
> The sessions will build on specific feedback we received after the November school-wide professional development. The emphasis of the sessions will be on modeling and "practicing" effective communication. All willing and committed members of the school community are welcome to attend. Participants must commit to attending all three sessions over the next four months.

They carried out the teacher-led action-oriented learning series in small teams. They theorized about the role of improving communication in improving school climate, relationships, discipline, and racial equity.

They used Kegan and Lahey's immunity to change mapping process to increase their awareness of their own thinking and tested their assumptions.[7] Ambassadors paired themselves with teachers to read, discuss, and map their immunities to change. They enacted their learning by taking on mini-challenges that required them to step into the discomfort of challenging the assumptions that held them from having meaningful authentic relationships, an expectation that was outlined in the invitation: "Participants will be issued challenges to incorporate what they learn into their practice with their colleagues and students." In the first session participants handed around a sack filled with unknown challenges (see figure 2.3). We observed and engaged alongside participants. We supported as needed and upon request.

They grew accustomed to talking about their experiences and taking on the challenges. They knew that after each session they would be challenged to work through something that was discomforting. People sat back. They laughed. And then literally accepted another challenge. As one teacher commented, "I think it's just great to have these conversations. I feel reinforced having staff members all on the same page. I don't get a sense of that in my day-to-day existence and coming here having these conversations is reaffirming." They found comfort in knowing several other people undertook the challenges and that the discomfort was

FIGURE 2.3　Sample mini-challenges

Challenge A: Start over with a colleague you don't like. Tell him or her you want to "start over." If needed, apologize (but be authentic and honest). Make a verbal commitment to her or him. Reflect. Come to next session prepared to share your experience and learning.

Challenge B: Start over with a student you don't like. Tell him or her you want to "start over." Apologize (but be authentic and honest). Make a verbal commitment to her or him. Reflect. Come to next session prepared to share your experience and learning.

Challenge C: Ask your three most behaviorally challenging students how they want you to *be* with them. Listen. Ask clarifying questions. Share what you learned in your conversation with at least 2 colleagues. Reflect. Come to next session prepared to share your experience and learning.

Challenge D: Use the talking guidelines for ONE week. Share your experiences with at least 2 colleagues or students. Reflect. Come to next session prepared to share your experience and learning.

curated, allowing them to try something dangerous by white standards, reflect on it, and return to make sense of their experiences.

> **Teacher 1:** What is our next challenge?
>
> **Ambassador:** If you get the same challenge you had last time, please exchange with somebody.
>
> **Teacher 2:** All the same ones potentially. I did do mine. I just have a good one this time. Oh, this is perfect.
>
> **Teacher 1:** I got the same one.
>
> **Ambassador:** Exchange with someone.
>
> **Teacher 3:** I can't exchange with you because I already had that one.
>
> **Teacher 1:** This one wasn't too good the first time. It didn't go well. You and I can practice.

Outside of the sessions, the school remained a site of unwieldy discomfort. The time ambassadors spent engaged in spaces of discomforting learning helped them to cope with the unwieldy racial experiences that happened both within and beyond the walls of the school. In one session, teachers' conversation turned to the problem of police-inflicted violence against Black boys and young men happening in the local community. The increased number of Black males attending the school meant the police brutality that, in years past, was easy to ignore was ever present in the school. The tension thickened as teachers discussed the racialized incidents and the effects they had on their own efforts to navigate the different corners that people used to make sense of police shootings. "Why do *they* run?" "Did he have drugs in his system?" And on and on down the abyss of white disbelief in Black and Brown people that justifies police shootings of Black and Brown people.

The self-study spaces evolved into opportunities to reflect on the shifting racial dynamics of school life. Teachers learned to relinquish power. They began to realize that students needed time and space to process police shootings.

> **Ambassador 1:** One thing that stood out to me is the intensity that we've experienced since our last meeting. We had two weeks in a row of

policing-related incidents. Three of our students were involved: two former and one current that I know of.

Ambassador 2: Then to have the shooting [a police shooting of an unarmed Black college student near the campus of a local university] the following week impacted the climate and students. On one hand, I could feel the desire to communicate differently and hope that the climate could be different. Then I also could feel that "Us, Them" and my reactions to that "Us, Them" is not wanting to accept that people could see these events differently. I mean that little small ego like "I'm right and they're wrong," that part. It's been a painfully perfect month to be conscious of others.

Ambassador 3: That's something that I was thinking about last night too. A lot has happened since we were last together. If nothing else, those kinds of things [police shootings of Black people] have provided opportunities to talk. I just fear that I don't want to slip back to old routines. Not only for myself but for us as a school.

Ambassador 2: I think that students appreciated. Wait, I'm making an assumption here. But I think students appreciated having those cards to write on. I think students appreciated, or felt like they had a little bit of a voice. I think it also helped us . . . well, it helped me to see the range of perspectives when I read the cards. Then thinking about our students represent our school and our community and our state as far as the spectrum being so wide. One thing I will say about myself is that when I read the student reactions, I did feel surprised but I didn't feel judgmental because it was just kind of eye opening. Wow, people really do feel that way and we have to respect that. We have to move from that point.

I never learned exactly what the cards said, what surprised the ambassadors, or what they found eye-opening. The important point was that teachers did the work of asking and listening rather than assuming. But asking, listening, and noticing generate more complex problems. Being conscious of what others think and believe is more problematic than not knowing. White people who experience the "pain of being conscious of others" find themselves in a dilemma that is par for the course for Black and Brown people. What should a person do when they know "I'm right and they're wrong"? Black and Brown people wrestle with this very question as a matter of life. Black and Brown students at CWHS wrestled with the question daily. Kevin did. "Should I tell Ms. Moore what this cafeteria worker did? Should I tell the cafeteria worker that she was wrong?" Janae, Tameka, Treyvon, and Yasmeen knew what happened in their class was wrong. "Should we tell Ms. Moore what happened?" The capacity to see racism and know white supremacy is a burden that Black and Brown people bear with great disproportion. The ambassadors' understanding of this perpetual dilemma grew. So did their frustration. They were in the discomfort of being damned if they did and damned if they didn't.

Unwieldy Discomfort

During the 2014–15 academic year, ambassadors, administrators, and teachers who volunteered to participate in the professional learning series routinely engaged in the kinds of collective reflection, critical self-appraisals, and commitment to undertake discomforting racial experiences for the purposes of learning. The commitments were not school-wide. The overwhelming majority of teachers and staff were not and did not want to be involved. In a stark break with years past, teachers made an effort to work with Elizabeth and the new associate principals. This was a problem. During the 2017–18 year, teachers, all White women, reflected on the various reasons they were not comfortable with the work ambassadors led:

> I had a good friend and colleague of mine go to the first summer retreat where everything blew up. It was really emotional, really intense, no guard rails. That sounded horrific to me. As a conflict avoider and someone who is new to the school, I wanted to understand what was going on before I went and put myself in the midst of that work. So I wasn't interested.

> At first it was difficult for me to buy in to the climate work that we were doing here, not because I didn't believe it, but because it felt so obvious

to me that it was almost . . . I don't know what would serve me well here. It was like duh! Aren't we all doing this? Aren't these everybody's expectations of how we should speak to each other and how we should communicate? And like good coworkers and human beings are like to each other? Like, isn't that just the norm? So sometimes I was frustrated sitting in these sessions thinking to myself, "I learned this in middle school." It took me a really long time to understand that, well, okay this is for me too. Like, I need to keep this in my mind, but again, like, we were all at different places.

The thing that was hard for me is some of the people who had spoke the bitterest words and complained the most and were the angriest in years past were suddenly in these positions of leadership as ambassadors. They were speaking out and moving us in a good direction and I appreciate that. I understand that that's a good thing. However, it was a quick turn, and so it was hard for me to really believe them and take it seriously. There were certainly people who had a lot of credibility and respect in my eyes who I believed were totally there for the right reason and really meant it. So that kind of put me off at first.

But again it's been a slow process of understanding that this isn't about me and this is about a community and a culture as a whole and just like with my kids in my classroom, like, unless I explicitly say it, we can't work towards treating each other better.

When one group of people in a school are learning differently than another, it creates a problem, especially for equity change, which ultimately requires schoolwide effort to take effect. When learning and knowledge are uneven, educators react differently to the prospect and reality of discomfort that stem from disagreement, racial conflict, and even feelings of incompetence. This possession of differential racial knowledge explains why Black, Brown, and White people "see things differently." More specifically, Black and Brown people often "see racist things" more clearly than White people. Many Black and Brown people develop racial literacies much earlier in life than do most White people. So by the time Black and Brown students get to high school, they are well past a stage of acknowledging racism, have some experience processing what it means to live in a white supremacist world, and thus are more inclined to want to do something to address racism. Some White educators fixate themselves on acknowledging and processing. At CWHS, the vast majority resisted or avoided the efforts as illustrated earlier. Others, like those who organized the effort to remove Elizabeth, tried to undermine the efforts. Some did multiple or all the above.

The educators at CWHS experienced unwieldy and unyielding discomfort. So they chose their corners. Ally. Resist. Acknowledge. Undermine. Question. Speak up. Call out. Prepare to exit. A historic number of teachers and staff prepared to exit. If the goal was to create a culture and climate that helped adults treat Black and Brown students better in the interest of their educational experiences and outcomes, safety and comfort could not be the primary value underpinning our design of adult learning opportunities. Yet, we also did not want to intentionally do harm. But Black and Brown students' well-being was as stake. And if we wanted educators to adopt practices that would affirm students' rights to educational opportunities, adults needed to think, believe, and practice differently. These concerns revealed a dilemma: how much white racial discomfort is too much? Is there such a thing as too much?

Learning from and Through White Racial Discomfort (or Not)

As the 2014–15 year wound down, the ambassadors grew more convinced that "they were right." The retreat was devastating. The data revealing. Students' influential presence pushed them. The Kegan and Lahey book study was transformational. The discomfort and learning they experienced were important for the entire school. New problems emerged. Several emergent questions began to shape our intentions and design of professional learning: Who requires more psychological safety to get better? And at whose expense? Who requires discomfort to get better? Is it okay if people leave? Is it okay to leave people? The ambassador group and administrators strategized on how to get more people involved, all the while holding these critical questions in mind. They found themselves in an awkward discomforting place, questioning their own capacities to lead others and growing more conscious of their own continued needs for racial learning. The following exchange occurred after the ambassador team lead a schoolwide professional development session aimed at helping their colleagues "see" the myriad forms of racism that operated in the school.

School administrator: We need to recruit more teacher ambassadors because your guy's capacity is stretched. I've been trying to invite people in.

Female teacher 1: I'll send another email today inviting people, and I'll reiterate that we would love to have more ambassadors.

Male teacher 1: Even if they just want to talk about it. Like we're not even asking you to commit to anything. Just join us and see what you think. But I agree we need more people.

Female teacher 1: We need to let people know what actions we take. What does it mean to be an ambassador?

Female teacher 3: I wonder about the structure with us supporting new people. We plan and lead professional learning, but are we ready to support other people? What do we need? I personally can't imagine asking somebody to jump into these shoes when I'm feeling like I need more.

Female teacher 2: What would that look like for each of us to get, say, two people to volunteer after today? You're well ahead of them, so this might be the good point to start talking about . . . you guys talked about it last time. What does the training for onboarding us?

Female teacher 4: I don't know . . . maybe this is like advanced for us or something. How do we not start being the "White know-it-all fixers" of everything? Do you know what I'm talking about? My son's been telling me, you're "whitesplaining" again and all this stuff all weekend. How can we not be the savior?

We're pretty much all White, you know, and we're here to do this [equity work], but can we be allies in that change, right? While at the same time bringing people on. 'Cause that makes me uncomfortable too, when I'm "whitesplaining" everything to people, which I've realized is my new favorite thing and, according to my family, I do a lot of it evidently.

Male teacher 2: I would put myself in a category of like having huge anxiety over, like, communicating . . . it's the fear of conflict, the avoidance of conflict. I have huge anxiety around, like, sharing anything about what I'm learning or thinking or questions I have, especially administrators about things that, like, I'm not happy with or that I'm struggling with. That's just super hard for me.

Female teacher 2: [To male speaker] If you still feel intimidated by some of this process, I think that's an honest thing to share with potential teacher ambassadors or people who you think might be good. You can just say, "This is still a process for me." It would be powerful for them to hear you say, "I don't have this title (of ambassador) because I'm done and I'm ready to teach it. I'm still going through it and I'm still not comfortable."

Just like standing up today and facilitating a schoolwide PD. We're kind of uncomfortable standing around and eavesdropping as our colleagues talk. And jumping in to redirect or whitesplain. But that helped all of us—ambassadors or not. Being honest might make it more palatable for that next teacher ambassador to say, "Alright as long as I know that other people feel what I'm feeling. . . ."

When White educators realize their discomfort and acknowledge their own learning needs, it can diminish progress and momentum. But the ambassadors did not try to overcome their discomfort, fear, or willingness to push their colleagues along to a more "right" place. They decided to acknowledge their discomforting experiences, process them with one another, and then explain them to others as a part of the enactment of racial equity change. Had they not chosen this approach, they could have become stuck acknowledging or processing. Both acknowledgment and processing are critically important aspects of equity improvement, not unlike what happened during the 2014 summer data retreat. But acknowledgment and processing are inadequate end goals for equity work. As they led racial learning, ambassadors found they needed to talk more about their own development. They synthesized the collective commitments from the retreat, what they learned from *How the Way We Talk,* and their increased focus on racial equity into a structure for sharing their learning experiences with their colleagues that featured the following elements:

1. *Incident/Problem*: What happened?
2. *Process*: What process did you engage to address the problem?
3. *Outcome*: What was the outcome?
4. *Personal Impact*: How did you feel about the outcome?
5. *Reflection*: Why did you approach the situation as you did?
6. *Commitment*: What was your commitment to the student(s)?

Through continued use of the talking protocol across multiple school spaces, school administrators and ambassadors began to increase their individual and collective capacity to be authentic and honest with one another and in front of faculty, staff, and eventually students. The protocol did not attempt to convey a master narrative about what creating a more equitable school required or entailed. Instead, the structure focused the experience of trying to create a more equitable school. And it allowed ambassadors to choose a corner they understood to be more right and to convey the reality of us versus them. They curated their white racial discomfort into a protocol that cultivated the capacity of people to offer powerful testimonials of their own efforts to become more capable of serving Black and Brown students.

As we all grew more authentic in the interactions that happened behind the scenes, we adopted an emergent practice of encouraging people to share their *corner comments* with a broader audience. At a planning meeting, Ethan confided in the group about how the equity work at the school was changing his perspective of how to manage the school's highly esteemed baseball program. In particular, he referenced his time listening and thinking about the first-year retreat when he was a part of a discussion group analyzing the underrepresentation of students of color in CWHS athletics and sports. For years, he explained, he thought that treating every player the exact same, being race-neutral, was the right thing to do.

After listening to his story, an ambassador said, "You've got to share that with the entire school staff. Say what you just said *here*. It was authentic and people need to hear what you said." Although we often had a general idea of what people would say, very little of what people shared in the actual trainings was scripted (although usually thought out in advance). At a whole staff meeting at the beginning of year three, Ethan recounted his experience of discomfort and change with the full staff. It was his first time publicly opening up about his own experience and the new ways of "how he approached things."

> Good morning. I'll try to be relatively brief, but *I want to talk about race for a second and I'm not trying to transform anybody here but this is some-thing that we need to talk about.* So we aren't the only ones that are going through some of this angst regarding what we're trying to do here in terms of improve school climate. This effort to improve our school climate, which includes staff and students, started three years ago. We collected information and gathered feedback. We came up with the things that we're doing. As for me personally, I changed.
>
> I've been coaching baseball for thirty-three years. When we [CWHS's team] went to the state tournament, I thought it would be a celebration, right? Well, I had issues with a coach throughout the entire season. I had heard things that he was saying about me, out in the community, to our athletes, etc. Eventually, it came to a head. We go to the state tournament. Instead of being able to celebrate, I have to fire this assistant coach because of the things that were happening.
>
> So the next week in the newspaper there's a letter to the editor ac-cusing me of being racist and that's the reason that I fired this coach. *I didn't really know how to handle that.* A couple more seasons passed, and I started to hear things again like "Look at the make-up of CWHS team." I thought we brought the kids in that deserved to be on the team. But I would talk to people in the community, and they would say, "Yeah, it's pretty much common knowledge that your program is a racist program. If you're Black, you are not going to play baseball in Central Waters." That was the narrative that was out there.
>
> My response was to defend myself. I'm not racist. How can any-body say that? [I'd defend myself by saying] I've done this (for Black athletes). I've done that (for Black athletes). I talked to my assistant

coaches and told them, "We're not racists. Look at what we're doing? We're trying to do this. We're trying to do that." But yet the accusations of racism continued.

When we started this equity work, it changed my thinking. I'm not going to stand here and say, yes, I was racist. *No, I wasn't racist.* But I have reflected continually on what can I do to make CWHS the best for all athletes, while keeping my core values as an educator and as a coach. For instance, in the past if you don't have that physical completed, you can't try out. Well, who are the kids that are not getting their physicals completed? The Black athletes. I was a major stickler on timeliness and attendance. You miss practice, you don't play the next game. I would only keep no more than fifteen kids on the team, period. It was unfair.

Does allowing kids to try out without a physical change my core values as an educator or a coach? In my opinion, no, it doesn't. I need to help those kids find a way to get the physical so they have an opportunity to compete for a position on the team. Lateness to practice or missing practice? If a student tells me "Coach, I'm sorry I missed practice this morning. I take the bus. My mom had to work. Or I had to take care of my brother" and I respond "tough luck," what message am I sending? Now, I'm different. I consider the circumstances. If I think that playing baseball is going to be transformational for them, I will do whatever I can to allow them to participate if they're struggling academically or behaviorally.

And I'm not saying this to pat myself on the back. I've changed how I look at things. And the way I look at it is, if this doesn't change my core values and my core beliefs, then I am going to make exceptions if I think it's going to help that young man who hasn't gotten the same opportunity as my son. Now, if my son shows up late, that's a different story. Is that a double standard? I don't think so.

In the past, when we—the staff—heard accusations of being racist, we would defend ourselves. 'I'm not bad. We're not bad. This is why we aren't. I'll talk to anybody about why we're not racist.' I don't do that anymore. I can't control what's said. All I can control is my attitude, my sphere of influence, how I approach things and how I deal with my kids on an individual basis as a team. I think a lot about the message that

I am sending Black students and the opportunities and experiences I want for them.

The increase in people's willingness to talk openly and publicly about their emergent behaviors, racial thinking, and beliefs, as exemplified here, proliferated during the 2016–17 academic year and beyond. People chose corners, and they moved to different ones. Ethan moved. Yet, he still remained unaware of the broader impact his transformation and positional authority could have on the school. When Ethan shared how he dealt with his "kids on an individual basis as a team," he noted some fundamental procedural changes that increased access and opportunity for Black and Brown students. He stopped short of suggesting such a change across all sports programs. In not trying to change anyone, he left a racially and socioeconomically transformative policy up for broader consideration. The approach—and the humility of it—has pros and cons. It seeds the possibility for change. It also waits for White people to catch on and catch up to a more racially equitable approach.

A DEVASTATING TRUTH: THERE WILL ALWAYS BE CORNERS OF DISCOMFORT

The discomfort at CWHS remained throughout the duration of the research project and beyond, albeit to different degrees. Avid resisters left. So too did avid supporters. The work was too fast and too slow, too much and too little. CWHS transitioned from the year of unwieldy discomfort that saw record numbers of retirements and transfers out of the school into a period that welcomed a crop of new faculty and staff who were eager to work with its increasingly diverse student population. The new faculty and staff's first day on the job was the 2015 summer relationship retreat.

By the 2015–16 academic year, CWHS educators started talking about their work in a way that reflected the danger, discomfort, and only the potential for improvement. The efforts and the best of intentions could possibly lead to nowhere. People who talked about their personal need to engage refrained from explaining direct benefits (for White adults) of getting involved in the efforts. They stopped selling promises of results and success to entice people's involvement and shifted toward describing equity work as imperative, voluntary, but impending. They also described their efforts to create a more equitable school as a learning process. Announcements and testimonials typically satisfied two curation elements of racial equity learning: they kept the school grounded in "proximal experiences and devastating truths" and "focused on adults' racial learning and students' well-being and benefit." During the 2015–16 beginning-of-year all-staff day, Elizabeth offered the following opening remarks to lay the groundwork for the year ahead:

> We started with the culture and climate survey and retreat. That retreat was extremely difficult for me. It was super brutal. The people who chose to come were very passionate about the way things are or were. They talked about how bad things were here [at CWHS]. I feel very responsible for everything that happens here. When I listened to people talk for three days about how bad it was, it really hurt me.
>
> I want this to be a school where all staff and students feel cared for and connected and do awesome things. I know that together, two hundred adults can do awesome things. But we all have to pedal in the same direction. It's more than just a vision or wanting the same thing. We have got to figure out how we get there together. That was the part where I really needed help. It's been an interesting journey and learning process for me. I don't even know that I see changes in me, but others tell me that I'm making improvements.

The opening remarks invited the two hundred teachers and staff who sat in the auditorium to join her in a collaborative process of identifying, studying, and strategizing to address the problems of racial inequity that persisted in the school. Elizabeth's quote signaled her increasing capacity for equity-focused improvement. First, she described her retreat experience as brutal. Her choice of words reflects the discomfort and cognitive dissonance of listening to her organizational subordinates criticize a school that *was hers*. When she expressed that she felt responsible for *everything* that happened at the school, she revealed her self-concept of powerful, in control, and all-knowing leader.

The outward expression of emotion and admission of self-concept were important. But the self-reflexivity she pivoted toward is noteworthy because it signaled an emerging capacity to lead and learn through racial discomfort. First, she admitted uncertainty. Second, she admitted needing help. Third, she announced that she was learning. Fourth, she left the mere possibility of her own improvement open for discussion, debate, and analysis. Throughout, her disclosure did not absolve herself or the educators who filled the auditorium of responsibility to "figure out how we get there." Elizabeth's acknowledgment of her struggle and aspiration revealed an ambivalent white racial identity that was tested and reworked over the duration of the project to the extent that people talked about "the old Elizabeth" and "the new Elizabeth," often referencing incidents and episodes where they observed "the old Elizabeth." The effect of curated discomfort was that many people at CWHS developed a capacity to step outside of their selves in ways that enabled them to partially see both their flaws and sometimes their potential. Indeed, White educators realized that "okay, this is for me too." This admission laid the groundwork for people to step into a new self.

PRINCIPLES FOR CULTIVATING CURATED WHITE RACIAL DISCOMFORT

Over time, people understood the learning benefits of racial discomfort to the point where they routinely said things like "As awful at it sounded, I think the whole staff should go through that sort of retreat experience," essentially wishing a similar discomforting experience on others and even themselves. This sort of understanding was not coincidental. Many CWHS educators saw and appreciated that the collective benefits and power of white racial discomfort reached these points as a consequence of learning. The method for developing the capacity to work through discomfort was to curate racial discomfort—to thoughtfully create professional learning experiences that gave White people opportunities to experience racial discomfort while learning from it in real time and in response to the racial learning demands of the local school context. Table 2.1 outlines the principles of adult learning design that curated white racial discomfort at CWHS.

TABLE 2.1 Cultivating curated white discomfort

CRITICAL PRINCIPLE	ENACTING THE PRINCIPLE	RACIAL LEARNING BENEFITS
Active and critically reflective learning is critical	Invite educators to learn about race and racism through the practice of "undoing" racism and challenging power relations in everyday work situations and environments. Bring their learning through practice back to the group for consideration, analysis, and critique.	Educators benefit from routine individual and collective self-reflection and follow-up opportunities for processing their learning experiences.
Continuous, compounding, and coherent learning is critical	Invite educators to learn through designing their learning based on previous experiences. Over multiple years, plan for new learning across different domains (classroom, team meetings, community). Focus on identified points of being stuck and anticipated breakthroughs will coincide with racial discomfort, problems, and areas for new learning.	Educators benefit from monitoring their learning and engaging in further learning experiences that are sufficiently challenging them to experience breakthroughs.
Dangerous, discomforting, counter-normative, and oppression-conscious learning is critical	Invite educators to learn through hearing dissenting and contradictory views, disagreeing, and engaging in productive conflict. Minimize activities that tokenize or require people of color to take risks or experience discomfort for the sake of White people's learning.	Educators benefit from knowing that racial discomfort, dissent, and disagreement are standard parts of racial learning.
Dual focus on adults' racial learning and students' well-being and benefit is critical	Invite adults to learn and work to "fix" problems within and amongst their selves. Draw from and center experiences from students of color to guide self-work: How do our efforts benefit (or not) Black and Brown students? What does racial perspective-taking teach me about my racial self? What, if anything, can I do to get better?	Educators, especially White adults, benefit from opportunities to disrupt dominant white racial narratives while thinking about the benefits of their growth for their selves, children, and families' vis-a-vis Black and Brown people.
Grounding learning in proximal experiences and devastating truths is critical	Invite educators to collect, study, and analyze testimonies, vignettes, and stories that draw on proximal experiences—events, episodes, stories, and problems from within the school and immediate community (rather than case studies or books removed from local context)—as primary data and texts for understanding race and racism.	Educators benefit from real texts, data, and stories of proximal experience—devastation, failure, fear, hope, growth, truth, transformation—that help them "see" patterns and gain insights that catalyze practices (behaviors), thinking, and beliefs transformation.

The first guiding principle is that the learning should be active (allowing teachers to learn while doing) and provide regular opportunities for critical reflection. This, like several of the principles, aligns with conventional race-evasive organizational improvement. Whatever teachers are learning must improve students' school-based academic experiences. Adults must have opportunities to learn by doing. Educators need repeated opportunities for individual and collective self-reflection and follow-up opportunities for processing learning experiences. Educators need opportunities to monitor their learning and progress toward effecting change. However, if a school's priority is to redress race-based power inequities to create racial equity, conventional race-evasive organizational improvement approaches are inadequate. By large measure, White teachers are responsible for the improvement tasks that are supposed to benefit Black and Brown students. Educators need to fully understand the task at hand as a racially disruptive one. As our understandings of what discomfort entailed multiplied and grew more sophisticated, we conceded that commitments to psychological safety for White adults and racial equity for Black and Brown students contradicted each other.

Because most White people fear a truly equitable racial order as well as the racial conflict necessary to bring forth such a reality, leaders must situate racial equity change within a language and context of danger and discomfort. In other words, learning must be dangerous, a second principle of curating white racial discomfort. For White educators, dangerous means counternormative and antioppressive and, in particular, antiracist. Ensuring learning is dangerously safe requires continually assessing what discomfort means for educators. Understanding what danger means allows facilitators and leaders to design learning experiences that turn people toward their discomfort as a site of learning (not evading it). Black and Brown students benefit from white discomfort. CWHS not only owned white discomfort as a matter of racial learning fact; it owned its inverse relationship with Black and Brown students' well-being.

We changed how we talked. Our early framing of the project was largely that it was "going to be good for the school." But when we sought to understand if the efforts were helping the school progress, the answer depended on the month, day, and time of day we looked at the data. It depended on whom we asked. Our belief in the potential for the equity leadership efforts to transform the school into a more affirming and educative place of learning for Black and Brown students became lukewarm. Our responses to "How is the research project helping the school?" sounded more like "This has the potential to be good for the school. But it may not feel good . . . at least not initially. Or maybe at all. Hopefully, it will be good. It's the right thing to do . . . but it's pretty scary. Are you nervous about what could happen?" We refused to confidently say that what we were learning would make a difference. Instead, we acknowledged and announced the discomfort, while not offering guarantees that it would be immediately beneficial, if at all. We began to explicitly state: "This is dangerous work." Not thinking, not reflection. Work. In short, we asked people to commit to actions that could be used as a source of learning and reflection.

To ensure discomfort, we mined for and collectively analyzed two types of data that made it less possible for folks to be race-evasive: (a) proximal experiences and devastating truths and (b) school-based episodes and stories of experience. These formed the basis of our professional learning "curricular content." Administrators', teachers', and students' stories—of devastation, failure, fear, hope, growth, truth, transformation—were the single most powerful data sources that helped CWHS educators "see" patterns and come to grips with their own roles in perpetuating the school's racial order. Specific school-based episodes unearthed a white racial logic that teachers were then able to actively resist and eventually work to disrupt. Elizabeth exposed her racial narrative of in-control, responsible, and all-knowing leader. Ethan's testimonial exposed a racial narrative of white innocence and denial. Throughout, they juxtaposed their old and emerging thinking and behaviors. Testimonials conveyed how discomforting experience and disconfirming information altered their practices, beliefs, values, and master narratives. The underlying structure provided a narrative frame for helping others make sense of the emergent or transformed ways of thinking about race and racism.

The square focus on "proximal experiences and devastating truths" and "focus on their own [White adults'] racial learning and students' well-being and benefit" introduced teachers and staff into the learning that discomfort invites. These data begged us to stop expressing a desire to create "safe spaces" for racial learning because the stories of change revealed the necessity of danger, discomfort, and anxiety as integral to change and improvement. The proximal internally derived stories formed a text that offered meaning and relevance to externally derived texts. We used what we learned in the first two years of the project to design and facilitate learning opportunities with the specific intent of making White adults uncomfortable with and critical of whiteness and its role in upholding racial inequity. Our decision to stop focusing on safe spaces created the possibility of curating professional learning that was more meaningful for achieving equitable change. We realized and acknowledged that equity reforms are not safe and likely will never be.

The evolution of how we racial self-talked and codesigned learning and what we asked people to do disrupted tidy white racial narratives of progress and inability to fail. It integrated trial and error, repeated failure, racial discomfort, and the potential to not get better as central to improvement. We also acknowledged the racial reality that, despite our effort, we may not improve. This is a Black and Brown kind of consciousness. Black and Brown people already know that the capitulation between despair and hope, failure and small wins, setbacks and leaps forward are part of progress. The deep irony is that White people needed repeated, seemingly too many, opportunities for individual and collective critical self-reflection. Too many follow-up opportunities to process. They needed time, which is at once deeply unfair and essential to disrupting the dominant racial order. Black and Brown people don't have time for White people to keep learning. Yet, White educators needed a long time horizon to make sense of their racial experiences.

Thus, the final principle is that curation of white racial discomfort should be continuous, compounding, and coherent. If educators cannot see how their learning coheres with other priorities (for example, how discipline reform, climate improvement efforts, and classroom instruction relate), the efforts are not as powerful as if these connections are visible and evident. Each principle is an interactive part that comprises the whole of a distinct organizational racial resource of curated white racial discomfort. The relative strength of the resource depends on the interlocking application of principles as illustrated in table 2.1. In other words, curated white racial discomfort is most powerful when it is designed and delivered with all principles in mind. For example, curation should not be only dangerous and discomforting. It should not be only grounded in proximal experiences as data. It should be all of the above. The application of each principle in isolation of the other results in a discomforting experience and a series of storytelling events rather than a cohesive experience that leverages discomfort and personal experiences into learning resources.

CONCLUSION: DILEMMAS OF SUSTAINING DISCOMFORT

Amplifying the importance of discomfort, anxiety, and cognitive dissonance as central to equity change demands that teachers routinely face evidence that disconfirms deeply held racial beliefs. White adults have immense personal and collective power to shape the learning access, opportunities, and experiences of Black and Brown students. The power generates from white supremacy, part of which offers White people the benefit of relative psychological safety. This investment in maintaining psychological safety translates into a demand for their professional learning experiences to be comfortable, immediately beneficial, and controlled. Curated white racial discomfort advances racially equitable change by disrupting a specific racial narrative and constructed reality: White people deserve to be comfortable, and thus they are. Black and Brown children do not benefit from White people's professional comfort. To sustain racial equity requires the unending curation of white racial discomfort.

We used the time we had to accelerate racial learning as an experience. How can we create a data retreat-like professional learning experience for faculty and staff who did not attend the retreat? How can the experience transcend time and space? Our goal was to establish conditions for antiracist practice, decision-making, and conversation to proliferate in the school. We planned discomforting racial learning experiences to span the duration of the school year. We wedged into the spaces of racial respite. We collaborated differently.

Yet much of what happened during the 2014–15 year was a mess. In subsequent years, almost everyone we interviewed conceded it was painful but necessary because learning experiences catalyzed transformed practices (behaviors), thinking, and beliefs. Understandably, many people avoided aspects of the work. Aversion took forms of initially engaging and then disengaging, watching from the sidelines, and leaving the school altogether. Central Waters administrators and staff found themselves stuck improving in the area of curating spaces of white discomfort in two ways. By year three (2015–16), many adults felt they "got it" and grew fatigued from having to continually address their own discomforts about race as well as those of their colleagues. They also realized their increasing capacity to work through discomfort applied mostly to spaces with trusted colleagues. While the adults were doing racial learning that they anticipated would support Black and Brown students, students' school life went on relatively unchanged. Their increased capacities did not expand into racialized spaces where they lacked control, such as hallways, commons areas, and even areas where they had too much control, such as classrooms.

We worked to achieve proliferation of racial learning through talking about CWHS in racial terms, collaboratively designing and leading professional learning, and using stories of race, racism, and efforts to redress inequity that stemmed from school and community as the primary text to learn from and about race, racism, and possibilities for change. But the curation of white racial discomfort varied over the duration of the project. The data retreat served a small group of teachers over the course of three days of learning. The retreat structure allowed us to apply all of the curation principles. In the second year, the structure, coherence, and opportunities for critical reflection were inadequate. Too much time elapsed between meetings. The teacher ambassadors were still building their capacity to provide teacher leadership for the learning. The school remained organized in a hierarchy of site-based management that handed down decisions to teachers without accounting for their wants and needs. The structures and people who could cultivate Black and Brown people's influential presence were woefully inadequate. Finally, there was the need to more fully develop an organizational culture that supported discomfort. As one teacher who knew Elizabeth for many years shared:

> I've worked pretty close with Elizabeth for five years, so I'm aware of most of her strengths and weaknesses. I imagine those initial meetings with the boss of the school is critical. I would imagine that helping any leader see their own blind spots is incredibly difficult.

She was right. When during our phone call Elizabeth said aloud, "I'm gonna have to trust the process," it was an indication of both her growth and the work she needed to do on herself. She was results driven, outcomes-oriented, decisive, and very much a leader who exercised control. It was time to articulate our own stances about the value of the retreat itself and the adaptive work we collectively agreed to undertake. This required courageous confrontation. And this was work that not only Elizabeth needed to do. Everyone did.

3

COURAGEOUSLY CONFRONTATIONAL SCHOOL CULTURE

You and you research team were like "Look . . . this is the issue. This is the problem. Here's what you all said you want to do to make it better. Do it. And if you all don't, it's on you all." You pretty much made that clear when we brought problems or solutions to you: "Tell your coworkers. You all got to work with each other. You all ain't got to work with me." Your approach put the mission back on us to do what we need to do. I think it makes people very uncomfortable in the sense that they are like, "Okay, I need to sit in this discomfort so that I can be better."

—BLACK MALE EDUCATOR (year five reflections)

Schools all over the United States go to great lengths to ensure they are free from violence and threats that pose dangers to students. But a narrow focus on physical safety ignores the immeasurable harms that racial violence does to Black and Brown students. Most educators consider disregarding authority, defacing or trespassing on property, and causing physical harm to any member of the school community complete violations of the sanctity of schools. Consequently, school communities expend vast emotional, intellectual, and financial resources to fight against disrespect and disregard of authority figures, physical altercations, hallway hanging, academic disengagement, and so forth. Educators give less effort to fighting the racist belief systems, organizationwide policies and cultural practices, and societal conditions that harm Black and Brown students and entire school communities alike.

The underemphasis on fighting the harms of racism and against white supremacy stems from vivid spectacles of physical and verbal forms of violence that overshadow mundane forms of cultural and symbolic violence that persist in schools.[1] Schools throughout the US would operate and feel very different if White educators abhorred and courageously confronted the inherent violence of racism and white supremacy as much as they abhor the vivid violence of Black students fighting. In this regard, White adults have much to learn from Black and Brown people's tragic and necessary need to confront the day-to-day problems of being racially subjected. In this chapter, I argue that the best approach to challenging all forms of school-based violence is the cultivation and maintenance of a courageously confrontational school culture.

Courageous confrontation refers to individual and collective practices of directly addressing episodes, events, incidents, and interactions as though they are indeed a consequence of racism and destructive forms of white racial socialization. Courageous confrontation demands critiquing racial ideas, taken-for-granted behaviors, and social structures that harm Black and Brown students.[2] A courageously confrontational school culture is evidenced in three routine occurrences. First, people routinely act within their sphere of influence to confront problems head on. Second, people default to racism and racial socialization as a central, but not singular, lens for analyzing the pervasiveness or emergence of school-based problems. Third, people leverage conflict and confrontation as a wellspring of learning. Learning from and through conflict offers the opportunity to at minimum acknowledge and move forward and at best to forgive, heal, and accept responsibility for the well-being of people who are often at odds with one another.

Educators working in courageously confrontational schools engage and learn about how to overcome their fears in a way that educators in congenial and collegial school cultures are not afforded.[3] Congenial school cultures refer to schools that privatize professional practice and learning but where the interactions that drive teacher learning and growth occur through "friendly" professional ties. Often, congenial schools operate with a façade of niceness and get-alongness that breed deep-seated racial resentment and misunderstanding by masking racism and racial conflict. Professional friendliness drives conflict underground, festers gossip and passive-aggressive behaviors, and seeds suspicion and mistrust. Collegial school cultures are characterized by high levels of teacher-to-teacher communication, collaboration, and problem solving aimed at adult growth and ultimately improved student experiences and outcomes.[4] Collegial school cultures are less toxic and more effective than congenial ones. Still collegial cultures lack an essential *practice of antiracist confrontation* that moves past collaboration for adult growth toward an end outcome of adults' transformation of practices that improve Black and Brown students' learning experiences and outcomes.

In this chapter, I tell the story "There's Definitely Way More Fights This Year" to show how Central Waters High School faculty expanded their focus and approach from fighting only against physical and verbal forms of violence to fighting against a school culture that disregarded, discarded, and damaged people for the ways they expressed their anger and frustration. I demonstrate how fear of confrontation is a racialized experience by analyzing CWHS's responses to student fist fights, teacher union fights, in-fighting of supposedly like-minded colleagues, and fights about the adequacy (or lack thereof) of CWHS racial equity change efforts. I chose the stories in the chapter because I want readers to know that school violence is more than physical and verbal in nature. I want readers to understand the differences between vivid and mundane violence and their differential effects on Black and Brown students and communities of color. Finally, I want readers to understand the dilemmas that emerge when administrators, teachers, and staff decide to confront violence in all of its forms. When CWHS developed a critical mass of administrators, teachers, and faculty who engaged in courageously confrontational practices, they created a school culture that was structurally and culturally better equipped to challenge its racist inclination to discard, dismiss, and damage people (of all races) and to extend Black and Brown students the resources of empathy and grace, forgiveness, and continued opportunities to heal, restore, and transform.

FIGHTING FOR WHOEVER COMES INTO OUR DOORS

Throughout the 2016–17 academic year, teachers remained peeved about hallway hanging, a culture of disrespect toward adults and authority figures, as well as student-to-student disrespect. Despite efforts, it seemed as though the culture and climate at CWHS remained unchanged. How is it possible to create a climate of respect absent clear rules and consequences? Before the project commenced, CWHS implemented Positive Behavior Interventions and Supports. They offered tickets and rewards for good behavior. They praised acts of kindness. They also created and enforced discipline policies, such as dress codes; hats and hoodie rules; and short, dress, and skirt length guidelines for female students. The goal was to create an expectation that students be serious about their education. Faculty and staff opinions about the necessity of such approaches diverged. Staff could never quite agree on the importance and need of such compliance-based efforts. Some contented the policies were necessary to regain control of the school's culture. Others were indifferent. Some considered the policies a distraction. When teachers and administrators did agree on specific policies, enforcing them for 1,600 students across a sprawling campus required more effort than seemed reasonable. Everyone agreed on one rule. No fighting. It was a clear rule with a clear consequence. If you fight, you get suspended. Still, every year, Black students fought.

> **Elizabeth:** We have some challenging young people this year, and it's really because we have some kiddos that are coming from different areas and are trying to assert themselves as a new gang, and that's caused a conflict with an existing gang here at our school. There's definitely way more fights this year than there ever has been in many, many years. Including with girls. We've had some pretty difficult situations on our hands. . . . There's no other way to say it. Every single student who has been in a fight has been Black. Every single one. We're sort of going back to where we were because now there's this kind of like, "If it wasn't for the Black kids, this would be a good school" kind of thing starting to happen.

Ethan: Like Elizabeth had mentioned, things that are happening in the community are spilling over into school.

Elizabeth: Our superintendent is meeting with the police chief today. Then tomorrow, I have to meet with the police officers. I know that our assigned officer is bad-mouthing us [administrators] to our staff. So we are dealing with all of this as directly as we can. The good part is that I don't think that his beliefs represents the staff's beliefs. What he believes is probably pervasive among maybe 25 percent of the staff.

Decoteau: Mm-hmm. Okay.

Elizabeth: There was one day there were three fights in one day here at school. Everybody got discombobulated about it. In one of the fights, none of the kids even made physical contact because all the adults were holding everybody back. The girl fight was pretty vicious, and it was caught on video. Another fight, no body intervened. We didn't even know it happened, but we got it on video. Anyway, ever since that rough day, everybody [corrected self] . . . not everybody, but quite a few of staff—

Ethan: [picks up Elizabeth's statement] The percentage I would say is a quarter or so are saying, "I don't feel safe here. What are we going to do to make this a safer place?" We actually had to meet with a couple of parents after the three fights because it was picked up in the local press. We did actually increase our police presence for a couple of days after that. Of course, the increased police presence made the paper too.

White parents and some teachers are saying they don't feel safe. But we know Black students and parents don't feel safe with increased police presence either. Arresting kids doesn't really help. We've been dealing with that, and trying to get people to understand that really we're trying to deal with things that are happening in the community with a small concentrated group of kids that are here at school.

Elizabeth: Friday, Ethan brought over a note that somebody put in a climate box. It basically said that she heard from the students that the kids that are involved in these fights are gang-involved. She's concerned because she doesn't know how to "teach gangsters." She's not comfortable having gangsters in her class. Which is really like saying all Black kids are gangsters. Because that's who is fighting, right? And how can she tell who is who. It's like, "Really?" Gangs are—Not all Black kids are in gangs. Not all of the kids who fight are in gangs. That's kind of where we are at. I don't always know what to do to push back on that.

Decoteau: Right. Yeah. When I'm not available, how are you processing and addressing these things as they were happening, if at all? I know that you're telling me about some especially chaotic days. But what are you learning from it and similar challenges about what you can do better?

Elizabeth: I'm struggling on how to not stigmatize students while also being very real about what we're dealing with. For example, we're not going to go on record about whether kids are in a gang or not gang. That's not what we're going to do. But we know. And some of what happened was gang related and is gang related. The rumors start with the kids, because some of the kids are on social media with a lot of guns. I personally was involved in the entire investigation for all three incidents, and not at any time was there a gun mentioned or threats of any type of weapon.

Decoteau: Was there any kind of way to process that day with staff? With students? I guess what I'm asking: is there any kind of space to have the conversations?

Elizabeth: Well . . . No. Because of FERPA [Family Educational Rights and Privacy Act], we have to be careful. As much as we want to be transparent and open, we can't do a big meeting about these fights. What we did is, the superintendent and I, along with our public relations person, created a note to parents and staff. After I met with the counselors, their office sent an email saying that the counseling staff was there if anyone wanted to talk or process. I did the same in my email to staff. I said, if you have any questions or concerns, please, you can talk to any of the administrators, and obviously, myself as well.

Decoteau: Mm-hmm [affirmative]. With the students who were involved, what was the kind of process like for them . . . consequences, or conversations, and how were they reintegrated back into the school community?

Elizabeth: They were suspended, and had readmit meetings, and behavior plans. Every kid kind of had their own special plan based on who they are. Like one of our girls has mental health issues. She's been hospitalized twice this year. Her plan looks really different than another student who normally isn't involved in anything. He's not had any problems before, you know what I mean?

Ethan: We've tried restorative approaches. We spoke at length with every kid. Had their parents involved. Suspension. Readmit. Behavior plans. After break, one of the girls came up and apologized on her own volition. Things seem to be a little bit better there. What's happening with these boys are actually issues that are going on in the community.

Elizabeth: Some pretty strong gang violence that's going on in the community. It's just rolling over into the school. It's not actually starting here. But it's here. Everyday. And we have to work with whoever comes into our doors.

Many teachers disagreed. "Violence strikes fear into everyone," they argued. They, as most people do, found the physical violence abhorrent. They often didn't know why students fought. Or why, for God's sake, fight at school. *"They don't care."* Teachers had been here before, frustrated by the disorder and climate of disrespect. Toward the end of the 2014–15 school year, teachers and union representatives organized themselves to fight. They secretly designed and survey-gathered data to demonstrate "how horrible the school was." Although the climate survey data from the previous year were equally damning, the secret survey offered an opportunity for teachers and staff to evaluate the school's leadership. Just before the next year commenced, they released their results. The response rates were low and skewed. About one quarter of employees completed it: 90 percent of respondents gave the school and leaders the lowest possible ratings.

Teachers delivered the results of the survey directly to the superintendent with hopes of having Elizabeth replaced as the principal of the school. To them, the results provided evidence that Elizabeth and her

administrative team were inept, leading the school in a fruitless and ultimately damaging direction. The school was getting progressively worse.
The data proved it. When Elizabeth learned about the survey, she was
hurt less by the results than about the timing and secrecy of the process:

> They gave us our results. Of course, the results were horrific. But the
> part of it that really bothered me was the timing. We met with the union
> the day before the staff came back from summer break. The very next
> day we had to go in and do our peppy welcome-back speech like, "Hey,
> welcome back. We love you. This is going to be a great year." Inside I'm
> thinking, "Okay, I'm going to apply for a new job next year."
>
> Before we went to the beginning-of-year meeting, we talked about
> it as a team. I'm a little fiery. I'm little salty sometimes. What I wanted
> to say to the union grievance lady during our initial conversation was,
> "Since you surveyed teachers, how about teachers surveying their stu-
> dents and gathering similar information? Do they [students] feel cared
> for, respected, and connected? Do they have good communication with
> you [teachers]?" What's good for the goose is good for the gander kind
> of thing.
>
> My team said to me, "That's not a good approach." So we decided
> that we would go in there and just make it a short meeting. Listen. Say
> thank you. Leave. But *I ended up spending probably a half hour telling*
> *them the steps that we were taking to improve things and why. It ended up*
> *as an opportunity to educate them.* And it dawned on me we need to help
> people know what we're doing. And to talk about outcomes. So, how
> often are we surveying? When are we surveying? Who? I would like to
> have some data to show improvement.

But teachers who participated gave their own critiques. The reforms
were not academically focused enough. They were narrowly focused on
Black students. They focused on race to the exclusion of socioeconomic
considerations. What about LGBTQ students? Latinx students? Few people openly expressed these sentiments. Most remained reluctant to get
involved for fear of being called racist. During interviews, they opened
up to members of our research team:

Leaderships' attempts at responding to diversity create bigger divides and more misunderstandings. The diversity efforts really refer to Black students only and ignore sexual orientation, Latino, and ELL students, and Islamic students. We're experiencing a racist backlash because there are unequal standards. And even what we are doing that is supposed to "benefit" Black students doesn't prepare them for the demands of real life. Relationships take precedence over learning, and so Black students are socially promoted. But why get involved and share my opinion because *people would call me racist. (Teacher being interviewed by White female graduate student)*

When people fight, there is always an underlying reason. Teachers fought administration because they did not feel heard, listened to, or valued as colleagues. They fought because they did not see the changes they so desperately wanted from Black and Brown students. They didn't feel safe. So they fought. They leaked information to parents who shared their beliefs. They created a closed Facebook site to share concerns and organize to challenge the school administrators. They weaponized data to fortify themselves. They used whatever means they could to protect themselves from too much damage. People's unwillingness to share opinions stemmed from a fear of retribution from the administration or, worse, being called racist. They did all of these things to get rid of Elizabeth as though she was the problem. Elizabeth, like it or not, had to confront these concerns. She reflected, "It dawned on me we need to help people know what we're doing," acknowledging her lack of clear, open, and direct communication. Based on our data-gathering and retreat experiences, we understood that the problems were not about any one person, but about the overall culture of the school.

Fighting to Be Heard, Fighting to Hear

The teachers' organized attempt to oust Elizabeth marked an important turning point in how she eventually practiced confrontation. Teachers had mixed feelings about the utility of the teacher and parent organizing. They preferred instead to bring their concerns directly to administrators and place them out in the open. But they felt the outlets were not there.

And if they were, expressing concerns led to no change. Most importantly, a practice of direct confrontation and conflict went against the
cultural tide of CWHS. CWHS educators were "nice." Or so it seemed.
Time revealed that people were not so much nice as they were with-
drawn, self-protective, and fearful. People kept to themselves and held
friendships with the people who behaved, thought, and believed as they
did. They avoided people who were different, including other White people who held different racial beliefs. They constructed professional lives
that were echo chambers.

If someone was angry, they shared their anger with a person who
would likely share their outrage. Conflict and confrontation occurred
through happenstance. Structures or routines that invited people to courageously confront interpersonal or organizationwide problems did not
exist. Having never had the opportunity to confront their experiences,
they carried anger, hurt, and harm with them from past interactions,
events, and episodes. At the beginning of the 2014–15 academic year,
our research team introduced two communication routines to the school
that aimed to confront these deep-seated white "Midwest nice" cultural
practices.

The first practice we introduced was the passing of "healing rocks."
We introduced them so that people would talk to people they were averse
to talking or sharing their concerns with. Most of the aversion stemmed
from past negative interactions or racialized speculations about what
bad would come if and when they shared their concerns. Healing rocks
were symbolic resources that offered people an impetus to seek out and
resolve past conflicts and harm.[5] The process worked as follows: participants passed the rock to people in the school. They could pass it to someone to express appreciation. Or they could pass the rock to someone they
wanted to apologize to or reset their relationship. They could also pass it
to open up a conversation about a perceived rift or distance. The initial
passing of the rock was not intended to resolve any problem or situation.
It was a gesture of acknowledgment, as in "Something doesn't feel right
between us." Or "I've been holding this feeling to myself. I just wanted
to share where I'm at."

When a person received a rock, that person had forty-eight hours to pass it to another colleague or student. At various points throughout early stages of the project, we invited people to offer testimonials of healing and restoration that stemmed from their "passing the rock." These testimonials became a powerful gesture of how direct communication created possibilities for healing and reconciliation within and across racial groups. In time, the central importance of the physical rocks gave way to the importance of the gesture and interactions of direct communication. The power of passing healing rocks was two-fold. It gave rock-passers opportunities to pause and think about who they needed to directly communicate with, about what, and why. It forced a deep level of introspection and, in the best of circumstances, catalyzed an act of courage they might otherwise have not taken. It offered rock-receivers the opportunity to listen. And to learn.

Some people learned that a remark or comment they made in a meeting, some five years ago, caused a rift between them and a colleague. Learning how they hurt someone offered receivers an opportunity to apologize, an opportunity they would have not received without the rock. People grew to appreciate the value and necessity to courageously confront their tendency to gossip and harbor negative feelings, and the apprehension to directly communicate to the people who, if they took the risk, would play a role in their healing and wellness. The continuous passing of the rock created a volume of interactions that gave people a common experience. After about a full academic year of healing rock exchanges, the application of being direct grew more clearly evident, even when rocks were not a part of the exchange.

Over time, people learned to expressed hurt, anger, or frustration. The person who heard the expression turned the hurt person toward confronting the source of the problem, including, as necessary, facilitating confrontation. A logic emerged that if the "offending" person had no knowledge, they would have no opportunity to learn or work to resolve the problem. If the "harmed" person did not confront the person or the problem, they would harbor resentment, take out frustrations in unproductive ways, and direct negative emotions and actions at people who lacked understanding or who were not directly responsible for their harm.

Second, we asked people to put their concerns on sheets of paper and drop them into a climate box. We initiated the practice during the first-year data retreat. Just like at the retreat, we encouraged teachers to share their concerns, complaints, thoughts, and ideas, no matter how acceptable or unacceptable, without fear of repercussions. The goal was to get teachers and staff to direct their concerns to the administration and to reduce the gossiping, behind-the-scenes organizing, and veneer of niceness that dominated the school's communication and problem-solving culture. The climate box worked as follows: administrators placed a message box in the copier room and placed sheets of paper and pens next to it. Administrators invited teachers to drop notes of their thoughts and ideas into the box. Teachers wrote and dropped comments. Administrators read the comments.

In a climate of deep administrator-teacher division, the box offered administrators a window into what people really thought and believed, in real time. It was common for the box to fill up when an episode or event occurred. Collecting the information was important for several reasons. One, it was a data repository that collected mostly dissenting opinions and beliefs. Two, it was a medium for teachers to communicate to administrators and laid an early foundation for their eventual willingness to talk. For months, the anonymous slips of paper offered mostly critical comments like the ones noted previously. Early on, administrators routinely checked the climate box but did not respond to the comments. For several months, administrators sat with the frustration of not being able to directly respond. They didn't know who dropped comments into the box. The content of the comments, their curiosity about who was leaving comments, and their own frustration functioned as a learning opportunity. Teachers shared their real thoughts free from repercussions. Reading them and having the comments *in writing* forced administrators to "see" opposing views.

But the climate box was a flawed structure. It offered a structure for expression but not confrontation. Specifically, it did not offer administrators or concerned parties the opportunities to directly confront those views. Climate box communication was one-way, mostly negative, and almost always directed at what administrators *should be doing*. While it was a major point of contention for administrators, teachers overwhelmingly thought it was a great medium. We asked questions such as "Why do you think people are leaving comments rather than talking directly to you? What does that tell you about the climate in the building? What are some things you can do to gather this feedback directly? What would you do or how would you confront the person who shared this if you did know who it was?" With our constant prodding, administrators begin to "see" the communication culture in the building. Rather than engage administrators in conversation about the specific content of the notes or appease their frustrations, we wanted them to think deeply about the meaning of the climate box and the need for it. Our point was: people placed comments in the box. What did their actions mean? People wanted to share their thoughts, even if they were grievances. Now that there was a place to confront administrators, free of repercussions, teachers were doing so.

Elizabeth despised the box. And the comments that it often drew. Associate principal Andrea adopted a more nuanced view of the box, seeing it as both problematic and important: "If teachers consider a box in the copy room as the best forum to share their thoughts, that's a problem. But a year ago, they didn't even have that. They are sharing. So that's good. My question is this: what can we do differently? And are we prepared to deal with whatever we hear." On our part, we continued pushing administrators to imagine a school where people offered their honest opinions to one another, *outside of the box*. Teachers who opposed the leadership directions believed administrators were aware of but not responsive to their grievances. In the absence of any other formal established structures for confrontation, the climate box directed confrontation toward administrators. Teachers and staff rightfully created their own paths for confrontation—closed Facebook groups, underground surveys, complaining and gossiping, and the like. Neither path was sufficiently conducive to a racial equity agenda. The administrative team decided to work outside of the climate box. Finding themselves talking in circles, they invited the ambassadors into the dilemma. What might it look like to move past this box? What is required to foster the kind of honest communication culture that will improve the school?

Given the school's congenial culture and low capacity for confrontation, the climate box was a forward step past the culture of indirect confrontation shrouded in niceness that existed before our research partnership. The box was one-way, antagonistic, and it did not yield the kinds of inquiry and dialogue that helped people understand or at best resolve conflict. Conflict was endemic, undergirded with thick racial undertones. Teachers versus students. Students versus students. Administrators versus teachers. Administrators versus parents. Latinx students versus White students. White teachers versus White students. White teachers versus Black students. My research team and I knew these conflicts existed. People talked to us about them both formally and informally. The problem was that they talked to us.

They needed to talk with one another. Conflict lingered unresolved and unaddressed because people refused to directly acknowledge the racialized nature of conflict or to courageously confront their problems. When Elizabeth expressed "We need to help people know what we're doing. And to talk about outcomes. So, how often are we surveying? When are we surveying? What are we surveying?" it marked a shift into using inquiry—asking questions, gathering information to answer the questions, and most importantly sharing the information gathered and lessons learned to confront the various issues of inequity in the school. At CWHS asking tough direct questions was confrontational. Giving people information was also courageously confrontational because it enabled people to confront their deeply held beliefs, see their practices, and problematize the outcomes that individual and collective practices produce. While the ambassadors took on the work of cultivating a culture of direct communication and courageous confrontation among their peers, we continued to ask administrators pointed questions about what steps they were taking to ensure lasting change. In a project meeting, Deirdre, from our research team, asked the administrative team how they were responding differently as a result of the issue:

Deirdre: I'm just curious to know how you guys are getting that feedback. If they're [teachers] not coming to you—I know the climate box was not a real effective communication tool that way—have you guys figured out a process for people to be able to get you feedback if they can't talk face to face with you?

Elizabeth: No. [pause] I would like to explore that. I'm just going to say one little wee bit. In addition to the work the ambassadors are leading on effective communication, all the admins are now assigned departments. We are contacting the department leaders to say, "As part of our commitment, we'd like to come to four of your department meetings this year. We don't need to be on the agenda. We can just sit and listen. You pick one that's good for you." That's another effort to try to get to a smaller group of people and be present.

It's interesting. When people say we don't have good communication, it makes me wonder, "Well, communication on what?" You don't understand the Common Core? You didn't get enough information about educator effectiveness? Is it when there's an incident in the building, you want to know more?

So we [admins] created a supervision grid. Each two months we are assigned a hall or a section of the building, and that's our place to have a really high level of presence and interaction. For example, September and October I'm the F wing. Whenever I can, I'm trying to be out and be visible. Then November and December I go to the G wing.

It's really about connecting with the teachers in those wings, so that they see us more and we have more opportunities to connect with them. But to go back to your point . . . No.

Although the administrators answered "no" to Deirdre's queries, her constant probing about the structures and routines required for an organizationwide practice of courageous confrontation helped them realize the need to create structures beyond the climate box. Although the climate box was a starting place for gathering ongoing feedback from teachers in a way that had never before occurred, it was but one approach. And a flawed one. Equity improvement required more substantial structural and practice changes.

Fighting Resentment and Indirect Criticism

As part of the second-year retreat, administrators and ambassadors agreed to use teacher tardy and attendance data to explore and unearth problems with the wide variability in how teachers documented tardiness and attendance. Administrators printed teacher data for inclusion in the data packet. But they did not de-identify the data. For each data set, a teacher's last name was atop the form. Some teachers felt violated. How dare the admin team share teacher data without first de-identifying it? Yes, they wanted the data to be used for learning purposes. But not at the expense of teachers' potential embarrassment.

Had we realized that many attendees considered this a violation of their confidentiality, we would have immediately remedied the problem by taking a black marker and blacking out identifying information. Instead, we learned that some teachers were frustrated as we circulated through the retreat to listen in on the table conversations that proceeded as participants worked through the data analysis protocols. "I can't believe our names are on this data for everyone to see," whispered Carver, who was particularly troubled by what had transpired. We asked Carver questions to gain a deeper understanding of his perspectives and listened as he explained how he experienced the decision as just careless. Still others at his table didn't consider it a big deal: if the goal was to learn from teacher practices for the collective benefit, it only made sense to know who engaged in what practices. Carver slowly disengaged. During a break, Kathy, a member of our research team, went to him to troubleshoot:

> **Kathy:** I hear you. I understand your perspective.
>
> **Carver:** I'm trying not to be judgmental. I understand that others don't see this as a big issue. But if a large part of what we are working toward is building trust, I feel like coming into a setting and seeing my name and my colleagues' names on data works against that.
>
> **Kathy:** Do you think we should bring your concern to the administrative team?
>
> **Carver:** Yes. I think they need to know.
>
> **Kathy:** Would you like to bring the concern to their attention? Would you like me to? Would you like for both of us to approach them?

Carver: I don't feel comfortable bringing it to them. But I don't mind if you bring it up.

Kathy: Okay. Can I share who expressed the concern?

Carver: I'd rather you not.

Kathy: Got it. I want to make sure the message hits the points that you believe are important for folks to hear. If you don't mind, I'm going to quickly practice what I will say. Will you please offer me feedback or guidance?

Carver: Sure.

With Carver's permission and guidance, Kathy shared Carver's and others' concern about the identifiable data with the administrative team. Kathy explained, "I'm sharing this with you after asking permission from the person who brought it to my attention: some teachers are troubled by the fact that identifiable teacher data is openly available. They would have liked to at least know this would happen. The teachers were caught off guard." The administrators were surprised and thought that given all that was happening, the concern was petty. From their perspective, seeing teacher data all the time, they reasoned that it shouldn't be a secret. Moreover, the retreat was designed for collective learning and improvement, and it was "just data." But it wasn't. Relatively quickly, the administrators self-reflected. "I can see how that would be offputting."

The capacity to engage in courageous confrontations stemmed in part from individuals and groups confronting problems within their immediate sphere of influence. The practice developed their confidence and skills to move beyond their immediate spheres as was the case when the administrative team's meeting with Black community leaders helped them realize they needed to engage more fully with community members. It was within Carver's sphere of influence to say, "I don't like that our data (or more specifically my data) is available for all to see. I understand why the data is useful. After listening, I can also see why it is useful and instructive to have teacher names associated with the data. However, I would appreciate the opportunity to explore those benefits (and cons) in advance of the retreat." As simple as it sounded, this type of directness was counternormative. Understanding the shortcomings of the climate box, the administrators and teacher ambassadors understood well the importance of getting teachers to take action to address seemingly small problems and large ones alike.

People in CWHS could address problems if they confronted the problems. This seemingly insignificant episode was a learning opportunity for everyone involved because it helped all to see an alternative to addressing problems. The approach was an alternative to holding a grudge, gossiping, withdrawing from participation, or sabotaging the efforts of others because of a problem. In this instance, multiple people's actions played a role in the creation and maintenance of the problem. Administrators brought identifiable data to the retreat without forewarning teachers. Teachers held their concerns to themselves. They did not go to administrators to express the problem they saw with having identifiable data at the retreat. Other teachers who did not have a problem with the availability of identifiable data did not take their colleagues' discomfort seriously. In other words, all parties played a role in the problem at hand. In the CWHS of years past, the problem would have lingered.

When people turned toward the problem or the people they perceived as the problem, everyone involved opened a window into a new way of being through cocreating new possibilities. This approach offered a chance to listen for loving critique. To reflect. And ultimately to clarify and relate to one another in a fundamentally different way than what their normative nice culture socialized them to do: be quiet, gossip, and harbor resentment. Instead, the group acknowledged the harm done, although unintentional. Carver felt heard. Teachers saw administrators admit they could do better. They continued to do this by creating structures that sustained courageous confrontations.

Structures for Courageous Confrontation

The administrative team confronted their own flawed approaches to dealing with and communicating about and through conflict in mutually reinforcing ways: dismantling their old structures, creating better structures, and enacting new practices within these structures. After consulting with the teacher ambassadors, the administrators kept but reduced their overreliance on the climate box. They acknowledged that teachers used it. They openly pointed out its limitations, in particular that it facilitated a one-way exchange of information and concerns. So they set out to create an organization in the school for transparent, continuous, and courageous flows of communication.

First, they adjusted their schedules to establish daily administrative open office hours. The administrative team experimented with building coverage grids that accounted for the importance of administrator *presence*, just being available and attentive to the moment for teachers, staff, and students alike. They stopped hovering over meetings and sat with teachers. They removed their earpieces when talking with teachers and students. They turned off their two-way radios during meetings. They developed and scheduled two one-to-one meetings with all faculty and staff to listen to their concerns.

They also confronted CWHS's restrictive governance structures. The administrators started dismantling the centralized, restrictive, and exclusive site-based decision-making structure that carried forward from years past. They replaced the site-based governance with school improvement teams and implementation teams. The school improvement teams included student representatives who were primarily students of color, to democratize decision-making and cultivate student leadership. They also included teachers, student ambassadors, and eventually expanded to include parent ambassadors. Administrators opened access to and democratized the use of school data, shifting from providing data in static summative forms to developing department leaders' capacities to use data systems and spreadsheets to generate pivot tables, charts, and graphs that responded to real-time concerns. Teachers began working to formulate questions and answers in collaboration with the school's data specialists. The newly created structures burgeoned into important sites where courageous confrontations occurred on a formal and routine basis.

Administrators soon realized an important contribution they could make, and which others could not: providing teachers with the space, time, and resources to engage in courageous conversations that would learn and lead to courageous confrontations about racial inequities. Ambassadors integrated their book study with their concerns about and commitments to racial equity. So rather than asking a race-neutral question such as "What is keeping me from changing my practice?" they explored race-specific questions such as "What is it about my White self that is keeping me from changing my practice?" Much of the ensuing conversations boiled down to fear of being called racist. As the ambassadors stepped more fully into their work, they found themselves in confrontations similar to what administrators often faced. As their actions forged their teacher-leader identities, many began to confront their selves and whether their efforts were worthwhile. The ambassador meetings became a place for teachers to explore racial emotions and beliefs, develop an antiracist lens, and practice new ways of relating to one another. The practices of being direct, talking candidly about race, and using data for purposes of learning and the structures that increased the frequency of the practices served the school well as they encountered increasingly higher stakes problems, especially with Black community stakeholders.

Fighting Against "CWHS Is a Racist School!"

During the 2015–16 academic year as CWHS administrators undertook the structural reforms, they found themselves embroiled in a conflict with several prominent members of the local Black community. It all began when a Black student who was expelled from a neighboring district petitioned for enrollment at CWHS. After reviewing the student's petition, the administration regarded his expulsion and history as too dangerous and disruptive to accept him into CWHS. They considered their decision a clear-cut "no" and moved on. So they denied his petition for admission. However, the decision caused a firestorm of criticism as the student's family and friends rallied behind him to fight for his admission. A local political leader and activist familiar with the student's situation and the overall tendency for schools to deny Black students opportunities to enroll disagreed with the decision. If they could not win in the court of a racially biased administration, why not take the fight public? About a week later, the social media campaign was full blast: "CWHS's racial inequities, here's the data. CWHS is racist!" The posts generated a flurry of immediate interest. Soon, organizers were planning a protest at the school, focused broadly on the school's racist outcomes.

The work of the preceding years provided CWHS with a different capacity and set of resources to draw from than in past years when they would have cowered under such threats. The administrative team turned directly toward the conflict. "Let's engage this for what it is." Only, they were constrained in three ways. First, the posts made no mention of the impetus for the accusations, that they stemmed from denying a student admission into the school. Because of student privacy policies, the administrators could not disclose any information about where the controversy stemmed from. They couldn't even explain the reason behind the decision despite having information that informed their decision. Second, many Black people regarded CWHS as "the racist school." Administrators knew this. They understood well why people believed it. The general sentiment was not untrue. But the specifics were woefully inaccurate. Where did the data in the social media posts come from exactly? Third, this situation was very much about race and racism. Black students struggle in the school. Administrators could not shy away from the racialized nature of the conflict and the crystal-clear allegation that the school was racist.

Drawing on their past learning and the capacities they had developed through within-school confrontations, administrators did not shy away from the problem (as they may have in years past). Elizabeth reached out to some Black community leaders with whom she had relationships and who were familiar with the school's racial equity reform efforts. She wanted to listen to the concerns people raised. Her immediate stance was to listen and learn not to argue against the accusations. After she talked with a well-respected Black community leader, he suggested they hold a community meeting. The meeting would be an opportunity to listen and learn. The administrative team also knew it would be an opportunity to tell the story of their efforts to do better. This conflict harkened back to the importance of telling their story. As Elizabeth stated previously, it was the leader's responsibility "to help people know what we're doing. And to talk about outcomes . . . to have some data to show improvement."

The administrative team invited me to a meeting. I read the social media posts. "What you can do is tell the story. The good and the bad," I said. For the first time, the team started to craft the story of their efforts in all of its complexity. The nature of the problem demanded they construct a racial story. Although their story was a racial one all along, the practice of gathering information, speaking, documenting, and storying their efforts to address the racial problems and racism for an external audience was an educative and developmental task. The process required they look very closely at the relationship between their efforts and the results the reforms produced over the three years. In preparation for the meeting, the administration, staff, and select teacher leaders pulled together information. It was fascinating to witness how seriously they took the community's concerns. And I was unsure whether the seriousness was a defensive posture or not. Was this an attempt to save face? To squelch a potential controversy? To cover their backs?

Associate principal Donnell took particular offense to the accusations. At the same time, he understood the community members' concerns. He shared his frustrations with me. "I get it. But they don't know the full story. And their facts are just wrong. I wish they had reached out to ask people who know our work before blasting us on social media." The summary sheet the school staff prepared revealed mixed results:

Black students make up less than 10 percent of the total population. Slightly more than 10 percent of Black students have been suspended. In 2016–17, there were 101 Black students. Twelve were suspended out of twenty-nine total suspensions. The twelve Black students suspended account for over 40 percent of all school suspensions.

In 2014–15, most suspensions for Black students were for objective behaviors (eighteen of twenty-two, 82 percent). Nearly all of the objective suspensions were for fighting, aggression, or theft (seventeen of eighteen objective suspensions, 94 percent). In 2015–16, more than half of all suspensions for Black students were for objective behaviors (nine of seventeen, 53 percent).

Nearly all of the objective suspensions were for fighting, aggression, or theft (eight of nine objective suspensions, 89 percent). In

2016–17, almost all suspensions for Black students were for objective behaviors (eleven of twelve, 92 percent). Nearly all of the total suspensions were for fighting, aggression, or theft (ten of twelve suspensions, 83 percent).

Close to 90 percent of Black students had no suspensions in the past three years. The category "Restorative / Peer Conference" is not included in the suspension data.

More problems emerged as they compiled information to construct their story of progress. Let the numbers tell it: their efforts to improve produced defensible but hardly brag-worthy results. Problems persisted. The story CWHS administrators needed to tell a group of disaffected Black community members was short of impressive. It went like this: we're trying.

The day of the meeting arrived. The four-person administrative team all attended. I joined by telephone. A highly regarded Black community leader who convened the stakeholders welcomed everyone to the meeting. He offered opening remarks about why the meeting was important and necessary and expressed his hopes that a deeper understanding, on both sides, would emerge from the time. A representative from the community coalition began by stating their concerns. The administrative team listened without interruption. With one major exception, the comments mirrored the concerns outlined in the social media posts. When CWHS team members responded, they started by acknowledging the concerns they heard. Donnell spoke first:

My very first day on the job, I attended a retreat that was exclusively focused on us acknowledging the very problems that you all have outlined. Before that, I'd never been a part of a school meeting that was so candid about race and racism. That was two years ago. Since that very first day, we've made an effort to ensure the school is a place that affirms and supports all of our students, but especially our Black students.

I take this work personally. I know our efforts. I'm not interested in refuting your arguments as I am with adding clarity and providing additional information that we admittedly have not done a very good job at making people beyond the walls of CWHS aware of.

In the course of about an hour, the conversation meandered through a number of considerations of race and racism, questions about access to opportunities, achievement outcomes, and how to foster a sense of belongingness. But it focused mostly on disciplinary mistreatment. It was much less contentious than I expected it to be. People listened, asked questions, and found common ground, such as "as much as we are working to increase faculty and staff of color, these are not situations we can hire ourselves out of" and "teachers have a professional responsibility to improve and adapt their instruction and management practices to support Black students." There was minimal posturing and little to no defensiveness. On most issues, the confrontation yielded clarity. Except on the issue of the school police issuing trespassing tickets to students. The administration knew about tickets but had not understood the severity of the problem.

Central Waters Regional police officers routinely issued students tickets for "trespassing" on school grounds after school hours. Disproportionately, Black and Brown students remained on school grounds early or late because they did not have transportation to get to and from school within the allotted school hours. CWHS maintained an open lunch policy that allowed students to leave campus for lunch if they chose to do so. Students who had cars often drove themselves and their friends to local fast-food restaurants. With a car, it was possible to leave and return before the lunch period ended. Leaving campus for lunch and returning on time without a car was more difficult. But it didn't stop students from wanting to leave campus during lunch time.

Administrators were aware that the school police could issue tickets. They also knew that officers issued tickets. But they considered it a low-occurrence activity and before listening to Black parents had not understood the violence of ticketing, the psychological and financial harm it caused students, and the ripple effect on their families and communities. For community members, low occurrence wasn't the issue. The students didn't deserve tickets. They posed no threat. They couldn't pay the fifty-dollar fee. They often hid the tickets from their parents. When they didn't pay, the penalties increased. A student who remained on school grounds after football practice (after hours) until a pick-up arrived could result in a ticket, increased fines, and court dates for families. Many students had accumulated hundreds of dollars of tickets and late fees. Waiting for a ride home after football practice was made into a criminal offense that could end in an arrest. As administrators listened to community members' concerns, they understood the long-lasting ripple effects and pervasiveness of the ticketing problem. It wasn't a small deal. It was a problem. And it reflected the broader problem of punitive policing of Black students. The administrative team committed to investigating the tickets at more depth and working to curb what was happening. They learned the troubling entanglement their school and district had with local law enforcement that encroached into Black and Brown students' everyday experiences.

Over the duration of the meeting, people talked and engaged differently than in years past.[6] They sustained a conversation about race and racism in a way that I had not seen before. They raised questions. They expressed curiosity over how to make things better. Their communication revealed a growing capacity to conduct race-specific data analysis, use race-specific language and concepts, sustain racial discomfort, and listen to Black people. CWHS administrators acknowledged concerns, they talked with courage and precision about the problems and opportunities that existed in the school and for whom, and they committed to working to fight against the harms Black community members expressed. In particular, the increased use of race-specific words and concepts correlated with more sophisticated problem identification and thus problem solving. The capacity to engage in problem exploration and analysis was distinctly different. The capacity to talk in race-specific terms and with a level of racial consciousness mattered. But talk, without actionable follow-up, meant little.

Everything Requires a Fight

At the end of the fifth year of the project, the school held another retreat. I listened in as administrators, teachers, and staff worked to make sense of Black students fighting, hallway hanging, and a culture of disrespect toward adults and authority figures. Really? They were back there *again*. Many teachers wanted improvements. They wanted to feel safe. They wanted to be respected, even if it was from students they didn't know well. Folks had long agreed it wasn't possible for teachers to know every student. And no adult should have to have a prior relationship with students to ask them to make their way to class. The days of pointing fingers were bygone. Teachers understood that administrators supported them. They appreciated it.

The school adopted many new practices for dealing with disruptions, disrespect, and the day-to-day annoyances of school life. Many of the school's responses were aligned with the most cutting-edge research on providing individualized behavioral supports, restorative approaches, and so forth. Elizabeth described the "readmit meetings, and behavior plans . . . and every kid having their own special plan based on who they are." Ethan explained they were using "restorative approaches. Speaking at length with every kid. Involving parents." Things seemed to be a little bit better. Until they weren't. The CWHS climate was fragile. It could shift from warm to icy cold in a matter of hours, triggered by a social media rumor or one bad interaction between students and teachers or between teachers. Or administrators and teachers.

Elizabeth had long been frustrated with teachers' unwillingness to collectively adopt practices and routines that might curb hallway hanging and disrespect, which were clearly within teachers' sphere of influence. Ask students, in a warm supportive way, to move to class: "If you're not in class, you gals are missing important learning." Ensuring students moved to class seemed straightforward. But it wasn't. Despite continued discussions about practices such as issuing a hall pass to visit the restroom, teachers never reached a consensus on whether or not that should be the way to curb hallway hanging. Small, seemingly simple actions required mustering the energy to fight. Take attendance. Start class on time. Stand in the hallways and interact with students during the passing periods. Offer gentle encouragement and reminders that arrival to class is important for academic success.

In a large, overcrowded school like CWHS, achieving schoolwide consensus on these sorts of issues was not easy. It was a constant fight, mostly of ideas. Teachers' uses of bathroom passes varied greatly. Some felt that writing passes was inconvenient. Others reasoned that high school students should be able to make choices about when they need to leave the room, and teachers trusted them to do so, within reason. After all, even when teachers issued a pass, students had to be trusted to go where they said they would and to return. For many, a lax reliance of hall passes indicated trust. And then, there were a number of teachers who just didn't have a problem with students coming in and out of their room during instructional time. Whatever the reason, the variations in practices translated into students in the hallways and prolonged passing periods. The fact that students were often "not where they are supposed to be" led to conflicts between students and teachers. Conflicts emerged with students wanting to leave class and the teacher not giving a pass. "How can you be teaching and students get up and walk out and you not address it?" administrators often wondered aloud. These cumulative experiences of seemingly small and mundane problems, those that are most visible to the people grounded in the day-to-day life of the school, deteriorated the culture and climate. A triggering event exacerbated the problems, especially the spectacle of Black students fighting.

More Violence, More Fights

By the 2016–17 academic year, violence still plagued CWHS. But, four years into the equity change efforts, a critical mass of teachers understood the violence of school-based racism. They knew that school was a safer place for students to fight than in the neighborhoods. They committed to stopping them, holding them back, and bringing them into peace circles and restorative justice circles. They wanted to support and welcome them back into the school community. They wanted to model proactive approaches to directly addressing problems before they reached a boiling point. One teacher explained what it looked like to both acknowledge the myriad forms of violence that students experienced and to help them fight against violence, by speaking up and taking actions, in ways that would not further harm themselves or others. A White female teacher, Emily, said:

> Students are speaking up because the communication approaches we learned, we're now using with students and they are using with us. I'm not saying things are great. We still have problems. But students are better at recognizing when something doesn't *feel* right, and they're starting to understand it's okay to question that or even to criticize that publicly.
>
> When students come to me, I simply tell them I don't really like teacher bashing or bashing my colleagues. I always tell them I'd hate it if somebody was talking behind my back. Then I always offer to relay the information in some way. Like "Do you want me to go with you to talk to Ms. So and So about the kid that's wearing the, you know, pro-life shirt even though you had an abortion?"
>
> There are these really personal things that are going on this year that can lead to bigger problems. So I've made that offer, like "Do you want me to go with you to do this thing, or do you want me to go with you to this meeting?" or things like that. I got it from the equity work and development because you used it with us at our meetings. You said, you know, when teachers come to me and they say, "Oh, I've got this problem," you kept saying in our department meetings "Okay . . . I can take that back to an administrator, but you know the goal is to get you to go forward yourself."
>
> That modeling in those meetings helped me a lot with trying to get kids to understand that their voice is really important for addressing seemingly small things. That it coming from me will not go nearly as far as if it came from them. Then if they need, like, that stepping stone that I'm willing to be part of that. So I've done that with students more.

Addressing the spectacular forms of violence requires courageously confronting mundane forms of violence, such as the retraumatization a shirt caused. Or a hectic home life that Black and Brown students may experience as a result of living in a white supremacist society. These sorts of underlying mundane conditions and root causes are difficult to discern, pin down, and point out. They require a closeness and insight into students' socio-emotional wellness that most schools take little to no time to consider. Instead, their best image of students is from social media posts. To many White educators, the day-to-day mundane violence of being Black and Brown in a white supremacist world is invisible. Unless Black parents explain it and educators actually listen, they will primarily concern themselves with fighting against and punishing spectacular forms of verbal and physical violence.

Educators who engage in courageous confrontation see and confront more than vivid violence. They pivot from "What happened?" to "Why is this happening?" Why? Why? They fight the violence of "Midwest nice" cultural practices that benefit no one. They help students fight against words that harm and traumatize Black and Brown students. They acknowledge that the violence of racism spills over into the school community and that the want for belongingness that draws Black and Brown students into dangerous lifestyles stems from racism. So, fighting for Black employees, student affinity groups, and a relevant and responsive curriculum are tools to fight racial oppression. In courageously confrontational schools, Black and Brown students have multiple and ongoing opportunities to be a part of community where they belong, where they can learn, and where they can become fighters for their own liberation.

In the summer of 2017, four years after the first union flareup, teachers were fed up again. They reached out to union representatives to demand that the administration redress the problem. Unlike four years prior, the union did not create an underground campaign aimed at ousting the principal. They didn't even take their issues directly to the superintendent of the board. Instead, the union representative went directly to the administration on the teachers' behalf. I wasn't a part of the conversation. But the teacher union representative attended the retreat. And the retreat agenda built in time for department chairs, administrators, and selectively invited teachers and staff to attend. They discussed. They explored. And they disagreed. It was not passive-aggressive confrontation. It was courageous confrontation. Colleagues pushing each other. Talking openly. And not shying away from the possibility that refusing to give a student a hall pass could result in an episode of racial conflict or a "You won't let me go to the bathroom 'cause I'm Black" accusation of racism.

Samantha was a teacher who did not experience the sorts of problems that the group discussed. So when Elizabeth asked the department chairs to convey to teachers the importance of adhering to the long-standing hallway pass policy, Samantha found it difficult to agree with the recommendations. She explained that "every teacher does not have the same problems with classroom management, so I don't feel it's right to overlay a blanket policy onto every teacher in the school. And I personally don't want to be in a position of having to make my colleagues comply with a policy that I don't even agree with." As the meeting wound down, the department chairs conceded the importance of trying something to abate the problem with hallway hanging. After all, the consequence of collectively not trying was crystal clear. There would be students in the hallways. There would be confrontations.

We adjourned, and Samantha expressed her disappointment one last time. She also said she would follow through as agreed, but that she didn't like it. Elizabeth and associate principal Andrea walked me out of the building, down the long corridor from the library toward the south parking lot. It was a slow walk. Elizabeth expressed frustration with Samantha's advocacy. After Elizabeth finished "complaining," Andrea replied in a very matter-of-fact tone, "At least she told us. She was willing to disagree publicly. We know how she feels and where she's coming from. Last year, we wouldn't have known. That's progress." "Well . . . I guess you're right," said Elizabeth. I nodded, thinking about what I witnessed over the course of the day. How Samantha was rightly frustrated. How Elizabeth was rightly frustrated. How Andrea was right. And how the interaction itself signaled progress. I witnessed a powerful well-planned day of professional learning about how to improve a school that openly recognized the pressing need to get better for Black and Brown students. They prepared for the coming year's fights, the spectacular and the mundane. Whatever those fights would be, I hoped deep down that it wouldn't be Black students fighting. I left wondering if White teachers at CWHS shared my concern for students' holistic well-being or if their anxiety stemmed from their racialized fears of "Black gangsters" fighting. Either way, I was tired of Black people getting hurt, physically and also by White people's racial fears, which were just as, if not more, damaging as any punch to the face.

COURAGEOUSLY CONFRONTATIONAL PRACTICES

Courageous confrontation, its principled practices and facilitative structures and routines, strengthened CWHS capacity to address racial conflict and problems. As we paid closer attention to the practices that reflected courageous confrontation, five important practice principles emerged, summarized in table 3.1.

Courageously confrontational practices require presence. Presence offered people whose voices were socially or organizationally marginalized the opportunity to be heard, felt, and seen. It enabled people in power chances to hear, feel, and see. Coming into a confrontation with presence is not a light task because presence requires standing between an offensive and defensive posture, withholding rebuttal and being curious while also honoring the convictions that compel the need for courageous confrontation. When CWHS administrators met with Black community members, all parties understandably came into the confrontation with a set of convictions. Black community members came in angry about Black students' experiences. Administrators came in angry that their efforts were unrecognized. They held on to these convictions while they engaged. They spoke from them, honoring why they were present. They used their convictions as confrontational tools to build greater understanding not as weapons to disregard, dismiss, or damage the people who sat across from them.

Being present in a moment and, in particular, in a confrontation does not equate to agreement or minimize dissent. It broadens considerations of what fighting for racial equity must look like, feel like, and entail. It was not surprising that CWHS administrators left the community meeting feeling a deeper need to strengthen and expand their partnership with Black community members if they were going to improve Black and Brown students' school experiences. The preparation,

TABLE 3.1   Cultivating a culture of courageous confrontation

CRITICAL PRINCIPLE	ENACTING THE PRINCIPLE	RACIAL LEARNING BENEFITS
Practicing presence is critical	Attend meetings and visit classrooms. Be visible in hallways. During important conversations, turn off or silence cell phones or walkie-talkies, remove earpieces, and minimize technological distractions.	People who practice presence (givers) benefit from minimized distractions, heightened in-the-moment experiences, and strengthened understanding. Receivers of presence experience feeling heard, valued, and supported.
Directing conflict to precise issues or problems is critical	Turn people toward direct confrontation with practices, policies, structures, and beliefs that are problematic. Give the person who is being confronted an opportunity to understand a different perspective (but not necessarily agree). Minimize gossip. Confront ideas and practices (not people).	People who are directly and not directly involved in a confrontation benefit from participating in and witnessing courageous confrontation, hearing diverse perspectives, and engaging in deliberative processes to address problems.
Using race-specific language and concepts to talk about problems is critical	Draw on race-conscious language. Use words such as Black, Asian, White, Hmong, Latinx, whiteness, racist, racism, race-neutral, privilege, and race-evasive to pinpoint problems.	The school community benefits because people can identify, recognize, and address what they are able to name. Race-specific and racial concepts transform race-neutral problems into racialized ones.
Proposing and taking actions within individual and collective spheres of influence are critical	A critical first step is to ask oneself the question "What can I do—as an individual given the resources, power, and people I have access to?" Teams, departments, and student groups can ask the same questions.	The school community benefits by activating agency. It reduces the tendency for people to harbor negative feelings and emotions. It helps people learn their own power and ability to effect change (or at least to try).
Engaging in confrontation in formal spaces is critical	Create and encourage educators to bring courageous confrontations into formal school spaces. Formalizing spaces for conflict allows people to prepare collective self-reflection, problem exploration, and problem-solving.	The school community benefits by partially bounding the problem so that it does not become all consuming. It creates a time and place for conflict and creates possibilities that conflict will be more productive.

presence, and capacity to learn from the community meeting stemmed from sustained learning and practice within the school setting. Countless times during professional learning sessions and meetings, we asked people to practice thinking about their thinking, what we referred to as gathering thoughts:

> Give each person in your group a full two minutes to speak. If the speaker finishes before the time elapses, sit in silence and think about what you heard or said until the time is up. No questions or feedback. . . . Now, take sixty seconds to think before responding. Use the sixty seconds to gather your thoughts.

Taking sixty seconds to gather thoughts and sit in silence became a routine that disrupted CWHS's façade of congeniality and culture of disregard and damage. CWHS's adoption of courageously confrontational practices and structures to facilitate productive confrontation did not stem the onslaught of problems. This process produced more problems. It was not that the problems were new. Each step forward revealed more problems and conflicts. It also helped them see the problems in their racial complexity. They had to confront the limitation of their practices and thinking and begin to reimagine how to address enduring problems.

CONCLUSION

Some people have to fight. And while some people fight, people who do not share their experience judge and criticize the people who have to fight in order to just be. At CWHS, Black and Brown students have to fight. So they walk out. And they sit in. They confront. They tell trusted teachers their problems. They curse. They take their time getting to class. And sometimes, not often, they make it a priority to physically harm a schoolmate. They know the consequences of fighting. Yet they do it anyway. They receive their punishment, and they come back to school yet again to learn. That is courage. The problem is that the capacity to be so courageous at fifteen or sixteen years old stems from coming of age in a racist society that cares nothing for Black bodies. Black and Brown students possess immense courage. They have to because being born Black and Brown into a racist society requires one to consciously and unconsciously fight. To be recognized. To be heard. To survive. To love oneself. Fights take many forms.

Many White people consider it their moral duty to condemn physical fights and in doing so absolve themselves of both the need to consider why the fight is necessary and what they are willing to do to stop them, other than express their fear. They absolve themselves of recognizing the daily fight of being Black and Brown students. Or considering that Black and Brown students who disproportionally bear the violence of racism and white supremacy need and deserve the same (and more) opportunities White educators want and need from schools—multiple pathways that enable direct confrontation to problems that cause them anxiety, hurt, and harm; multiple and routine pathways to express grievances with those with positional authority and power; opportunities to heal, forgive, and seek reconciliation; and opportunities to build community with people they are not like.

I never met a person at CWHS who expressed interest in or excitement about courageously confronting White parents who were appalled that the school "supported" Latinx students and their allies who walked out of school to show their disapproval of Donald Trump's election to the presidency of the United States. Or from fielding phone calls from White parents who want the school to "respect the United States flag and troops" by reprimanding students' solidarity with Colin Kaepernick.[7] I once sat in the front office and listened to an administrator explain, "We're not going to make students stand or recite the pledge of allegiance in class or at athletic events if they choose to not do so." It seemed a simple enough stance. But not to White parents.[8]

But when White students arrived to school wearing pro-Trump and "Make America Great Again" paraphernalia and chanted "Build that wall" to Latinx students, White people did not respond with the same force as when Black and Brown students pointed out the racism and xenophobia of such hateful speech. "If students can stand with Kaep, what's wrong with standing with Trump to make America great again?" White people reasoned. Taking a public stance required a confrontation that many

CWHS educators were happy to avoid. In the emergence of a culture of courageous confrontation, these questions and the confrontations that they compelled are unavoidable. In the best of situations, they are taken up directly and formally.

Fighting these forms of mundane violence in the context of a courageously confrontational school culture breeds possibility and the potential for substantial improvement. It also breeds uncertainty and occasional hopelessness that stem from an emergent racial consciousness of how much more work is required to become a school community where Black and Brown students thrive. As people listened, actively sought, or accidentally gained exposure to information about racism or other marginalizing experiences, it created a dilemma. As CWHS's White staff encountered information—school data, stories, varied interpretations of national events—experiences and racial learning about race and racism, the question "What now?" continually emerged. A courageously confrontational school culture is not for everyone. And so people left. Or withdrew. Others broadened their fight. Usually, before people decided on a course of action, they had to have a talk with their selves. The confrontation with oneself—emotions and beliefs—was often the most important ongoing fight of all.

4

COLLECTIVE AWARENESS OF RACIAL EMOTIONS AND BELIEFS

E ducators who want to disrupt racism need to understand how they individually and collectively think about race and racism. They must also develop an understanding of the racial emotions and beliefs of colleagues, students, and parents. Most people don't have a deep understanding of the racial emotions and beliefs of the people they work, teach, and learn with on a daily basis. Developing such an understanding within a community of educators who are at different places on their journey toward racial consciousness is highly complex and challenging. White people learn very quickly not to share their ideas and thoughts about race and racism. They learn to not ask questions for rightful fear of being laughed at, ridiculed, shamed for being racist, and told they don't belong. "If you don't understand that race is socially constructed, you just shouldn't be teaching science." "If you don't believe in racial equity, you shouldn't be leading a school." "Anyone who voted for Donald Trump is racist, xenophobic, and shouldn't be teaching." Black and Brown people learn to not share. "Get over it," "That's not true," "I can't believe you don't know that," "How is he qualified to be a principal?" and "You're angry today." Year after year, experience after experience, fear and defensiveness crystalize as the predominant racial emotions that guide educators' interactions, shutting down the talk practices and open dialogue that are foundational to organizational racial learning and awareness.

Awareness of racial emotions and beliefs is a racial resource that provides people in a school with the opportunity to challenge their own thinking and behaviors. Increasing a school's capacity to engage in racial equity work requires that people continually become self-aware and collectively aware of the racial emotions and beliefs that shape day-to-day school life. Awareness of racial emotions and beliefs stems from meta-cognition. *Meta-cognition* refers to an awareness of one's thought processes and the emotions that underpin a particular way of thinking. A person who has a high level of meta-cognitive awareness has the capacity to make sense of situations, notice patterns, and engage in self-regulated decision-making because they can pinpoint, in the moment, how they are thinking and feeling about the situation. Across a range of settings and among numerous Central Waters High School community members, I learned people developed a meta-awareness about race and racism by self-talking about their racial emotions and beliefs and through listening to other people self-talk about their racial emotions and beliefs. Unlike what many scholars argue, talk is not *merely* talk. Speaking is action. Speaking yields outcomes, generates consequences, and creates possibilities.

Racial self-talk is a developmental process whereby people openly wrestle with their own thoughts about racism, racial dilemmas, and their own role in perpetuating racism. Racial self-talks are internal dialogues made public through the act of speaking. When people at CWHS self-talked, it was done as a practice of convincing themselves to take some position on a matter—to double down, to acknowledge the trouble with, or even to affirm they were justified and right to challenge their own beliefs, practices, or patterns of behavior. I grew attuned to racial self-talk when people said things like "I could hear [Black or Brown person's] voice in my head" or "I'm thinking this" or "My thinking may be wrong here . . ." or "This reminds me of what I read and makes me think. . . ." In some instances, people self-talked to me. In other instances, people self-talked to others. This self-talk was usually deeply personal and emotional and used to make sense of a specific racial experience. In some ways self-talk is akin to personal racial narratives. But, unlike personal narratives, it is grounded in real time and references proximal problems and dilemmas. To the unrefined racial ear, racial self-talk can sound like incoherent speech, rambling, stupid questions, and complaining. I want to challenge this inclination to write people off as though they do not know what they're talking about. If a person of color can't quite "put into words" why they hate police, it makes their disdain and critique no less legitimate. People's "ridiculous" talk is a learning resource. If a White person can't quite put into words why they hold the police in high regard, it does not mean they cannot or will never achieve an understanding of why US policing is racist and problematic.

Critically, racial self-talk does not intend to sway or convince *others*. It confronts the self. It questions the self. Its incoherence is a search for racial understanding that creates possibilities for consciousness raising. The invisibility of racial emotions and beliefs gives them profound power because disrupting or changing what is not noticeable is very difficult. Publicly sharing one's thinking about racial emotions and beliefs is critical for organizational improvement because when individuals make their thought processing available for others, it becomes a resource for collective racial learning. Racial self-talk is a critically important practice because it cultivates self and collective awareness of racial emotions and beliefs that in turn enables people to challenge their own racist thinking, recognize their racial knowledge gaps, and hopefully try on ways of thinking and behaving that support racial equity changes.[1]

In this chapter I demonstrate the power that developing an awareness of racial emotions and beliefs has for "The Races We Ran" toward making CWHS a school that better served the educational needs of Black and Brown students. I present different self-talk episodes that demonstrate people's emergent ways of thinking about their own actions, stories, and experiences that constitute increased racial consciousness. I analyze how seemingly insignificant increases in racial consciousness intersected to benefit the broader school community. At Central Waters, people's willingness to racial self-talk aloud about racial emotions and beliefs was an indicator of the school's capacity to make more racially equitable decisions as part of their school improvement efforts. Specifically, sometime throughout the third and fourth years of the project, White people began to talk aloud about race and racism—to themselves, to one another, and in groups—in ways that I had not at all witnessed in years past. People's public racial self-talks were often contradictory, incomplete, or framed as problem-posing curiosities about how racism works and their role in perpetuating or challenging its workings. At the core of their talk was the question "Who belongs?" Throughout the chapter, I amplify the dilemmas that stem from letting people belong even if they don't share beliefs. I suggest that treating people like they belong is a radical act because it assumes that all people possess redemptive qualities. I also attempt to demonstrate what happens when people who are assumed to not belong act like they indeed should and do.

RACING HOME: WHAT AM I DOING OUT HERE? (RACISM AND BELONGING)

In the 2015–16 academic year, school board meetings were a flashpoint for confrontation. The district was under intense scrutiny for its improvement efforts. The previous year, the district quietly adopted a districtwide equity and continuous improvement policy. Advanced Placement classes had been integrated at the highest rates ever. Teachers who left the school still lived in and around Central Waters. The high school was the talk of the town. Parents and local media crowded into the Central Waters district office boardroom to demand answers: "What are you going to do to get control of the school?" The divisions that surfaced within the school a year earlier now existed in the community. The debates, divisions, and corners were identical. The people having them differed.

Without saying it directly, parents, armed with anecdotal accounts from students and teachers, determined that CWHS's problem was Black students' misbehavior at school. A newly elected board member, a White male, who had been a student at the school corroborated their claims. The dominant white narrative went like this: Administrators coddled disruptive Black kids who would benefit from punishment, not support. The good students deserved support. Making the school more orderly and safer required removing bad students. The packed room of impassioned White parents regarded clear rules, consequences, enforcement of rules, and application of consequences as the keys to getting things back in order. So when the district's new equity director, dean, and school administrators asked me to offer the board expert testimony about CWHS discipline and climate reforms, I halfheartedly agreed. I wanted to be a team player. And be supportive. Yet, I anticipated that none of the research I was prepared to present would matter.

The problem was that although a preponderance of research evidence countered White parents' claims, their experiences and the ways they made sense of their experiences mattered more than any research study. Black and Brown people who could offer an experiential counter to their positions did not routinely attend board meetings. I sat in the front row with administrators. I looked back and noticed a Black woman and Black teenage girl in attendance. For better or worse, and although I had never met or seen them in my life, I found comfort in having them there.

My presentation was well put together. Had I been at an academic conference, it would have likely been well received. Elizabeth and Ethan provided an overview of the discipline culture and climate reform efforts underway at the school. I piggy-backed by laying out the research on the harms of zero-tolerance era reforms as well as the potential for restorative approaches to pave a new path for the school. I concluded by telling the board that in many regards, the work underway at CWHS was cutting edge, it would take time, and it was aligned with what was regarded as developmentally appropriate. As soon as the board opened the floor for attendee comments, it was clear this was not an academic conference. The public testimony kicked off; parents and community members unleashed a furry of white rage. We sat and listened. "My kids don't feel safe. What are you *doing* about it? This used to be a good school! You're letting those kids ruin the school. What are you going to do? This is unacceptable." I expected all of the racially coded comments. What I didn't expect was that the three-person *Black community* I imagined minutes earlier would become three Black people at a board meeting.

> My name is Camille. I'm a tenth grader at CWHS, and I'm here to talk about the problems at CWHS. There are students who are disrespectful to teachers. They curse in the hallways and have no respect. *They don't care* about school. And the administrators don't do anything. They know they won't get into trouble so *they don't care*.

I exchanged glances with Elizabeth and Ethan. What was happening? We sat stone-faced and contemplative listening to this courageous young Black CWHS student speak her truth. As the racial universe would have it, Camille, one student out of more than 1,600, just happened to feel so compelled to speak that she convinced her mother to bring her to a board meeting. She put her name on the comments list as she rightfully can and should have. And she used her two minutes to speak with passion and eloquence.

> Most of the students who don't care are Black. I care. They're probably not bad people. But maybe they just need some more help or something. I don't know. But I just wanted to say that I think something should be done because they ruin the school for those of us who want to learn. And they make Black students like me look bad, like we don't care. I do care.

"Students, speak your truth." "Your voice matters." Well . . . we ate our own words, swallowed our own actions, and tasted our own recommendations. We never collectively processed Camille's comments, so I can't speak for Elizabeth and Ethan. But I personally was annoyed. I appreciated Camille's initiative. But I was annoyed at the chance of it all. Why now? Why Camille? Why, why, why? How inconvenient a time, place, and audience for her remarks. After the board meeting wrapped up, I didn't stick around for small talk. It was later than I usually remained at the district, and I had a long drive ahead of me. I thanked people for listening to my remarks and proceeded to quietly sneak out to the parking lot. I was more than halfway to my car when I heard a voice behind me:

> Excuse me, excuse me! . . . I just wanted to tell you that we are not racist. We are NOT racist. And you're here making my kid think she's a racist and she's not. This school used to be a good school. I raised my family here. We've been here. We work hard and we're not racist.

As more people trickled into the parking lot, they slowed their steps to listen in. Some kept moving. Some stopped to give their full attention.

Those who stopped nodded in agreement, cosigning her words. I stood and listened. She continued, inching closer and closer to me: "It's not true. You think that you know something because you read a research study. Well, I know I'm not racist. And my daughter is not racist." She put her head down and started to cry. A White man put his arm around her to console her. As I stood, I glanced up to see Camille's mother standing a short distance away. The White woman looked back up and pointed her finger at me, and pronounced to the onlookers, "He needs to stop his lying." She looked at me. I calmly replied, "I appreciate that you shared how you're feeling." And turned to walk away.

I scanned the parking lot and caught eyes with Camille's mother. She maneuvered through the dispersing crowd. "That was an interesting exchange," Camille's mom said, now within arm's reach. "She's drunk as hell," I smugly responded. The other woman had been close enough for me to smell her breath as she talked. Camille's mother and I shook our heads at the absurdity and giggled like old friends. The three seconds or so of mutual laughter eased the discomfort and pain of the prior interaction. It was just enough to make room for affirmation.

> **Camille's Mom:** Dr. Irby, I want to thank you. I'm glad you're here. And I appreciate the work you are doing at the school. The school has a lot of issues, and I don't think they could do it alone. Your presentation was spot on. They are benefiting from you being there. I do not agree at all with my daughter. And I try to help her understand how her thinking is part of the problem. But she has her own mind, and I encourage her to use it. I support her in expressing her voice. I'm interested in talking more with her about tonight. She'll get it as she gets older. At any rate . . . I wanted to thank you and encourage you to hang in there and keep up the good work.
>
> **Decoteau:** Thank you. I really appreciate it.
>
> **Camille's Mom:** Safe travels on your return home.
>
> **Decoteau:** Thank you so much.

About five minutes after I left the building, I was in my car, finally. It dawned on me that I was drained.[2] As I buckled my seatbelt, self-doubt, disbelief, and frustration flooded my emotional well. "Did this White lady just confront me in this parking lot?" I turned my attention to the oncoming traffic as I waited to turn right out of the parking lot to race back home. I couldn't get out of Central Waters fast enough. "Yes. She did. She definitely confronted me in the parking lot." My internal dialogue was scattered. I felt disrespected, angry, and embarrassed. Then I felt exhausted. Then inadequate. Over the duration of my drive home, I felt defeated for a span of ten minutes. Then, for the next five, I laughed at the whole situation. Perhaps my attempt to find humor in the episode was a means to smooth over the hurt—to keep myself from crying or being overcome with hatred. I remembered the warmth of Camille's mother and the way she, a Black mother, knew exactly what to do to offer me respite in a moment of racial duress. So I felt appreciative. Anger crept back in. "White trash," I thought. As much as I wanted to find calm, my emotions and thoughts refused to be still. It was unwieldy racial discomfort. I pondered, "Why do I keep driving all the way out *here?*" I told myself, "I don't have to do this."

RACING TO STAY: AM I BEING WHITE? (RACISM AND HIRING)

"I applied for other jobs. We've been doing this great work since 2013–14. It's now 2015–16, and I want to see this work through. But I can't deal anymore." I was surprised that *Carla* was sharing this with me. Over the course of the project, numerous people confided in me that they wanted to leave CWHS. Some told me when they were leaving. With some I would return to the school and learn they were gone. I never had the chance to bid farewell. Others shared their dreams of being somewhere else but, for numerous reasons, couldn't or wouldn't leave. Hearing someone say they wanted to leave wasn't a new message. But "Not Carla," I thought. She was a stalwart contributor to the school's racial equity efforts. She connected well with students. She had the respect of her colleagues and administrators alike. She exuded a rare blend of confidence and humility, patience and urgency. She was short in stature but had a commanding presence. She aligned her feet and shoulders directly to whomever she spoke. In the midst of a hurried school day or meeting, her gripping eye contact suggested to whomever she was speaking that what they said mattered.

I found myself gravitating to Carla when I visited the school. She was the person who offered reassurance that the "work" and the journey were "right." That was the reason I knocked on her door shortly before she revealed her efforts to leave. I expected I would pop in for two minutes of small talk. "May I sit?" I asked. She replied "yes" and nodded toward the door, signaling her preference that I close it.

> **Carla:** I'm exhausted. My workload has doubled. People are leaving, and I feel like I'm treading water to stay afloat. I'm so torn about leaving. I love the kids, and I never imagined working anywhere but here.
>
> **Decoteau:** Is your mind made up? It sounds like you'd rather stay here and work under better conditions.
>
> **Carla:** That's about right. I would rather stay here. I don't feel like my work is done at all.
>
> **Decoteau:** I appreciate you telling me this. Have you shared any of this with Elizabeth? Or any other administrators? They are the people who are in a position to do something.
>
> **Carla:** I've shared my frustration and concerns with Elizabeth. Numerous times. She's not willing to fill the vacant position in our department.
>
> **Decoteau:** But have you told her you're at the point where you are considering leaving?
>
> **Carla:** No.

We both paused. What would be the courageous next move to make? I think we both understood where the conversation might go next. The thought of alerting Elizabeth to the seriousness of Carla's potential decision to leave CWHS was daunting. Carla's face flushed red.

> **Decoteau:** Do you think it would benefit you for her to know?
>
> **Carla:** It would. But that terrifies me.
>
> **Decoteau:** Do you mind if I tell Elizabeth that the two of you should talk? If so, I'll go get her.

Carla's challenge was not singly a matter of confronting Elizabeth. It also required her to confront herself. To confront the privilege of being able to leave. To confront the present condition of being understaffed and overworked that diminished her potential to see a better future for herself at CWHS. Carla did not want to leave. But from her vantage point— an increased workload, colleagues leaving left and right, the constant chatter of things getting worse, and an administrator she regarded as unresponsive—she had no choice. But, in truth, she did have an alternate choice: be courageously confrontational enough to move past the racial practice of inaction and invite the administrative team into her problem. I left Carla's office to find Elizabeth, but she wasn't there.

On my way back to Carla's office, I ran into Andrea. "The administrative team should make the time to talk with Carla," I said. "I have time right now," Andrea replied. We returned to Carla's office, where they talked for about three minutes. Andrea mostly listened as Carla recounted our earlier conversation. She thanked Carla for sharing and committed to pulling the administrative team into the conversation. Andrea left. "That worked out well," I thought to myself. But there was more.

> **Carla:** That was terrifying. Very uncomfortable. But good. Okay . . . I feel conflicted about saying this. I need to know if I'm being White here. I'm interested in your thoughts because I do feel like this is me being White. But it seems unfair. Here it goes.

Carla explained that the administrative team's commitment to hiring more teachers and staff of color was causing her staff to become disenchanted. As so many White people often explained, she was fully on board with hiring more people of color, but only in a way that she deemed "fair." Remember, White people get particular racial outcomes because they control the processes. Her argument was the people who were willing to come weren't qualified for the position. At first Carla implied that she didn't have a problem, but that her colleagues and "the department" did. As she talked aloud, she started to explore her own emotional struggles with preferential hiring:

Carla: The person who the administration wants to bring in is Black. But he will be straight out of college, and his degree and credentials don't exactly match what is required. My department feels that's preferential treatment. I am committed to making sure we bring in people of color to fill openings. I agree with that. But I understand my colleagues.

Decoteau: Okay. So, how are you responding to them?

Carla: I guess I feel some type of way too. You need the proper credentials.

Decoteau: I probably wouldn't be talking with you if I weren't offered a scholarship to attend undergraduate. I attended College of Charleston on full scholarship. In high school, I was an average student. I finished high school with a 2.67 GPA. That scholarship was specifically for Black males who demonstrated potential to do well in college, financial need, and who otherwise might not finish college.

When I got to college I had people—professors and mentors—who supported me and helped me figure out how to succeed, as a first-generation student, in an academic environment that I would have likely not succeeded in without that support. I'm sharing my experience because I went to college and am here, not solely based on my own meritorious performance. Once I was in college, the wisdom, selflessness, and generosity of people with knowledge and experience cultivated the success I achieved.

This may all sound like I got an upper hand. We could debate about whether I deserved the opportunity. Or if I earned it. Or deserved it, right? I don't think it's a straightforward answer. I could see it many ways. But here's how white supremacy works. White people are born into a society that gives them the upper hand. Again, we could debate about if it's deserved or earned and so forth.

The point is that just like I gladly accepted the scholarship, White people gladly accept whatever they get. And all of the benefits—all of the upper hands—that White people gladly accept are invisible. That's my analysis. I'm all for reparations and my scholarship was that for me.

So, here's the question: What was your upper hand, if you had one? How did you get here? What helped you? Who helped you?

"Go back to the past three jobs you've had and tell yourself a critically honest story of how you got those jobs," I requested.

Carla: You know what, I started off as a teacher's aide. I was able to go back and get my degree and certifications while I was working here. So when this position opened, the job ad was basically mine. It just made sense that I would be hired. I had the inside information and relationships. I don't know that I competed with anyone for the job. I had never taken the time to think about the advantages I had to get where I am.

As I think more about it, I've gotten almost every job I held from someone inside recommending me and advocating for me to be selected. And I also was welcomed with open arms and supported as I learned on the job. That helped me get better at what I do.

And that aspect of support is important because that's the number one reason the very few Black people who have come to CWHS have left. They talk about how unwelcoming, hostile, and unsupportive the workplace is. As a White person, that seems foreign to me. But if I'm a White person who has a chip on my shoulder because I don't feel a person of color deserves to be here, I'm sure they sense that in our interactions. Multiply that times one hundred White people. I know they experience disdain whether I think I'm being supportive or not.

I get it. In my mind it makes sense. I'm embarrassed because I still am experiencing a range of emotions I can't quite explain. I'm a bit embarrassed. But I'm also afraid, because thinking differently means I should act differently. And be supportive. I shouldn't only support hiring a more diverse staff. I should be supportive of them when they get here to ensure they last past the typical one or two years. Advocating for them amongst White staff who think like me. Extending support. That's the work.

It's scary. I'm thinking through how deeply conditioned I am as a White person to think a certain way. And to feel this perverse sense of injustice when people of color get opportunities that I think should be earned. But they are not earned . . . This is heavy. But it is clear. Students and staff will benefit from hiring more Black and Brown staff. It's that simple.

Decoteau: So the question for me is about more than hiring. Because the people of color that get hired here tend to leave. What role will you play in keeping whoever is hired here for longer than others stayed?

Carla and I learned right in the moment. Her self-talk revealed that she did not feel valued or heard. She didn't have the resources she expected or rightly deserved. It also revealed her racial disdain for the *possibility* that someone she regarded as not fully qualified to work in a particular role—a person she did not know—might be hired as her colleague. She worked her full career in a resource-rich school. The level of work-related stress was taking its toll. As her workload increased and resources waned, so too did her stress and well-being, respectively. These were experiences of racial exhaustion born from a sense of entitlement about what counted as adequate work conditions. Her self-talk also revealed frustrations that working in conditions of relative material abundance is a white racial experience. Many underresourced schools have one counselor.

In a white supremacist society, people who hold meritocratic beliefs presume Black and Brown people are where they are professionally and otherwise solely because of effort or lack thereof. White people are where they are because of their effort, ingenuity, and talent. There is no such thing as white mediocrity. Everything is earned and deserved. The CWHS teaching staff was predominantly White because that's what good teachers, good counselors, and leaders were. Hard working. Appropriately credentialed. Timely (except to all staff meetings). They believed in all kids. They were fair. They treated people not by the color of their skin but solely on their effort. After all, they worked at CWHS. Anyone who did not fit the bill did not deserve to work at CWHS. Anyone who did therefore deserved the absolute best working conditions. In a white supremacist society, White people find it difficult to see their lives as shaped by a string of taken-for-granted "breaks" because they imagine their lot in life derives solely from effort, intelligence, and hard work. Carla, without elaborating it as such, played right into this line of thinking.

And then our racial self-talk disrupted it. She analyzed her own racial thinking. And I shared my racial thinking. Carla's willingness to get curious and think aloud revealed to herself the sense of white entitlement and expectation that she kept wrapped up in her unexplored emotions. Once Carla admitted she "was feeling some kind of way," her self-talk invited her to look into her white emotional baggage. A meritocratic ideal wasn't merely an idea stuck in Carla's belief system. It was a belief system that nearly kept her from supporting a person of color. It was literally emotional baggage. She moved past noticing it. She named it as best she could. And that offered her an opportunity to peek into her baggage. Her belief in meritocracy lent itself to racist thinking and nearly led her to behave in a manner that would preserve a racist system. Instead, her emergent racial consciousness and opportunity to talk it through caused her to pause and change course.

RACING TO NOWHERE: "IT'S A POWER MOVE" (RACISM AND POLICING)

When it came to police relations with students, CWHS was racing to nowhere. The conflict and problems had no end in sight. So when Dontae tagged *F.O.B.* all over the school, everyone wondered, "What does that mean?" Officer Blaine was fed up and he let the administrative team know it: "This is all your fault because you haven't done enough with these kids to show them there are consequences for their behavior. When are you going to learn? If we don't start doing things differently, it's just going to get worse. I'm not here to babysit." He gathered himself and returned to the school's police liaison office. The outburst was a long time coming. CWHS was trying to do things differently: restorative justice circles, peer court, and peer mediation. "Soft" stuff. To Officer Blaine, the ongoing problems were unacceptable.

> **Officer Blaine:** Dontae stole five things from the school in one year. You have him on video stealing. He looked right at me and said, "I didn't steal that phone." I said Dontae, "I've got the video." After I showed it to him, he said, "I didn't say that." And now this kid is walking

around threatening me saying "F.O.B." Writing F.O.B. all over the school! That means "F--k Officer Blaine."

Elizabeth: I hear you. We are continuing to work with Dontae. We have a meeting set up with him and his case manager. We'll make sure we address this again.

Donnell: It's been challenging. We've been trying really hard to stay focused on building relationships, and not just suspending kids out. Teaching them new behaviors and really talking through things. But it's a struggle. We have students with serious needs. The process takes time, patience, and effort. And people want swift reactions.

Dontae transferred to CWHS in 2015–16, and he did not like the police. So, he didn't like Officer Blaine. They encountered each other when people called Officer Blaine to respond to Dontae's occasional outbursts. He punched doors, cursed at teachers, and made a scene out of seemingly minor interactions. Ask Dontae to go to class. It could turn into an episode. CWHS was supposed to be a fresh start. Dontae transferred into CWHS after being expelled from his three previous schools for fighting. Because he transferred from several states away, administrators had limited information about how to best support him. Why was Dontae so angry and confrontational toward Officer Blaine? They talked with him several times. Each time, they believed that maybe they broke through. And then, another confrontation. And then another. Conferences, restorative circles, and calls home became routine.

Elizabeth: Help us understand why you don't like cops? Why are you so mad at Officer Blaine? What's up with that? What's up with this F.O.B. stuff?

Dontae: F--k this school.

Elizabeth: Do you want Officer Blaine and me to leave so you can just talk to Ms. Lanier [case worker] by yourself?

Dontae: You [Elizabeth] don't have to leave. He can [referring to Office Blaine]. He's a liar.

Elizabeth: We're both going to leave. You have Donnell here. You have your case manager. I'll check in with you tomorrow.

Was Camille right? Maybe the parents who attended the board meetings were wrong. The administrators self-talked aloud with one another,
trying to make sense of their changing, more racially just and affirming
practices. They became increasingly attuned to the complexities of figur-
ing out how to support students differently in a system that was punitive,
stacked against them, and retributive. Yet, while their continued practice
of talking through problems, counseling, and racial consciousness expanded, Dontae remained unpredictable. And Officer Blaine remained
unhappy at their responses. Why Dontae? In the following exchange, the
administrators talked through what transpired after their meeting with
Dontae, their problem with Officer Blaine's response, and their frustrations with their local police force. They accepted the racist practices of
US policing.

> **Elizabeth:** Before I was able to reach out to get his take on the outcome of
> the meeting "What do you think Dontae says to Blaine? . . . F.O.B."
> He never told us that's what it meant, but I'm sure it does. Blaine
> comes up here, and he is pissed as hell. He is like "I've had it."
> Enough of this disrespect. So Donnell and I bring both of them up to
> talk about everything. First, we talk to Dontae alone. Then we bring
> in Officer Blaine, because we are trying to run the intervention like
> a circle and convey "we're here to help you and I'm not trying to be
> in your grill," and other stuff. They both agreed it was a good step to
> participate. Then, we're in the circle and Dontae is just sitting there
> lying. I know him pretty well by now. He just repeatedly denies the
> behavior. So I said forget it. The circle is pointless.
>
> **Ethan:** So the next day, we said forget the circle. I went to find Dontae.
> All three of us and the case manager were there. We basically said to
> him: "It has to stop. It's unacceptable." We had a long conversation
> with Dontae and his case manager. Then I called up Blaine. And we
> talked. I explained we're doing things differently, and we're learning
> how to not be punitive.
>
> **Donnell:** And just like that, it all stopped. Dontae never said F.O.B. again.
> He's never disrespected Officer Blaine like that again. He's done a
> 180. No problems.

Ethan: So, you know what? At the end of the day, was that approach effective? Yes. It stopped the behavior.

Decoteau: Mm-hmm [affirmative].

Elizabeth: But now, the problem is that Officer Blaine felt very disrespected. Basically, he could not believe that Dontae was not suspended. Or expelled. So he goes to his police chief (he's not a district employee) and says that we are basically incompetent, and it's our fault that there's so many fights because we aren't doing anything. Do you see how this is working out?

Ethan: You know what, there's no way to win.

Elizabeth: I left that initial meeting to support Blaine and not look like I was coddling Dontae, you know what I mean? Dontae's fine with me. He was okay if I stayed. But I left. Now, Officer Blaine is on the radio badmouthing us and saying we aren't doing anything. It's not enough that Dontae stopped acting out.

Donnell: Yep, it's crazy. So you know we had the community meeting. One of the things that caught us off guard was when we learned Central Waters Police Department and even our own officers were giving students trespassing and disorderly conduct tickets. So that's been another problem. It's a problem that we don't have a handle on because we don't know how pervasive it is. We just have to go off what the folks at that meeting said.

Elizabeth: Right, that's not data that we collect. So we requested it from the district, who then requested it from the police chief. We want to answer some basic questions: How many tickets were written? Who's writing them? What students are being cited and when? And then we found out the district doesn't have it either. Long story short, it turned into a back-and-forth between the district and local police. The superintendent is involved. We still have no information. I think they are withholding it.

Donnell: We can't respond to or work with the community to solve this problem. And it looks bad on us that we can't answer basic questions.

Ethan: You know what? I'm so damn frustrated. It's not hard for them to provide that information. It's just a power move. It's all about power.

Elizabeth: It's another story, but I think it's a good representation of the challenges we're having with our school police officers. Like, I'm responsible for what happens at the school. If students are getting tickets, we need to know.

Ethan: I think a lot of this has got to do with race. They have the data. But they want to show their power. That's it. It's a power move. We're damned either way. Can't win.

The administrative team explored their challenges mediating Dontae and Blaine's conflict and happened upon the racial ideology of policing and punishing Black people. In each case, the capacity to discern racial emotions and beliefs correlated with a capacity to see some alternative ways of behaving that disrupted dominant narratives. Many of these epiphanies, some that came in the form of questions or self-admissions, were not readily available for organizationwide racial learning. My own racial self-talk was private. Carla talked only to me. The administrative team racial self-talked among themselves. Others within the school community would have benefitted from hearing this thinking.[3]

THE PRESIDENTIAL RACE: I CAN'T STOP FEELING SUSPICIOUS (RACISM AND POLITICS)

"Good morning. I want to accomplish what we have planned for today, but I also want to acknowledge the discomfort I'm feeling." In November 2016, a few days after a sizable portion of US voters made Donald Trump the president of the United States, I drove to Central Waters to cofacilitate a morning professional development session with department chairs. Ironically, I was there to lead department leaders through a process of breaking down barriers and appreciating one another's differences. A month earlier, we trialed the session with the administrative team. I had data in hand. Leadership-style results ready go. But this particular morning, I was in no mood to embrace differences. Donald Trump was president.

Facilitator: Why don't we go around and just put our feelings out on the table. We don't have to respond or react to one another. If everyone's okay with this, that's what we can do to get started. If you don't want to speak, that's okay. Just say "I'll pass."

One by one, we listened to one another.

> **Decoteau:** I went to dinner last night, and I just felt like all the White people were super happy. I know that's not true. But I'm just frustrated as hell with White people right now. I don't get it.
>
> **Speaker 1:** It's very awkward for me because I know it shouldn't matter, but I feel a really strong urge to want to know "Who voted for this guy?" Maybe so I can just ask "Why?" I mean it shouldn't change my relationships with any of my colleagues, but it's just this big secret. I can't stop feeling suspicious.
>
> **Speaker 2:** Students are scared, a lot of our students who have parents who are immigrants here, just mainly fearful for them. You know our LGBTQ students are distraught.
>
> **Speaker 3:** I didn't realize the impact this election would have on people.

Although they were not prepared for the election results, the CWHS community had the capacity and structures to process the election. They did so through leveraging the myriad resources they had cultivated over the years. When Jennie jumped in to facilitate our process, it was a bit of a relief. Everyone participated. By the time I arrived, CWHS had been processing the election fallout for several days. White students proudly sported "Make America Great Again" hats and shirts.[4] They walked through the hallways, emboldened by a Trump victory, taunting their Latinx peers by whispering out of earshot of adults: "We're gonna build that wall."[5] Branden, a Black school counselor who joined CWHS several years after the project began, elaborated on the election fallout:

> It was a shock. When everybody learned that Donald Trump became president, students were heavily impacted. There were also staff who was caught off guard like, "Oh my God, what happened?" I had to remain neutral in my role no matter how I was feeling. I was able to have a little, not a circle per se, but more like a space where staff can even

come and to express their thoughts and how they were feeling. They used the space to talk their thoughts and everything.

Like, oh man, the campus here was just in complete awe. The election coverage went so long the night before, so people just kind of shut it off, went to sleep, and then woke up to the results like, "Gee, did this just happen?" For the staff the worry was about where they personally stood on things politically regarding this country. They also worried about students they had great relationships with, who they knew were going to be impacted by some of the decisions and outcomes of the elections and family members as well, you know? They were just shocked and stuck not knowing what to do.

First, students protested. So we respected the students' petitions to protest. We didn't bash them about walking out of class into the halls or even leaving the building to go to the neighborhood park. We just asked them to protest in peace and don't disturb those who are in class. They were respectful to that request.

We opened up student services for any student who wanted to come to just be in a space of support. Some used it as a space of quiet. It was whatever they wanted. So student services opened to both students and staff.

A teacher in the social studies department opened up his room as a spot for students. He just reached out and said, "Hey, you know if students and staff want to come for support or just to talk about their thoughts, they're more than welcome." After he did that other departments and teachers started opening up space. What that then allowed is for student services to spread out rather than be concentrated in one area. We adjusted our approach and began rotating to classrooms to ensure that teachers in those rooms felt supported there.

After school, Elizabeth asked all the staff to report to the auditorium so we could plan for the next day. It was kind of reactive. But it was proactive in a sense, because nobody expected the election outcome to be what it was. I thought it was good that she brought staff together to come and then voice how they were feeling. She modeled what we saw happening. She created a space for adults to express their thoughts and, you know, similar to what we did for the students, allow the space for us adults to have that time and have that moment. 'Cause again we were feeling just how the students were feeling, but it was tough to voice your opinion without a designated space to do so.

CWHS has students who are pro-Trump. We have students who are anti-Trump. We have to support both. We have students who were wearing their "Make America Great Again" hats. And other students rolled up like "Take that hat off, take that shirt off." Even if I don't agree with those students, it's like how do we now protect both students and make sure that everyone is safe and all of that good stuff? So I think allowing that space for students and staff to come in and say, "Hey, this is how we're feeling" is important.

So the next day we provided the same opportunities again. But we were intentional this time. We had different spaces for students to report to if they needed that support. The previous year we started the Black Student Union so we had space there for our Black students. And Latino Nation for our Latinx students and so forth. That worked because students and their advisors talked more and shared their thoughts or their opinions and how they felt. It was well received.

At that Black Student Union space, a lot of staff came to support. They listened to students. And they also shared how they felt too, you know, and their frustration and their confusion, and I think it helped close the gap a little bit between staff and students. 'Cause you sense that large gap that happens about race. Students saw teachers at a vulnerable moment. So I think it closed up some of that gaps we have in our school. I think it helped us move forward a little bit.

We weren't prepared, to be quite honest. We didn't prepare for any type of results. In hindsight, we as a school dropped the ball. We should have held a staff meeting before the election took place and said, "Hey, here's the game plan for if it's yay or if it's nay." We should have prepared for whatever outcome. Our initial response was impromptu. It was one of those things you have to do on the spot, which is perfectly fine. That's what we're hired to do sometimes. You've got to go with the flow.

THERE IS NO FINISH LINE: HOW COLLECTIVE
AWARENESS CREATES POSSIBILITIES

Throughout the 2015–16 year, I was ready to abandon the research project. Carla was being White. And the administrative team thought it might make sense to abandon their commitment to restorative discipline approaches. And then we each, in our different ways, racial self-talked ourselves into staying in the race. When I asked Carla "What role will you play in keeping whoever is hired here for longer than others stayed?" she understood what I was asking. I was essentially saying, "Are you going to be *that* White colleague? Or are you going to be a colleague who is White?" Elizabeth, Ethan, Donnell, and the other administrators were problem-solving and working to meet students' needs. And trying to honor the concerns of the community about the problems with the long-standing problem of Black community-police interactions. In the meantime, the district and school administrators were recruiting Black and Brown people to the district, including Branden.

> When I was called for the interview, I interviewed with the principal, Elizabeth, and the Director of Student Services at the time. They were just honest and straightforward. No fluff. They were like "Look, these are issues we have as White people. We've found it hard to relate and hard to connect with our students of color on certain things. We need more staff of color who will (a) help us (White people) understand how to support students and (b) connect with our students so they successfully graduate out high school."
>
> Many people have told me there's been a dramatic and drastic change at this school. In the past, there were folks who were ready for that change and who would make attempts and strive for that change but were met with a whirlwind of resistance from teachers and staff who were just stuck in their ways and stuck in their mindset, not willing to step outside of what they were used to. I've heard some crazy stories. Hearing some of the stories I've heard of staff who just didn't get it and who would say and do racist things. I can imagine what it was like five years ago, and I don't think I would have stayed at that time. So it's very humbling and it's an honor to

be here at this time when this change is happening and to be a part of the change.

Our department chair, Carla, she's been here about eleven years. She's great by the way. She's said many times that this is by far the best team she has experienced. I've heard other staff say the same thing: this is best that they ever experienced being here, since they were here. And that's humbling. I think it speaks to the change that has occurred over the years.

CWHS would likely be very different if any one of us remained where we were—believing I didn't belong, believing in racial meritocracy, and believing that restorative discipline approaches aren't worth the effort and criticism, ambivalent about school counseling. There is more to the through line between people at CWHS than meets the eye. There is a through line of racial emotions, belief, and experience that is difficult to appreciate if one does not look closely: we believed CWHS needed to be better for students of color. We each acted on that single belief. But this belief was substantiated through the act of talking. In other words, we talked ourselves into behaving in ways that reformed our beliefs.

CULTIVATING AWARENESS OF BELIEFS AND EMOTIONS: THE POWER OF RACIAL SELF-TALK

Racism thrives when people do not talk about it and through it. Carla talked herself into letting go, making space, and supporting Branden. Dontae resisted. Ethan mediated. Donnell recruited. CWHS created positions. Human Resources called. Branden interviewed. Students formed affinity clubs. Staff members advised. Students protested. Elizabeth created a space for staff to process: "Even a year ago, I wouldn't have made time or space. I just would have not thought of it. I would not have had the ability to even understand the need." But it wasn't all on Elizabeth's shoulders. Many teachers opened their classroom doors. Racial self-talk produces a collective awareness of racial emotions and beliefs that differentiates the old CWHS from the new.

Racial self-talk is a learning practice that if cultivated becomes an organizationwide routine that leads to powerful racial learning by establishing collective awareness of racial experiences, emotions, and beliefs. Racial self-talk is not a group discussion or debate. It's also not a courageous confrontation. It does not sound like "If you don't or can't behave like a, b, and c, you shouldn't be here" or "If you don't believe a, b, or c, you don't belong. You have no business teaching or leading." When a person makes it their right to evaluate and assess who should or has the right to belong or be, they reify a white supremacist logic that creates a racial hierarchy of who can belong. Deciding that some people belong and some people do not is a racial belief. The White woman who approached me in the parking lot thought I did not belong at CWHS. Carla initially thought that someone she had not yet even met did not belong at CWHS. Officer Blaine thought that Dontae did not belong at CWHS. For a second I felt I didn't belong. And then I talked to myself.

Racial self-talk does not intend to sway or convince *others*. Racial self-talk is a practice of self-exploration that, because it is expressed aloud, offers layered opportunities for self and collective learning. It sounds like "I don't understand the disconnect between Black kids and police. Why do Black kids hate the police so much? I need to understand that." It sounds like "I don't like it. I find it offensive, but I don't know what to do when a kids wears a 'Make America Great Again' hat or shirt." It sounds like "Am I being White?" Racial self-talk causes people to pause, self-evaluate, and self-reflect. When it doesn't do that, it is not self-talk. Self-talk statements are invitations to explore. When shared publicly, they create opportunities for others to learn through gaining access to how people think and believe.

Racial self-talk is most powerful when people learn to "read" the ideological underpinnings of their own and others' racial emotions. Racial self-talk is a window into our selves that allows us to question the racial ideologies that are somewhere in the racial stuff. I peeked into the house of my childhood to examine my sense of belonging and purpose. In her stuff, Carla found her beliefs about meritocracy. If one fails to develop an adequate understanding of racial emotions, beliefs, and the experiences that shape them, it is nearly impossible to manage one's racial emotions, change beliefs, and create new experiences and ways of being. A range of racial self-talk practices, outlined in table 4.1, benefit racial learning.

TABLE 4.1 Cultivating racial self-talk

	CRITICAL PRINCIPLE	ENACTING THE PRINCIPLE	RACIAL LEARNING BENEFITS
SEMI-PRIVATE SELF-TALK ALOUD	*With trusted colleague (confidant) is critical*	Encourage members of the school community to self-talk in the presence of one other person, usually a trusted colleague or workplace confidant (e.g., research team member).	Creates potential for deep self-exploration and racial learning. However, this form of self-talk is not by default available for broader organizational learning.
SEMI-PUBLIC SELF-TALK ALOUD	*In team setting is critical*	Encourage members of the school community to self-talk aloud in the presence of a team—a group of people with whom the person routinely collaborates and works (e.g., administrative meetings, department meetings).	Creates potential for deep self-exploration that catalyzes racial learning and cogenerative recognition of emotions and beliefs. This learning is often closed off to people who are not members of the team. It creates uneven organizational racial learning and development.
	In group setting is critical	Encourage members of the school community to self-talk aloud in the presence of a group of people with whom they may or may not routinely collaborate or work but which was established for a particular purpose (e.g., professional learning, retreats).	Creates potential for self-exploration that catalyzes racial learning and cogenerative recognition of emotions and beliefs. The nature of group settings often yields surface-level self-talk and reflection. It creates broad but shallow racial learning and development.
PUBLIC SELF-TALK ALOUD	*In schoolwide setting is critical*	Encourage members of the school community to self-talk aloud in the presence of people who participate in the daily life of the school.	Creates potential for shallow, broad self-exploration similar to group settings. Requires well-established norms that allow facilitation of thinking aloud and dialogue. Speakers willing to self-talk aloud are highly vulnerable in this setting.
	In community setting is critical	Encourage members of the school community to self-talk aloud in public settings, which takes the form of a moderated panel or testimonial.	Creates potential for self-exploration similar to the group setting and is usually prepared forms of self-talk aloud, such as recounting a past line of thought or emotional response. Requires a well-established structure and places the speaker in a position of vulnerability.

continues

TABLE 4.1   Cultivating racial self-talk (*continued*)

CRITICAL PRINCIPLE		ENACTING THE PRINCIPLE	RACIAL LEARNING BENEFITS
PRIVATE	*Internal dialogue is critical but no learning benefits*	Encourage members of the school community to think about feelings and thoughts without asking them to verbalize or share.	Does not benefit anyone because unshared internal dialogues do not create learning conditions.
	Self-talk is critical but no learning benefits	Encourage members of the school community to self-talk with people outside of the school community (e.g., family or friends).	Closes off learning opportunities to students and colleagues and is not available for others to benefit from.
	Journaling is critical but no default organizational learning benefits	Encourage members of the school community to keep journals containing their feelings and thoughts.	Individualizes learning opportunities but they may be more expansive if members of the school community share their journals with other members of the school.

Public racial self-talk benefits organizationwide racial learning and improvement because the spoken word becomes a resource for other people to learn from and explore with other members of the school. This public aspect is critically important and should not be understated. Table 4.1 outlines the types of self-talk that happened in CWHS, which gave people access to experiences, emotions, and beliefs.

Leveraging racial self-talk as a resource for learning and improvement is quite simple: people who talk aloud to themselves about their own beliefs and experiences and offer their own analysis benefit from their own self-talk. Talking about racial experiences and beliefs is a risky practice. People reveal racist, even hurtful, thoughts. People express anger. People reveal their ignorance. A White person may say, "Why do Black people not like cops?" Someone listening may think that is a stupid question. Any educator should know why and get it. But they do not. At one point, Elizabeth didn't get it. Elizabeth had to see Officer Blaine's disdain for Dontae up close and personal to develop a deeper understanding of why Black students might hate cops right back. Blaine had it out for Dontae, even after Dontae stopped his behaviors. In order for Elizabeth to "get it," Black parents told her about the injustice of tickets. For White people, learning from Black and Brown people is discomforting but necessary. For Black and Brown people, explaining what seems like basic experiences and pointing out routine indignities of racial violence are annoying but necessary. As hard and hurtful as it may be to hear a person make a racist statement, be it covert or not, that statement makes the racial ideology visible.

Racial self-talk is powerful when it happens in courageously confrontational rather than congenial school contexts. It benefits when affinity spaces are present in the school, when White teachers have high capacities to sit with discomfort, such was the case when social studies teachers opened their classroom spaces. As demonstrated by Branden's narration of CWHS post-election fallout, the capacity to operate in courageously confrontational ways coincided with CWHS's rapid deployment of numerous racial resources—Black and Brown people's influential presence (Branden's leadership, students' protests, affinity space), impromptu but nonetheless curated space for white discomfort (all-staff meeting, research project meeting), and the practices of courageous confrontation. By drawing on its own racial resources, CWHS *learned* in the moment and from the moment.

CONCLUSION: SUSTAINING RACIAL AWARENESS AND LEARNING

The most powerful way to develop racial awareness of emotions and beliefs is to talk or use some medium to express oneself in a manner that allows others to bear witness. Thinking is important. Speaking is more important. So too is hearing. Racial self-talk allows people to hear their selves and thus offers opportunities for self-reflection. It is an act of sharing, which makes one vulnerable. Hearing one's own thoughts and hearing others', be it in real time or later, usher one into vulnerability and community in ways that thinking about racial beliefs does not and cannot. I spoke into my audio recorder, trying to capture my experience and connect it to research questions. "*This* is the part of Central Waters that is ugly. The parent engagement literature doesn't address racist White parents. How should they be engaged?" It was racial self-talking. I used my research to mask my raw thoughts. People in CWHS were ugly, unruly racists—drunk, entitled White people. Threats to black bodies, willing to insult Black people's intelligence. Inadequate, just as I expected them to be. Had not my life experiences and study of racism taught me this was going to happen? And that this was who they are? Was this how White people treated students of color at CWHS? Did Black students feel like I felt?

My self-talk revolved around an experience that made me ask myself the question "Why am I out *here*?" It was a question that was deeply mired in racism, racial experiences of belongingness, and the existential crisis of not having a firm place in a white supremacist world. I relearned that I was *Black*. I knew it all along. But as I drove from the parking lot, I felt Black, as in "I do not belong" Black. Not Black as in Black and proud. I felt present. But not influentially present. There's an experiential difference. The emotions that overcame me took me back to Southside Christian School in my hometown of Greenville, South Carolina, where I first learned that I didn't belong. My sister and I were two of the handful of Black children who attended the predominantly White conservative school. It's where I developed a manner of speech that earned me the Black neighborhood infamy of "talking like a White boy." It was a place where I ran across the neatly manicured athletic field as fast as my little Black legs would carry me. Winded, I basked in my White classmates' awe: "He's soooo fast!" You see, I could win a race at Southside Christian. My neighborhood friends and I were more equally matched. So I won or lost, dependent largely upon who was outside on a given day. At school, the validation was in the win. At home, the joy was in *the race*. Win or lose, I belonged.

At CWHS, I tricked myself into believing I was an important contributor. Enough White folks convinced me I had something of value to offer their school community. And I ran the race: "He's an expert." Then, out of nowhere, parking lot Patty broke my Black stride. A woman I didn't know and will likely never encounter again told me I wasn't an expert. I was a liar. I didn't feel threatened so much as I felt hurt. Maybe belittled. As I listened back to my rambling audio recording, I wondered to myself why I was so caught off guard? Why had I not stood up for myself. Why did I stand there? And of all things, why did I thank her? Why did I liken myself to students? I started questioning whether it was worth subjecting myself to the ire of a White community. My degree didn't matter.

I was equally frustrated that Camille stood in front of a school board meeting, packed with White people, and dogged the Black students. *Sister Camille, what are you saying to these people? Young sister, why here and now?* "I'll be damned," I thought. Perhaps because of embarrassment, despondency, or anger, I never shared this defining moment in my time with CWHS. What was the value in what people would have learned? What would I have learned? Public statements, however clumsy, incomplete, or profound, created collective opportunities for learning about race and racism and the emotional responses each evokes that would not be otherwise available if people did not self-talk aloud. In other words, whatever people said and however problematic, it was a learning resource from which others, given the right organizational culture, could benefit.

But on another level, not sharing my emotions and beliefs makes sense. White supremacy seeks out racial authenticity and attempts to stamp it out with hostility, violence, and hatred. So I think I've become socialized to not share. I've experienced silencing critiques too many times over the course of my life. Silencing critique discourages, dismisses, and suppresses racial self-talk. Silencing tells Carla, "Yes, you are racist. And you clearly don't like Black people." It tells Latinx students, "Trump won. Get over it." It tells fifteen-year-old White students that "if you want to build a wall, you are racist as hell," as though they are unredeemable. Silencing feels right and I want to believe it's justifiable. People's self-talk suggested something about the capacity for racial equity improvement. It enabled people at CWHS to connect people's actions to the emergence of racial awareness.

But racist ideologies and beliefs cause tremendous harm. The dilemma is that silencing critiques diminish the potential for the awareness of racial emotions and ideologies to openly flourish. In contexts where awareness is continuously cultivated and leveraged, organizational racial learning grows. But at whose expense? As with all aspects of antiracist and equity work, practices and routines that cultivate a collective awareness of racial emotions and beliefs create a dilemma of "letting people belong" even if they don't believe the same. Treating people like they belong, even when their actions are harmful and their thinking and beliefs deeply flawed, is a radical act. It assumes that all people possess redemptive qualities. It raises a question that Black and Brown people must grapple with: how can we treat White people with love and grace, despite their continued insistence to marginalize and oppress the people they encounter? Is love and grace the answer? Despite our knowledge of oppression, Black and Brown people treat White people graciously as though they belong, asking for space, demanding justice, and prodding them to be better. Almost never seeking retribution or revenge.

Here I've attempted to make one resource—racial awareness of emotions and beliefs—visible and plain. I've suggested racial self-talk as the lever that cultivates the resource. I hope I demonstrated its power and suggested it as a resource that should be cultivated for the purposes of improvement. The fact that people talked aloud about their racial emotions and beliefs, in naturalistic settings, was a leap forward from the CWHS of yesteryear, where race-visible talk was relegated to the structural and social margins of school life, when it happened at all. CWHS's increased capacity did not happen as a matter of luck or happenstance. Deep racial understanding stems from radical questioning and inquiry into one's own racial beliefs and actions.

5

RACE-CONSCIOUS INQUIRY
CYCLES (LEADERSHIP)

Race-conscious inquiry cycles refer to a collaborative inquiry-based leadership practice that combines principles of leadership for continuous organizational improvement and antiracist leadership.[1] As with cycles of inquiry in general, race-conscious inquiry leadership relies on formative data collection, collective data analysis, and data use in a broad sense—climate and culture surveys, student outcome data, teacher and student feedback from formal focus groups, listening sessions, community meetings, and observations—and explicitly seeks to discern and amplify the racialized nature of school problems, patterns, and practices. Race-conscious inquiry cycles include the influential presence of Black and Brown people, make use of race-specific data that accounts for racial experiences, and uses the school setting as the primary text for ongoing analysis. A culture of racial humility and curiosity is also essential to ensuring genuine race-conscious inquiry cycles occur.

Race-conscious inquiry leadership is multifaceted, a situated leadership practice that merges principles and practices of continuous school improvement, antiracist, and social justice leadership.[2] Race-conscious inquiry is distinct from both race-neutral cycles of inquiry and racial data analysis typically found in schools. Organizational improvement science research, for all of its power and insight, is race-evasive. It fails to cut to the racial core of the organization. Race-neutral inquiry cycles assume that race does not matter. Traditional cycles focus on identifying problems, planning, doing, and assessing as though race and racism are not baked into every stage of the cycle. Through omitting the ways that racism and race shape schooling, conventional race-neutral cycles reify white supremacy by generating problems, plans, action steps, and so forth, suggesting that many things might be problems, but none of them are necessarily rooted in racism. Starting with a premise that racism is not a problem ensures that solutions will be inadequate to address the problems of school-based racism that Black and Brown students experience in their day-to-day school lives.

In this chapter, I tell the story of how Central Waters High School moved from a compliance-driven to an interest-based leadership approach that leveraged race-conscious inquiry cycles to drive their enactment of racial equity improvements. I trace CWHS from the time when the school wanted to know "How do we reduce suspensions?" and "How do we get students to take off their hats and put away their cell phones?" to asking "How do we create a sense of belongingness and academic curiosity for students of color?" I do not attempt to answer these questions. Rather, I illuminate the significance of how the questions evolved; the implications of the evolution; and the methods CWHS administrators, teachers, and students used to answer them. I demonstrate how a continually broadening range of racial perspectives and representations enabled them to "see" problems anew. As CWHS learned to race-visibly see problems, they also envisioned new possibilities for how to address them.

By centering the experiences of teacher leaders and staff who held formal administrative, department-level, and schoolwide team-level leadership positions, I illustrate how CWHS educators uprooted racism and white supremacy through proliferating practices, posing questions, and working to continually understand their progress (or lack thereof). I hope to convey a leadership practice that is complex, unbounded by conventions of time-based planning, but nonetheless iterative and powerful in its ability to create emotional, intellectual, and practice breakthroughs. I argue that learning breakthroughs are an essential data point that is mostly invisible and therefore leaves school communities unaware of the progress that individuals, teams, and groups make in the efforts to enact racial equity change, and thus feeling stuck.

Throughout, I point to several dilemmas—for example, I explore the difficult mutually reinforcing interactions of solving oneself and solving school problems. Many people commit to one or the other. They create policies, develop processes, and direct people on how to solve their problems. They work to fix everyone else, especially Black and Brown students or colleagues they are not like. Or they work on their selves, close off to collective learning, close the door, and keep their head down while not extending or accepting help. People decided for themselves when and if to get involved. This created uneven development that led to variations of professional learning and outcomes. I pose the dilemma of who to involve at what points and when to make everyone get involved. Through presenting the iterative leadership practice *race-conscious inquiry cycles* that partially fostered CWHS's capacity to improve, I show the emergent learning-leadership work that drove iterations of CWHS equity improvement efforts.

CURIOSITY AND LEARNER'S STANCE

The marketplace of educational ideas is filled with solutions, models, and programs that are designed to fix the perennial problems of schooling. In July 2013, I attended a national leadership conference where I presented a breakout session called Rethinking School Discipline. I posed big, broad questions about shifting societal values, the racialization of space, and the social construction of deviance. I offered critiques of race-neutrality. I pointed out the problematic behaviorist underpinnings of Positive Behavior Interventions and Supports (PBIS). I suggested frameworks for thinking about how zero-tolerance, punitive, and exclusionary discipline policies shape students' disciplinary experiences in school and how they adversely affected Black boys and girls. I asked participants to consider multiple viewpoints. I asked, "Would this particular policy change create a net-widening and net-deepening effect in your district?" It was the same day I met Ethan and Suzanne, the district director of student services who was in charge of districtwide PBIS implementation. Ethan introduced himself.

> I'm from Central Waters Regional District. I'm one of the associate principals in charge of behavior. We've been working to implement Positive Behavior Intervention and Supports, but after sitting in for this breakout session, I realize that we never sat back and asked the deep questions about if our approach is what we want and believe will work best for students. The focus on different discipline philosophies is what's missing in our work.

As Ethan spoke, Suzanne stood next to him nodding her head. She broke her silence, "I agree. You gave us lots to think about."

I was supposed to be an expert. But I didn't have a neatly packaged remedy. People described my research and presentations as thought-provoking but not necessarily practical in terms of "tools I can take back." Instead, I said things like "Thanks for asking me that question. I don't know. I hadn't thought of it that way. I could see it a few ways. What are your thoughts?" "I'd need more time to think about it. I want to know more before I decide." "I've seen this work at another school. It may or may not work in a different context." "That's my best thinking right now." My favorite: "It depends. . . ." "What kind of 'expert' am I?" I often thought to myself. Real experts were supposed to offer immediate, practical, and results-oriented remedies. Tools to take back. Not questions to take back. I had no immediate answers, packaged behavior programs, or models to share. No quick fixes. CWHS had racial disparities that required immediate remedy. Who had time to think? To ask and answer questions? Or to explore? CWHS needed action.

MAKING RACIAL PATTERNS VISIBLE

In August 2013, Ethan left me a voice message. "I told my principal about your presentation. We are having a whole school professional development day in October. I'm wondering if you are available to present the same presentation you did at the leadership conference to our staff?" I arrived that October to a small classroom in CWHS. I cued up my "Re-thinking Discipline: What's theory and philosophy got to do with our discipline data, policies, and practices?" PowerPoint presentation. I neatly stacked my handouts and organized my demonstration materials. "We'll give a few more people time to show up," Ethan said. I waited while he walked in and out of the room a few times. I believe he was trying to round up a few more people so maybe we could get to ten participants. Elizabeth entered: "Hi, Dr. Irby, nice to meet you. Welcome to Central Waters, friend. Thanks for making the drive." We shook hands. Ethan returned and said with a slight air of frustration, "I thought some more people were coming. Maybe they changed their minds. We should just get started." And so we did. I explained:

> Our first activity is a writing activity. Write about a discipline success story. Use the following prompts: Incident/problem—what happened? How did you address the problem? What was the outcome? How did you feel about the outcome? In your eyes, what made it a success? Why did you approach the situation as you did? What does your success story suggest about your commitment to the student(s) who were impacted?

I walked around the room to read the responses, windows into people's thinking. After people shared in groups of two, I invited them into a whole group discussion. I listened to their stories. When they finished, I said, "Thank you for sharing. Let's move forward." Before providing an overview of the session, I shared a quote from Henry Giroux's newly released *America's Education Deficit and the War on Youth*: "Critical pedagogical practice does not transfer knowledge but creates the possibilities for its production, analysis, and use." We exchanged thoughts about what this quote meant and what it suggested about how the workshop experience might unfold. I then shared why I accepted the invitation to present.

> I'm here because I would like for Black children to be able to attend any school in the US and thrive. I'd like to feel confident that I could move

wherever I wanted to move, including here, and not have to worry about if my child will be treated with dignity and get an education that affirms who she is. I hope my time with you today will help increase that likelihood.

As I rotated to hand each participant an 11-by-17-inch sheet of blue paper and "discipline analysis workbook," I explained the workshop objective was to expose them to different ways of thinking about discipline. "Today we will explore different approaches to discipline: Compliance (behaviorist), Relational (restorative), and Interest (educative order). We'll use these lenses to rethink what discipline is and how it can be cultivated (see table 5.1). We'll ground our exploration in values of social justice, equity, and educational success. If we meet the objectives, you will leave with a more expansive framework to address discipline-related problems in schools." I spent the day exploring four claims:

Claim 1. Discipline is not a bad thing. The problem is how discipline is cultivated, why, and to what ends.

Claim 2. Black children and youth, boys, and Latinx students are disciplined differently than their White peers. They are disciplined more often. They are disciplined in ways that are harmful to their growth and development.

Claim 3. You use a method of cultivating discipline that reflects your belief in a person or group.

Claim 4. Your school would look different if your discipline philosophy and code of conduct used interest-based discipline as your primary focus.

Throughout the lecture, we stopped for different activities that explored the ideas and connected them to the stories they each wrote and shared. "What do the actions and assumptions exemplified in your success story suggest about your commitments?" One "success" story ended

TABLE 5.1 Perspectives on school discipline

DISCIPLINE PERSPECTIVE	EMPHASIS AND GOALS	SOURCE(S) OF AUTHORITY	LOCUS OF CONTROL	CAPACITIES AND COMPETENCIES
Compliance-orientation	Establishing and maintaining control, order, and obedience through positive and negative reinforcements.	Legalistic and procedural authority (rules, due process), established by people in positions power.	Located outside of the individual and/or community—assumes dependence.	Control students, conform to expectations, clearly communicate, deduce rules from values and expectations, be consistent, see people as the same, take objective stances, and be firm and decisive, etc.
Relational-orientation	Building, nurturing, maintaining, and restoring healthy relationships and communities.	Moral authority, cultural norms of community.	Located at the nexus of individuals and cultural norms as embedded in communities—assumes interdependence.	Share control with others; remain emotionally aware and self-regulate; be mindful, self-reflective, and empathetic; take alternate perspectives; listen deeply, accept feedback and criticism; forgive and apologize; facilitate (re)connections and healing among others collaborate, etc.
Interest-orientation	Cultivating and supporting learning through creating relevant and challenging learning opportunities that interest learners.	Expertise and experience, persons with high level of content and process mastery.	Located within the act of learning or doing something individuals or members of a group deem valuable—assumes independence and existence of internal locus of control.	Generate interest from students, facilitate learning and educative order, master subject content, engage in life-long learning, take a learning perspective, be culturally responsive and competent, take direction and coaching from multiple sources, experiment, take risks and adapt to change, find creativity and purpose in "disorder," etc.

in a suspension. Recurring patterns reveal underlying structures. Compliance dominated. So I continued to mine their individual stories for recurring patterns. I polled them and asked them to share their responses publicly so they could see patterns their actions and beliefs produced. "In your story, what was the student's race?" Black. African American. Black. Black or African American. Do you see the pattern? I continued. "If Black students comprise only a small fraction of the student population, why might they be overrepresented, almost 90 percent, in the stories about discipline? Mind you, I asked about the successes." They get in trouble more. Why? They aren't as engaged and that leads to problems. Why? Why? Why?

After lunch, we conducted a rapid review of CWHS data and policies: "Compliance, Relational, or Interest? What perspective underlies this particular policy?" Overwhelmingly, CWHS policies foregrounded compliance and "safety" concerns. Why? The code of conduct contained almost no references to relationships. Why? Aside from "having a safe and orderly school is essential to learning," it contained nothing at all about learning or education. Why? At the end of my workshop, I explained, "I hope that our time today raised some questions for you to consider moving forward. Thanks for inviting me."

RIGHT SOLUTIONS, RIGHT QUESTIONS

The core problem: racial disparities. The goal: eliminate the disparities. For each problem, CWHS had a solution. Integrate Advanced Placement. Reduce referrals and suspensions. Implement PBIS with fidelity. These "fixes" to racial disparities would certainly make the numbers look good. Many teachers called the reforms Band-Aids that failed to address more substantial problems:

> Everything we do is a—they say equity, like the diverse population and the diverse kids in AP classes. Yet, they don't focus on equity, you don't focus on what is like the heart. I think you should put the emphasis on fixing bigger problems like the kids feeling welcome, teaching

strategies, and culturally responsive practice. They don't put the emphasis there.

If kids don't feel connected to me, and if kids don't feel like I care about them or that I am representing them in my curriculum, I could teach literacy strategies all day every year, and they're still not going to learn them because they're going to shut down. So, I feel like we're just putting Band-Aids on all these huge problems, it's Band-Aid, Band-Aid, Band-Aid, Band-Aid.

—WHITE FEMALE TEACHER *(Year One Focus Groups)*

Teachers were angered by the Advanced Placement and discipline reforms. They claimed the reforms were done to them. The process was cold turkey. They had no say in choosing the reforms or rolling them out. They struggled to adapt to the changes and to teach students who were "not prepared for Advanced Placement." Teachers asked, "What are we supposed to do if students can just walk out of class with no consequences? Are we not suspending students?" A smaller group of teachers claimed the reforms didn't go far enough. "Change the curriculum so students see themselves in the learning." Regardless of their perspective, they blamed administrators for the problems: "Administration won't do anything to help. There's no consequences for bad behavior. Students run the school." The general sentiment was "Just tell us what to do? What are we supposed to do?" But such questions were rhetorical, questions asked in jest, frustration, and critique. They were angry because there was no time for a whole school of teachers and staff to figure out what to do. The consent decree was clear. Eliminate the racial disparities. Elizabeth blamed teachers: "They refuse to embrace our new policies that will eliminate disparities. They don't do basic things like take attendance, start class on time, and write hall passes. These are basic things that all teachers should be doing. They should be in the halls. Instead they complain and resist. That's the problem."

While White teachers and administrators pointed fingers at one another, students suffered. Some sat through classes with growling stomachs. Some listened to racist lectures, read racist books, and were required to participate in racist learning activities. Students like Leemai sat in silence. White girls—Sarah, Jenny, Becky, and Susan—cheated. CWHS culture and climate deteriorated. It was going from bad to worse.

> **Suzanne:** We're looking for a consultant to work with us to improve our climate. We have support from state PBIS team, but we're really missing the racial equity part. PBIS does not address that. And I appreciate the candor in which you point that out. It lines up exactly with what we saw happen here. We reduced suspensions overall, but the racial gap persists.
>
> **Elizabeth:** We're working with an organization from out of state who is doing the work on the academic side. They use a formula to identify students of color who should rightfully be taking Advanced Placement courses. I'll introduce you to our local consultant. She's great.
>
> **Suzanne:** How much would you charge to support this kind of work?

I couldn't think of an amount. The problems were so vast and deep. The picture they painted was clear. On one hand, I understood the conditions. I had read the books. But I could think of no organizational and school improvement books that accounted for the centrality of race and racism as the underlying factor that impedes improvement. On the other hand, antiracism and social justice education research focused more on teacher improvement and antiracism, not whole school reform or organizational leadership. Neither bodies of research spoke to one or the other. I didn't have clear examples of the racial improvement work that would help CWHS. A training series would not suffice. A book study wouldn't matter without supportive organizational conditions. I didn't know how to help. But I did know that the people in the organization were best positioned to "fix" this mess. I admitted to them:

> I have no point of reference for where this sort of process has worked well in a school like yours. So I can't confidently outline deliverables or outcomes I feel you can achieve. Based on what you described, I'm not confident that this school can or will improve. I'd be lying if I told you I know how to help you, so I wouldn't feel right consulting.

Here's what I do know. It will take four years or so, at minimum three, before you start to see any changes. You'll have implementation lags for a year or two in the process. My best guess is that the fruits of the work will show up in year four or five. But again, none of the organizational change and school improvement books factor race or racism into the mix. I am curious about what it might look like.

I think you would benefit more from a research partner to colearn with and ask you questions, collect data, etc., than a consultant to offer solutions. What if we approached the work as an opportunity to try to figure it out together?

In the next few weeks, I codeveloped a memorandum of understanding with the district and school administrators. I formed a university-based research team. We were set to begin the work of colearning and initiated our first race-conscious cycle of inquiry.[3]

LEADING WITH RACE-CONSCIOUS INQUIRY CYCLES

Race-conscious inquiry is a collaborative leadership practice that aims to make racial patterns and racism visible within organizations. Visible practices can be disrupted and transformed to produce affirming and positive experiences for Black and Brown students. Like inquiry cycles in general, race-conscious inquiry relies on problem finding, data collection, analysis, and data routines but differs in its intentional goal of discerning and amplifying the racialized nature of school problems, patterns, and practices for the purposes of organizationwide racial learning and improvement. This approach to inquiry makes sense only if educators regard their schools as racialized organizations.[4] Openly acknowledging that racialization and racism are endemic to organizational interactions enables inquiry teams to generate racial data and learning opportunities that enable members to identify antiracist improvement strategies. The inquiry process works best if team members engage in race-specific talk and use race-specific concepts throughout the inquiry process that enables more robust problem identification.[5] Leaders, teachers, and students can only address problems they talk about. Figure 5.1 depicts a race-conscious inquiry cycle.

FIGURE 5.1   Race-conscious improvement cycle

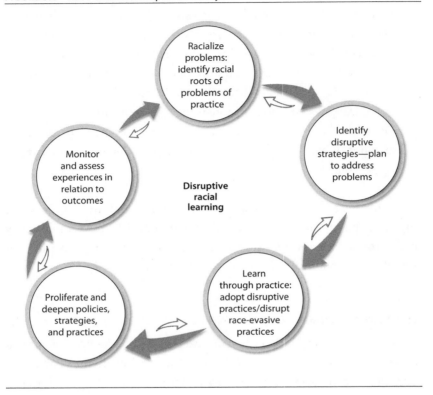

Racialize School Problems

Racializing school problems refers to the process of formulating, asking, and answering questions that deepen a school community's understanding of race and racism. Racializing school problems requires intentionally mining the school for stories of white racial privilege and racism that are ubiquitous, routinely erased, and therefore invisible. At CWHS, our goal was to make the racial stories, patterns, and structures that existed in the school visible for analysis. We initiated the inquiry process by administering a comprehensive school climate and culture survey. We purposefully made it a big deal. We gathered almost 1,300 student responses. Next we conducted focus groups and interviews with teachers, students, and administrators. We used the data from the survey as a focus point for the conversations. We asked focus group participants to "help us interpret and make sense of the survey results. Why these results?" The final stage of racializing problems was a summer data retreat that focused on identifying and framing root racial causes of culture, climate, and discipline disparities reflected in the survey and focus group data. Retreat participants crafted a statement of the root problems that the school needed to address.

> Unequal access to school based opportunities is the primary problem the school must address.[6] Unequal access persists because of relational and structural inequalities.[7] Relational and structural inequalities persist because of a communication problem . . . increased communication would reveal and require the school to confront racism—the belief that white middle class values, norms, beliefs, and ways of being are inherently better than those of "others."

The data itself and the administrators' and teachers' extensive role in the data-gathering process—as collectors and participants—breathed life into the equity efforts by generating curiosity and more nuanced questions. People grew curious. As more questions emerged, so too did CWHS's ability to see more problems. Administrators and teachers didn't find the quantitative data novel. They expected the results. They learned the most from student focus group data. The students talked to us about the day-to-day school life in an unfiltered setting. Most teachers had not paid close attention to the stories we listened to. We transcribed them and asked teachers to read students' accounts. Reading the students' stories offered a new perspective that listening did not. After we wrapped up the data retreat, we prepared a report to share with the broader school community. Doing so was a racially disruptive process because it forced people into corners and engendered a level of discomfort that caused the racial reckoning of 2014–15.

Identify Disruptive Strategies—Approaches to Addressing Problems

Disruptive strategies refer to the processes of intentionally going against the conventional organizational norms for the purpose of disrupting whiteness and making racism visible. After the summer data retreat, we transitioned from data collection to the sense-making stage of the project. In the fall of 2014, we released a summary report of the data retreat to all members of the school community. The report created a fury. Michael, a teacher leader who did not participate in the retreat, conveyed in his year five interviews what many teachers thought, himself included.

> The staff didn't agree . . . the staff didn't write those problem statements or goals. Twenty or thirty people who were at the meetings set those goals for everybody else. If you want the collective buy-in, there needs to be the collective process to go through that hard work and to accept that we all have a role to play in this process of change.

Michael was correct in that there was no schoolwide buy-in. We realized this. The goal at the point in time was not buy-in. Releasing the retreat summary report to the full school community was a mode of communication that disrupted the racial status quo. It communicated an acknowledgment of racism in a radically open way that countered the school culture. Although it did not offer recommendations or solutions, the act of releasing it and its content was a solution in itself. The summary report and statement resulted from a radically inclusive learning process that achieved a small breakthrough of "people being real for the first time." But Michael was right. It was a breakthrough for some of the people who participated in the retreat and who crafted it. For many adults in the building who did not participate, the statement was nonsense. We realized the limitations of the retreat almost as soon as we finished. Teachers were upset. Suzanne and Elizabeth were confused and upset. The situation was discomforting. And it laid the groundwork for a radically open communication culture that is essential to racial equity change. I created a vital feedback loop that offered still further insights into CWHS culture and climate of racial resistance.

On the surface, the book study appeared to be a shallow form of racial equity action (see Figure 5.2). Had CWHS studied the book as an isolated strategy of consuming information, it would have been shallow. But they leveraged the book study to disrupt the congenial race-evasive

FIGURE 5.2   Circle of racial equity actions

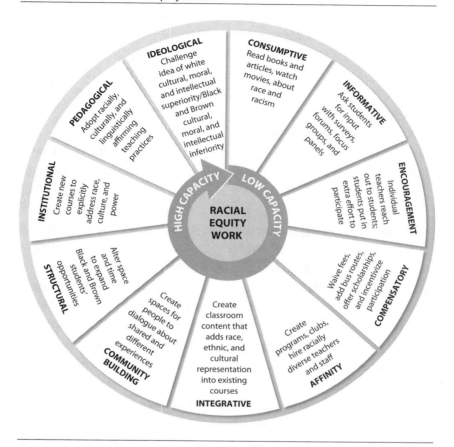

relational culture, which undermined the school's teaching and learning culture, and allowed racism to fester unchecked. Ambassadors critiqued and modified the summer data retreat protocols: "These prompts could be improved." "This activity requires more time." "We need to clarify this set of directions and objectives." They also integrated practice challenges into the book study process, which pushed the inquiry cycle into active learning through practice. For ambassadors, the planning process and facilitation itself deepened their racial learning and strengthened their leadership practice. But the book study was not intended to teach about racism. Rather, it was used to foster a language and communication practice that would create the organizational conditions in which they would be able to address the racial roots of school problems. The important point is that the design of racial learning must integrate inquiry, study, practice, and reflection. Racial learning design must draw on and combine a range of racial equity improvement actions into a broader strategy for change.

Learn/Adopt-Learn Disruptive Equity Actions

When teams at CWHS established a shared understanding of a practice that might address a racial equity problem, school community members learned to adapt themselves and the organization so that they could disrupt their past practices and adopt new, more equitable ones.[8] The key point here in this segment of the cycle is that learning and adopting new practices go hand in hand. Figure 5.2 outlines various types of racial equity actions that individuals, teams, and groups took, ranging from reading books, seeking student input, and modifying the structure of class schedules to spatially reorganizing the school into "houses." Some equity actions require substantially more capacity than others. Shallower actions require less effort and can usually be accomplished by individuals. Deeper equity actions require collective action and capacity. None of the racial equity learning actions are "wrong." Indeed, school communities committed to deep systemic change must welcome all of these actions. Indeed, a higher capacity organization will see multiple people engage in myriad equity actions. Even people who are most "advanced" should engage in continued consumption, seeking out information and input that will contribute to their learning and growth. Everyone must commit to active and action-oriented learning.

Leading-adopting disruptive equity actions requires not doing one or another equity action. It demands a collective view of progress. A community can undertake many actions at once—reading books, changing the school schedule, creating courses, sponsoring affinity groups—to continually deepen the inquiry toward a systemic understanding of racism and actions that disrupt its institutional and ideological roots. Thinking comprehensively about equity actions offers everyone in the school community "something" to do and leaves no one out. It fosters learning opportunities that accommodate each person's individual capacity for enacting equity actions, ideally pushing them toward the outermost edge of discomfort. When a critical mass is taking on varied actions, it increases the school's capacity for equity change.

For example, after we completed the first stage of data gathering, teachers agreed that understanding the nuances of students' racial experiences required more than focus group summary reports and disaggregated data. Administrators and teachers realized that student influential presence was critical yet minimized in the improvement efforts. Their capacity to improve was limited as long as students' voices were not more influentially present. During the second year of the project, administrators and teachers included students in teacher professional development and in doing so disrupted the racial conventions of almost exclusively white decision-making and learning.

During the 2015 summer relationship retreat, teachers, administrators, Black and Brown students, and old and new staff collaborated to understand problems and formulate solutions. Put differently, they leveraged Black and Brown students' influential presence as part of their improvement planning and learning. Doing so required equity actions. Teacher ambassadors strategically invited students in large numbers. Teachers and administrators anticipated challenges and thus worked around students' schedules to ensure they could attend. One student kept her five-year-old sibling during the summer break. "No problem. Bring her. She's welcome. We'll make sure she has plenty to do, and we will include her participation where it makes sense." Students lacked consistent transportation. "No problem. We are going to organize a car pool." The efforts reflected informative, encouraging, pedagogical, and ideological equity actions. The new practice of collaborating with students leveraged actions that disrupted conventional planning practices of the past.

The result was that almost thirty Black and Brown students inquired, colearned, and planned with teachers, staff, and administrators. The experience created new conditions and thus possibilities for antiracist learning for everyone involved. Students fully participated and even led some segments of the retreat. Still, students were not as deeply involved as they could or should have been during the academic year—at least not early on. Creating continuity between the intentional design of learning spaces and day-to-day teacher and leader practice proved more challenging. The structural and ideological constraints that bifurcate teenagers, young adults, and adults into distinctly different groups of people exclude students by preordaining when and where professional development occurs, with whom, and what content is most appropriate. Michael, a veteran teacher, shared his concern about the lack of student involvement over the duration of the project, in particular students' role beyond the colearning spaces:

> I've really been disappointed in the student piece of the project. . . . Somebody gave me an analogy a couple years ago. Our community is a triangle between the admin, the teachers and staff, and the students. If all three of those points are not touching, then there's no stability in the triangle.
>
> The student body is not *hearing* the message. If one part of that triangle doesn't work, then the whole triangle itself doesn't work. That's where I feel like we really miss some key points. That if this is truly an important thing for us to do, then we should be doing more with students.
>
> The work with Dr. Irby has been more focused on the admin/teacher/staff relationships and learning. It's year four, and we're finally bringing in the student voice more regularly. But yet I don't understand how we can bring that student voice more together and then collectively *disperse* it as well.

When considering the spectrum of possible equity actions, who was involved in what learning-actions, and their depth of involvement, Michael rightfully noted our prioritization of adult learning and ineffectiveness at reaching students. But it was teachers' responsibility to reach students and even other adults who were not involved. This process happened through transformation of practices in the day-to-day work of leading, teaching, and learning that I refer to as proliferation of equity practice.

Deepen and Proliferate Equity Practices

At CWHS "dispersing" ideas and practices took a different form than whole staff professional development, top-down mandates, or coercive attempts to compel compliance. Increasing the influence of the work occurred along two dimensions—proliferation and deepening—that constituted improvement.[9] Deepening refers to the learning process whereby individuals, teams, and groups developed more complex understandings of what actions and changes created a more equitable school. Deepening practice moved people at a pace of learning, growth, and action that kept them at the edge of their own development, both at the individual and team level. It was evidenced when a person or group of people learned—read enough, invited enough student feedback, and so forth—their way into a sharper vision of what deeper or more expansive equity actions looked like. They also "noticed" when colleagues were not as far along, could place them at a point in their journey, and could pinpoint learning experiences that might benefit people who were "stuck."

Administrators encouraged deepening by giving teachers the support and latitude to test out new, more equitable, approaches. But doing so created a problem amongst teachers who did not try new approaches. Deepening practice resulted in variability in practice across the school and over time. For example, some teachers adopted classroom circle practices, introduced climate feedback boxes, and coconstructed classroom commitments. Others dictated rules, meted out consequences, and held tightly to past ways. For some people, their knowledge of the problems was only deep enough that they could work toward surface-level equity actions. As they progressed through inquiry cycles and thus understanding of problems, they envisioned more deeply equitable responses to the problems. The people whose knowledge and understanding deepened grew frustrated at having to continually justify their new practices and explain what they were doing. The adoption of restorative practices and peace circles was a case in point, as Ethan noted during a Behavioral and Emotional team meeting:

> For me, it's a wear-down type situation. People are saying we are not communicating what we are doing. But it goes two ways. Every person

in this school has been repeatedly invited to participate in every activity to make this school better. Every single one. Everyone gets the same invitation. We share the same data. Everyone gets the same report.

People have got to receive it too. It's not that we're not doing anything [responding to student discipline problems], and it's not that we're not communicating. It's that people aren't receiving what we're communicating too. Maybe they block it out because they don't agree with what we're doing. Whatever it is, I don't know what more I can do but show you and tell you. It's up to you to receive it.

Ethan experienced frustration because he was much further along in understanding and practicing relational discipline approaches that create a more racially equitable school. He split his energy between deepening his own practice; collaborating and supporting others to deepen their practices; and defending, rationalizing, and explaining the importance and effectiveness of restorative approaches and peace circles to those who were not "on board."

One thing Elizabeth continually made clear: "The train is out of the station." Her priority was forward movement. So the continued dilemma throughout the project was how to know when to go deeper and with whom. So the challenge and opportunity became keeping everyone moving forward without holding back the progress of people who moved at a more accelerated pace or who developed more ambitious visions for change. The administrative team and teacher leaders understood that expending energy to earn "buy-in" invited immense resistance, pushbacks, and step-backs. Yet, the very people who resisted, pushed back, and stepped back criticized those who expended energy on imagining and trying equity practices. Some argued that continued forward movement without buy-in wasn't collaborative. Others were critical of the approaches themselves. First attempts often failed. As did second and third ones. But trial and error, combined with seeking and taking feedback to heart, was essential for deepening practice. This give and take worked best in teams who made their commitment to improve visible. Adrienne, a leadership team member, explained:

In the process of making a new schedule, we had a couple of community events to share with parents. At one event, the parents started asking these really tough questions. Right in that meeting, I realized, "This isn't going to work." The meeting ended and I was sweating and red and thinking "no" . . . I went to Elizabeth. She said, "Let's rework it." We had to go back to the drawing board and basically make a new schedule and do the whole dang thing over. So I guess what I'm trying to say is you make mistakes and all you can do is own them and revise and do it again.

As Adrienne did the work of trying to adopt-learn how to implement structural change, she experienced insecurities and struggles in the process. People felt incompetent. They experienced embarrassment. But failure, mistakes, and incompetence masked a reality that deep learning was also happening in the same moment. Confirmation and vividness bias masked the latter, obscuring the experiences of racial learning and equity change. As the "let's try this" ethos proliferated throughout CWHS, so too did equity practices. Meredith, a teacher leader in the world language department, described how nervous she was to try out a cell phone "hotel" practice that essentially eliminated the need to address student cell phone use on a student-by-student basis:

I was really nervous about making the kids put their cell phones away. I created the story in my mind: "they're going to hate it." But I thought of how Ethan really takes the time to care about people around him and sort of studied from him what that looks like to establish relationships with students and families. If you have a problem with a student, how do you express that in a way that's going to be positive and coming from a place of wanting to benefit the child instead of get the child in trouble?

So I approached it from a point of positivity and I told them, "I as an adult have times in my life where I want to text . . . and others where I'm deciding I'm going to put my phone away." That was it. They actually did it. The cell hotel is basically a pocket thing that students check their phones into. Students put their phones in "cell hotels." I tried it and then shared. All of the teachers in our department started doing it. It's been amazing. Fewer kids are missing work. And kids never give me a hard time about it.

How did Meredith decide to try this out? Proliferation of equity practice refers to a hybrid of formal and seemingly informal practices of transferring knowledge, skills, and competencies through leveraging personal relationships on one hand and the modeling practices via means of conventional school structures on the other. Proliferation of practice constitutes a highly complex web of continuous learning and social interactions, whereby equity practices emerge in various spaces and times. Equity practices often emerged from teachers and administrators trying out a practice and sharing their success with colleagues.

Practice adoption proliferated from top-down, bottom-up, and horizontal influences. The proliferation process often hybridized practices that both solved problems and treated students with care, consideration, and dignity. Meredith hybridized the cell phone hotel idea with what she learned in her interactions and "study" of Ethan's relational work with students. Ethan's relational work stemmed from his deep learning about different discipline philosophies and their associated practices. He used his influence as a school administrator to convey the practices, both through modeling and testimonials. Meredith took note. She applied her learning to address a problem that she knew had long caused racial conflicts in the classroom. She used her influence within her department to proliferate the hybridized practice, as in "How do we introduce this to students by conveying its practical benefits?" The proliferation of the practice did not stem from a schoolwide workshop or the effort of administrators to enforce a policy or engage in coercive tactics of getting "buy-in."

Proliferation is difficult to track. The process remains invisible because teachers and administrators rarely announce when they plan to try something new, because it might not work. Most people share their equity practice change successes after they deem them a success. While tracing the roots of a practice's proliferation is highly complex, designing and facilitating intentional proliferation are not. Intentional proliferation occurred in two forms: inviting and embedding.

Inviting proliferation began when administrators and teachers identified an equity practice or routine that they speculated would benefit the entire school community and expressed a desire to share it. Whoever learned from their own adoption of the practice considered to whom and when to invite colleagues of students to try the practice, primarily within their own sphere of influence. The introduction of the idea usually involved a racial-self talk (this is how I thought about my fear of what would happen), an experiential explanation of the practice change (through modeling, demonstrating, or explaining), what practices it replaces, and the myriad effects of the change. Next, the proliferators made a concrete invitation for the people whose practice they hoped to influence to "try" the new practice for a period of time. Invitational proliferators followed up as needed to check in and process how the practice worked during a trial period. The invitation usually generated from the proliferating teacher's awareness that the practice could potentially help their colleague solve a direct problem, often one they themselves encountered.

For example, teacher ambassadors proliferated the communication and confrontation practices that built the school's capacity to address racial conflict and otherwise. Ambassadors recruited their colleagues' participation in the book study by each inviting two people: one person they believed would appreciate and embrace the work, and one they thought would be critical of the work. Ambassadors focused on inviting people they had established strong relationships with: lunch colleagues, people they considered friends, and so forth. They collectively shared whom they wanted to invite to reduce duplication. This intentional process increased the number of people who tried and eventually adopted new policies and practices. Teacher ambassadors' direct invitations were critical to increasing the number of people willing to pay attention to the school's equity efforts. So too was the way that they embedded their practices into well-established school structures and routines.

Embedded proliferation occurred when CWHS administrators and ambassadors strategically positioned themselves within meetings and other decision-making spaces and structures. When Elizabeth required all staff to attend professional developments, she consulted teacher ambassadors on group breakout composition and content design. Over time, we developed a shared understanding that one-time workshops would primarily provide informational learning opportunities. We didn't expect anyone to adopt a practice or change their beliefs as a result of attending. If they did, that was fine. Continued exposure to ideas was enough. With tempered expectations, CWHS administrators and teacher leaders did not worry that professional development sessions offered breakthrough experiences.

FAR PAST CURIOUS: DILEMMAS OF PROLIFERATION AND DEEPENING

By 2015–16, it was clear that many people were not going to do anything on their own accord. Extending to people the grace of entering the "journey" on their own terms slowed CWHS's efforts and ultimately upheld the racial violence that students experienced. The school began wrestling with the tension of requiring involvement or not, being directive or collaborative. Deirdre, a member of the research team, joined Elizabeth and Ethan for one check-in where they described embedded proliferation practices that hybridized their courageous confrontation and restorative practices. These approaches were aimed at reducing punitive practices that dominated in the past. The question they continually faced was how to integrate newcomers and latecomers into their equity efforts. In the following excerpt, the tensions are clear. So too are the intentions of proliferation.

> **Deirdre:** How's the school liaison officer integrating into things?
> **Ethan:** He's doing okay. He's raised a couple of red flags with some comments that he made. There was an incident the first week of school, where a couple of kids . . . I don't remember exactly what happened. He was inferring that he thought maybe a battery charge should be made against a student . . . We were all meeting together. We all raised our eyebrows at the same time like "What? This is not anything near a battery situation." Donnell talked to him and said, "No we're not doing that." He was fine with it.

Deirdre: Okay, wow, yeah.

Ethan: I don't know if we talked to you since we had our late start and where we went back in circles and revisited commitments. Elizabeth scheduled an hour and a half for us to do our restorative practice overview. I thought that went really well. A lot of the staff were not happy initially, because they thought they wanted time to do their own classroom planning.

Not all of them, but some came in with a little bit of an attitude. Anyway, myself and members of our restorative practices team presented an overview. The session before that was dedicated to reviewing the commitments that we did at the relationship retreat. I did a brief overview of what that process entailed and then we divided up.

Before we met, Jan Braves, a teacher ambassador, sent a survey out to staff so they could choose which of the six areas they wanted to be part of. Each of the teacher ambassadors took one of the groups and we divided up into circles. The intention was to review the commitments and see if anybody had any thoughts about changes, or additions, or editing that. We spent probably close to an hour in our groups. The feedback was generally very favorable. I think staff felt really good.

Elizabeth was not involved. . . . She wanted everybody else to take the lead on it, so she could, as we talked about, hand it off and not make it an administrative compliance type of issue. We had a couple of little snafus and a couple of groups, but nothing major. All the feedback from staff was very positive.

What we're going to do for the October 19th session is combine our restorative practice group and our ambassadors to review our restorative practices. We had some classes, situations where people have done some restorative groups. We had the conferences that I talked about. We had a few student circles. But we want to make it a more common practice.

So we're going to have staff members who have gotten involved in circles that share their experiences and then we're going to devise staff circles again and we're going to go through the complaint to commitment process, in groups of circles of probably twelve to fifteen people. All the teachers, ambassadors, and restorative practices people are going to lead the design and cofacilitate that.

Elizabeth: With student ambassadors.

Ethan: Yes. We're inviting student ambassadors.

Elizabeth: We've practiced the circles using retreat topics as the subgroups—hallway behaviors, climate of respect, and so on. It was talking about those areas where we are struggling. But the primary learning objective was to share and practice effective communication. For example, I was in Jan's group, and she was the teacher ambassador. The administrators were distributed, so I was just a participant. I didn't do any leading. We had students in all these groups.

Jan and the students were leading them in a circle approach and modeling effective communication. Somebody was saying, "Well, we think. . . ." They would say, "Are you open to me offering a loving critique?" It was about a topic, but it was an opportunity for ambassadors to practice and others to learn the practices through experience and seeing others do it.

Elizabeth: Now moving into October 19th, we know we need more practice than that. We can't say, "Okay, now we're good." But we were sort of looking at restorative approaches and ambassador work as distinct and Ethan's great idea to say, "Can't we really combine restorative practices and effective communication?" So we put those groups together to coplan. That group is coming together I think is a really great idea.

Deirdre: That's wonderful.

Elizabeth: I'm telling you, friends, Ethan has been the lead superstar of this. I was not involved in the planning. I trusted Ethan to make sure that there was a quality control piece, because if people found it was unorganized, a waste of time, a bunch of bullshit, we would lose traction. I went into that day as a participant and I left thinking, "Hey, that was really good." Ethan did a fabulous job along with teacher ambassadors and student ambassadors.

Embedding proliferation included activities such as arranging chairs in circles to ensure people faced each other, removing tables that would otherwise disrupt the flow of energy, transparently acknowledging the thinking behind group composition; establishing commitments, democratic facilitation protocols, and racial-self talking; and using established communication guidelines. This intention benefitted the proliferators. Deep learning occurs when connected to day-to-day practice in multiple professional settings, where novel problems emerged. As ambassadors modeled, facilitated, and participated, they gained opportunities to learn. They gained opportunities to see new approaches in action, which expanded opportunities to learn as they "sort of studied" their colleagues' behaviors.

Assess Outcomes in Relation to Practices and Experiences (Data Reviews)

The final stage of the race-conscious inquiry cycle is processing experiences and assessing outcomes. Race-conscious assessment processes are more expansive than the typical inquiry cycle process focus on outcomes and goals because it focuses on making the relationship between self and experience, practice change, and outcomes highly visible. Outcomes and goals are important. But a sole focus on answering "Did we achieve the intended outcomes, and are we progressing toward our goals?" risks leaving important lessons learned and opportunities for deepening practice off the table of consideration. It also invisiblizes and erases practice change breakthroughs, which is an experiential data point that is important to notice and name but which is overlooked in conventional assessment practices. Race-conscious inquiry must be concerned with understanding how an organization's culture and practices inscribe race, gender, and positional power. Power arrangements yield organizational outcomes—fear, failure, erasure, discipline gaps, academic achievement patterns, and so forth. Since a substantial part of our efforts was to disrupt extant power arrangements, it required that we make analyzing such arrangement a part of a monitoring and assessment practice.

As Elizabeth shifted her practice from dictating decisions and "fixing" problems to inviting people into problem solving and listening, we made these practices and their consequences visible. After a circle meeting with teacher ambassadors to discuss Elizabeth's disdain for the climate box, members of our research team and associate principals Andrea, Donnell,

Owk, Ethan, and Elizabeth debriefed. We focused on Elizabeth's practice changes and how they reshaped power relations. We also focused on the solutions that emerged as more democratic space emerged. We started the meeting by going round robin to process experience and to understand how people made meaning of the circle conversation:

> **Andrea:** I'm still reflecting. But it was really powerful for me to hear the discussion about the climate box and where people were at. I heard two themes. First, people said it gave an opportunity for people to have voice. Second, the climate box reduces people's fears of repercussions. They said the climate box is "a way for me to speak my truth, have my voice, and not feel like I'm going to be in trouble."
>
> **Elizabeth:** For me, it was the first time I heard people except for the team say that it's not just the admin's responsibility. I heard multiple people say that today and wanting to be a part of leading improvement. They felt like they need some more skills to lead. But that's okay because I feel like we do too.
>
> **Andrea:** What was interesting is you asked the question. You asked them that question. You put it to them. You invited their responses, which I think is really something you need to acknowledge.
>
> **Elizabeth:** Okay. I didn't realize I did that.
>
> **Owk:** That's something I noticed too. It's important to see your own practice. Here's what was powerful that hasn't been mentioned. You started asking questions aloud, really to yourself, but the group heard your own questions. In the past, you would have done that with me or with us [researchers and administration team]. I've not seen you do that in front of teachers.
>
> **Donnell:** You let them answer. It was an invitation. It wasn't like, "What do I do?" It was a genuine kind of like . . . "I don't know necessarily how to work through these challenges. What are some possibilities?" In the past, we probably would have just made the decision. It would have not went like that before.
>
> **Andrea:** People are giving different ideas for ways to structure it, and then Kathy ended up saying, well, she sees some value in the box itself because some people are scared to give feedback. Some people who

are in a different place. Even if people are in a place with fear, they should be able to have a place to have their voice heard. She ended up saying, "I'm scared too. I'm scared of repercussions. I'm scared of what happens if I put myself out there because I've had it happen to me."

Allison had an idea of taking comments out of the box, reworking them, and placing on a board. If you put a sticky note where other people can put ideas, they can weigh in with ideas and express solutions. It's really open and transparent. Then there could be a group of teachers who field solutions from colleagues that folks who have the problems can try. Maybe an administrator is a part of the conversation, but it's not that they're there to solve the problem.

Donnell: What this process did was it asked the staff. The fifteen people who were in the circle tried to answer that question "What do we do now?" It was really a powerful brainstorming of ideas on how to communicate and have a table for discussion. I felt that they heard what Elizabeth was saying, and then also was able to say, "Okay and this is what we're saying. How do we get to where we want to be?" There's some ideas about how to still continue the idea of the climate box and maybe structure it a little different. I felt that it was good.

Elizabeth: Well, what's interesting is that it's an evolutionary process, right? We're all growing and changing and doing and being differently, very slowly, but you may not necessarily recognize what's changing or how you're being different. But if you behave differently, people respond to that. I am a fixer. I'm a problem solver too.

You know, Decoteau and Kane often attest to the idea "the solutions are mostly in house." I'm owning that more through reflecting on the readings and these opportunities to process. I was really struck by Sally. First of all, I was shocked that she attends any of this because she has said that she's very scared, very fearful. And we were in the circle talking about the climate box; that is scary for me. It's very hard for me to own my fears too.

In conceptualizing the practice of progress monitoring, we expanded beyond mere attention to quantitative data. We sought to understand experience. During debriefs we prioritized reflective feedback to amplify practices and make visible the ways of disrupting power. Owk pointed out Elizabeth's practice breakthrough. Elizabeth's recognition of how her own seemingly small behaviors shaped possibilities for teacher learning and engagement was just as important as the solutions that emerged during the circle conversations. The fact that the conversation was structured as a circle was itself novel. If we'd focused only on meeting outcomes, we would have missed the subtle practice breakthroughs that produced them. At the end of the meeting, I shared my own key takeaway: "It is especially important for you all to be conscious of your growth and your development in the process. If you are by default a fixer, then letting people help you and supporting people to help themselves should be a part of how you define your success." That is exactly what Elizabeth did in the following year.

WHY ARE STUDENTS FAILING? DEPARTMENT CHAIR'S INQUIRY CYCLE

By 2016–17, people who had a historical memory of CHWS in years past noticed "something" was happening. Elizabeth's leadership practices changed. She encouraged creativity and made an effort to provide platforms for teachers to proliferate promising practices changes. She listened. She collaborated. She invited people into and embedded her new practices within her spheres of influence, which expanded far beyond the school. Elizabeth's emerging practices were not lost on faculty and staff, who over time started to refer to her as "new Elizabeth" and "old Elizabeth" to distinguish her leadership practice. She too often made similar self-reflections: "The old me wouldn't have thought of that." Black and Brown community members often asked me, "What's going on at Central Waters? Ethan seems like he's changed. He used to be racist as hell." The race-conscious inquiry and learning enabled people to create themselves anew. Relationship ambassadors were doing their part. Administrators were doing their part. Student ambassadors started doing their part. The restorative circles, conferences, and student clubs were great. The late buses were too. The practice of codeveloping classroom commitments proliferated.

But the school's white-dominated curriculum and culture of teaching and learning remained systemically untouched. The equity efforts were not transforming the school's academic program in ways that benefit Black and Brown students. The train was out of the station. But not everyone was on board. Department chairs, not teacher ambassadors, were most influentially positioned to lead the kind of instructional and teaching improvement that would create a school that intellectually and emotionally engaged Black and Brown students. It just so happened they were the least involved group of leaders in the building. With a few notable exceptions, CWHS department chairs sat on the sidelines of the school's equity efforts for the first three years. Most had not participated in summer retreats. Elizabeth assumed they did not support the improvement efforts, which we later learned was partially true. But she didn't know. She had never asked.

We all understood addressing the school's discipline and climate problems would be nearly impossible without addressing the culture of teaching. This begged the question: how could we get all formal school leaders involved? With Elizabeth's blessings, we asked them. During the summer before year four commenced, two White graduate students, Kane and Robyn, conducted interviews with department chairs.

> We're broadly interested in why you and other department chairs have not participated in the formal efforts associated with the culture and climate improvement project. We noticed the pattern, but rather than speculate about why you were or were not involved, Elizabeth thought it would be good to ask you. That's why we're here. What's kept you from engaging? We're here to listen.

We learned the highly regarded and respected teacher leaders were not actively participating for numerous reasons. Some wanted to, but the time and space did not allow them to. Others had no intention of getting involved. They offered explanations for not being involved such as "The scheduling doesn't work for me" to "The work is not valuable because there is no direction in terms of what can be done to be proactive." As much as the energy had shifted, we all understood that without the support of teacher leaders who held formal leadership positions, the school's teaching and instructional culture would not change. One department chair who had not been deeply involved, but nonetheless was supportive of the efforts and new energy, explained the importance of getting department chairs involved:

> The bigger issue at this point is that we [department chairs] need to adopt a capacity-building approach to operate with our administrative team on a more as-needed basis. They can help. But we should be leading too. Admins are too overwhelmed to offer the intensive support that we need to get better.

This was a sentiment that administrators and teacher ambassadors expressed much earlier in the project. As we had done many times over the years, we summarized responses and submitted them to the administrative team. By the time we started the department chair professional development sequence, the administrative team and I were much more confident about what learning needed to happen to compel teaching and instructional practice changes. We understood from the trial, error, and learning from years past how to design and lead the learning: draw on data and research that reflected Black and Brown people's perspectives and experiences, sustain curated racial discomfort, cultivate courageous confrontation, and get people to self-talk aloud—*a lot*. The overall year-long learning plan and the individual session agendas we designed contained each of these elements.

We also realized that we needed to make the learning experience a mirror for this group of powerful teacher leaders to "see" their own practice. The outsized amount of influence that department chairs had at CWHS meant that if they changed their leadership and instructional practices, improved their work with students of color, and took on a more racially conscious approach to their work, so too might others. Noting this, we started the learning series by introducing an inquiry cycle on leadership practice, the problem that they cited as wanting support on during the inquiry interviews:

How do you run your meetings? For next time, everyone bring in your department meeting agenda; be prepared to present and critique it. The question is "Are you using the meetings to focus on instructional improvement?"

After that initial quick inquiry process, the department chairs realized that they had some things to learn about leading their departments. I offered readings about the instructional core, leadership for learning, and other instructional leadership materials. As I offered those readings, I critiqued the race neutrality of the literature. We explored the authors' philosophical assumptions and asked questions about what kinds of schools they conducted their research in. What where their aims? I invited them into the problems I saw. And they invited me into theirs. Drawing on the Kegan and Lahey work that the school took up years earlier, I asked, "What eats away at you, that if we solved right now, would make the school better?" They were invited and encouraged to talk about race and racism. By now, CWHS's racial resources worked in our favor. Put differently, the school had the capacity to take on race-specific improvement work that it had not in prior years. The established organizational conditions, increased cultivation of racial equity resources, and extant capacities welcomed the race-specific exchange I started. After our quick cycle of meeting practices, I invited the department chairs to pose their own burning questions, from which we developed the following frame for initiating a race-conscious inquiry cycle:

- Improvement area: Using data to identify areas for instructional improvement
- Organizational problem: The gap between *your collective vision or standard of excellence* (performance and outcomes) and the current state of affairs (performance and outcomes)
- Current focus: Understanding and describing grade and Pass/Fail data and patterns
- Questions and curiosities: We have several interventions in place to help students with specific instructional deficits. But I believe

students with multiple failures (three to seven *F*s) have unique needs and as a school we have never really addressed their needs. What supports and strategies are effective in helping students with multiple failures? What can we do to address their needs?

Using these questions as a starting point, we racialized the problems of "who fails?" by getting leaders' racial assumptions out into the open. Black and Brown students didn't do well in math. Under the logic of white supremacy, there had to be a *good reason* for their widespread underachievement, usually a simple one. They aren't engaged. They don't want to be at school. *They don't care.* Even in the face of contrary evidence, white supremacy demands that teachers bias themselves to confirm rather disconfirm their racial beliefs. So we collectively probed the racist roots of these assumptions. They aren't engaged. Why? They don't want to be in class. How do you know? Why? Well, they don't see the relevance of what we're learning. Why? Why? Why?

Quickly, department chairs reframed their questions. They pivoted from "Why do students fail?" to "Why do Black students not succeed in my class, our department, our school?" to "What would improve Black and Brown students' sense of belonging and learning opportunities in my class?" Race-conscious questions began to proliferate. CWHS formal leaders were getting curious and cultivating self-initiated racial-conscious inquiry as a distributed leadership practice. So it was time for me to leave. When I withdrew from the in-person data collection, the reason wasn't that CWHS had the right answers. It was that they started asking the right questions.

When department chairs grew curious about the roles curriculum, teacher practice, and their own instructional leadership played in producing racial disparities, the stage was set for transforming the core of CWHS racial equity work to include major modifications to course options, assessment practices, and other curricular, teaching, and student learning matters. I knew going in that it was not enough to tell White educators at CWHS that their explanations about why students failed were wrong. Because white is right until White people discover for themselves it's not. There has to be *good* reason for a cafeteria worker to close the line in Kevin's face. It's impossible for there not be. After all, her shift *was* over. He could have gotten in line earlier. If he waited, clearly he was not that hungry. He'll be okay. It was one time. Maybe it taught him a lesson: get your lunch before socializing with your friends. His priorities are mixed up. And so on and so on, into the abyss of white disbelief in Black and Brown people and erasure of their experiences. Race-conscious inquiry asks White people and to consider the white supremacist inclination to erase Black and Brown people's experiences and explanations on one hand and to quickly rationalize White people's racism on the other. It asks them to stare white racial beliefs in the face, post them to sticky notes, and speak them aloud. Making them visible puts them on the table to learn from and potentially to disrupt.

RACE-CONSCIOUS INQUIRY LEADERSHIP PRINCIPLES

Over the duration of the project, we used race-conscious inquiry cycles to develop a clearer sense of how to codesign an inquiry process to accelerate leadership for racial equity improvement. So when Elizabeth expressed concerns about getting department chairs more involved in the equity reform efforts, I knew what we needed to do. We had already completed multiple inquiry processes at multiple scales—whole school, leadership teams, and so on. As Central Waters adopted and integrated racial equity problem identification and framing into their standard organizational practices, absent our involvement, I noticed four principles that guided race-conscious inquiry leadership, as outlined in table 5.2.

Starting from a place of curiosity and questions about how to make the school more equitable is important for two interrelated reasons. First, every school is distinct enough that its problems warrant localized improvement strategies. It's not the absolute case that any imported solution or strategy can't or won't work. They can and they do. Yet, they often do not because educators prioritize fidelity of implementation over tailoring for local contexts and conditions. In contexts where fidelity rules, teachers experience imported solutions and strategies as compliance mandates that undercut the professional discretion, experimentation, and learning that are so important for creating a culture of improvement.

TABLE 5.2 Cultivating race-conscious inquiry cycles

CRITICAL PRINCIPLE	ENACTING THE PRINCIPLE	RACIAL LEARNING BENEFITS
Racial curiosity and exploration are critical	Lead with questions that seek to unearth the multiple layers and complexities of racial structures and patterns.	Individuals, teams, and the school community benefit from creating a culture of inquiry and learning which concedes that racial learning is complex and difficult.
Collective problem solving is critical	Lead by inviting people to coexplore, problematize, and problem-solve as a group.	Individuals, teams, and the school community benefit from deepening and broadening their understandings of racism and the myriad ways to challenge the patterns that reflect racism.
Cultivating and leveraging an organization's racial resources are critical	Expand Black and Brown influential presence. Curate white racial discomfort. Create a courageously confrontational school culture. Cultivate collective awareness of racial emotions and beliefs.	Opportunities for racial learning are expanded and sustained, allowing racial equity changes to proliferate throughout the organization.
Using one's own school setting and self as primary text for learning is critical	Lead by sharing one's own self-exploration, experiences, and knowledge while using episodes, data, and patterns from the school as a tool to promote inquiry and learning.	Individuals, teams, and the school community benefit from using local stories, data, and experiences because they can continually explore the local in real ways that are not afforded through other means.

Over time, this experience leads to initiative fatigue. Teachers who are asked to do racial equity work and retort "Tell me what to do" are fatigued, resistant, and fearful of appearing incompetent. They don't know what to do. But in actuality, they do not want to be told what to do. So, second, they want to be invited to solve problems. There is an element of empowerment that accompanies the invitation to solve complex problems, of course with adequate supports. Inviting teachers, students, and even community members into problem solving empowers people.

Michael explained how he changed as a result of the school's efforts:

On a personal level I've come to realize that I can effect change not only within my own classroom, but within the structure of our staff and our building, and I try to mirror and echo those statements to everyone so that collectively as individual teachers we all have a voice, we all have ability to raise this thing up. That it's not the responsibility of a certain few people to do these things. . . . I complained about this work for the first year and a half of it. It just made me feel ugly on the inside when in the end those problems that I'm complaining about are things that I can change. I feel that's been a tremendous thing for me.

It's helped me feel more excited, more at ease, more at peace with what I do. It's helped me to broaden my shoulders a little bit more and try to take on some of the responsibilities that I maybe necessarily didn't want at times, but I feel like I can do now. It's helped me to be more aware of obviously with race, ethnicity, cultural differences within my classroom. It's still an area that I think every teacher can improve upon, and I don't know if any teacher can ever say that they're really good at it. I think there's always . . . that spectrum will always continue to keep moving, but I think it's something that I've gotten better at as a result of working with him [Dr. Irby] and the process.

Michael's reflection points to the importance of self-awareness and racial consciousness as an integral part of race-conscious inquiry cycles. This aspect of race-conscious inquiry leadership demonstrates the potential of change that occurs when the school itself is and remains the primary text of inquiry, analysis, and learning. It took time and numerous repeated learning opportunities for Michael to get arrive at the place he described. Formal structures facilitate the continued study of the school itself. By the 2016–17 academic year, a newly formed Culture and Climate School Improvement team composed of administrators, teachers, and staff subsumed the tasks of gathering, analyzing, and presenting formative and summative student and teacher data for use in discipline, culture, and climate decision-making and practices. It was in this space that inquiry cycles took root as schoolwide practice. Arielle, a White teacher who was critical of the improvement efforts, explained that she began to see the benefits of the inquiry-based approach to leadership when it was formalized as a structured process:

Well, I was asked to be a part of the continuous improvement team, which is department leaders and admin. And so that also means that

I would be an IT team member, which will be the implementation teams, and I'm on the climate and community team and so you know I work with staff members and I work with student and *parent ambassadors* to forward our mission. Last year was a big data collection year for us to see, you know, how kids are feeling and how staff are feeling on a bunch of different topics and so this is the year where we make the change.

Let's say, for example, a subcommittee developed a strategy to promote positivity; we walked through our halls to observe and collect data. We develop ways to enhance the visual culture, the interactions, and so on through promoting positive messages to students and staff too. So it will be our job this year to kind of make that real. I'm in a leadership position for that. So that's also changed.

As CWHS sought help to solve its problems, we—my research team and I—sought to continuously put a mirror up to whoever at CWHS was willing to look into it to see its perils and possibilities. We did not want to fix CWHS. We wanted CWHS to see its potential to fix itself and to take hold of its own equity improvement. The tools my research team and I brought were racial consciousness, philosophy, theory, data collection, a willingness to listen, and the willingness to invite others into the process of thinking and asking questions about CWHS as an organization and community of learners. Likewise, CWHS leaders invited me into their thinking and questions, which were grounded in the day-to-day problems they experienced. The best text to understand race and racism was to develop a capacity to see how it played out in real time, in the here and now at CWHS. In any school improvement effort, the school community itself is the most important source from which to identify learning opportunities for growth and improvement. The school community itself is also the source that impedes its own growth and improvement. Holding on to both of these truths so that the truths don't counterbalance each other is tough. The capacity for a school community to "see" itself as its greatest hope and hindrance for achieving racial equity is essential for its improvement. This ability to see itself with a broader context of racism increases racial consciousness.

CONCLUSION: SUSTAINING RACE-CONSCIOUS INQUIRY

CWHS administrators, teachers, students, and our research team used cycles of inquiry that informed both structural reform as well as leadership actions that responded to the individual and interpersonal needs of faculty and staff. Because inquiry drove the improvement process, CWHS administrators plus formal and informal leaders catered their leadership approaches to address racial problems that emerged through their analysis of school outcomes, conditions, culture, and climate. The inquiry process reflected a commitment to formative data collection, collective analysis, and use in a broad sense—climate and culture surveys; student outcome data; teacher and student feedback from formal focus groups, listening sessions, community meetings, and observations—but with an explicit emphasis on discerning the racialized nature of school patterns and practices.

CWHS leaders adopted different leadership approaches at different points to advance different aspects of the school's equity work. For example, during the first year of the project, administrators prioritized listening and learning, and sought to extend opportunities for the school community to make sense of its experiential and outcome disparities. In the 2014–15 academic year, in response to the understandings and racial politics that emerged from taking racism head on, administrators and a new group of teacher leaders who called themselves relationship ambassadors spent much of their time and energy attending to the racial anxieties and racial politics that were reshaping the school. That year was tumultuous. Teachers and staff resigned. Teachers organized a campaign to oust Elizabeth. White parents showed up en masse to school board meetings to shout down Elizabeth and other administrators. Having weathered the tumult of the 2014–15 year, the administrative team began in 2015–16 to initiate the kinds of structural reforms that are associated with transformative leadership.[10]

They restructured days into block schedules to increase instructional time, created A-plus periods to enable students time to receive additional supports during the school day, formed "houses" to personalize the school experience by allowing groups of teachers to work with a more manageable number of students, and continued their quest to expand college and AP course access to students of color. In 2017–18, Elizabeth arranged monthly release time to develop department chairs' skills and capacities to engage in equity improvement at the departmental level. The year's efforts focused on accelerating department chairs' leadership for equity, with an emphasis on how to apply an equity lens to review student performance data and lead similar collegial explorations at the department level about classroom instruction. At the same time, school administrators engaged in equity efforts that required they interface with external stakeholders. By 2018–19, the racial equity work pivoted toward instructional practices, and the departments started redesigning the school's curriculum and instructional approaches to better meet students' wants and needs, including introducing new courses, such as

- 2015–16: Cultural Perspectives in America (Social Studies)
- 2016–17: Rock and Roll Society and American Culture (Social Studies)
- 2017–18: World Drumming (Music)
- 2018–19: Modern Revolutions (Social Studies)
- 2018–19: Area Studies—Latin America (Social Studies)
- 2018–19: Area Studies—Africa (Social Studies)

Race-conscious inquiry is not a panacea. There were times that called for decisive action, not inquiry. No students should write *nigger* on the wall. The deeper question, however, is why such an act is tolerable. Inquiry driven racial equity leadership builds organizational capacity for racial equity improvement that answers questions and generates solutions to improve Black and Brown students' educational opportunities, experiences, and outcomes. Racializing problems; "seeing" whiteness, racism, and white supremacy; and proliferating and adopting disruptive equity practices take time. Our reports offered considerations, not recommendations. "What are we going to do to fix this problem? How does this report help us fix the problem? Or improve our discipline practices?" The reports were not intended to put forth any solutions or recommendations. Only to provide new information to deepen understanding. So many grew impatient with our research team, their colleagues, and especially the school administration. Some grew impatient with the pace of change and my research team's commitment to inquiry and insistence that CWHS answer its own questions. Some White teachers experienced the cognitive dissonance of coming to terms with the reality that the CWHS of yesteryear was no more. But curiosity coincided with impatience and discomfort.

Race-conscious inquiry leadership assumes educators are curious, willing, and capable of collaborative inquiry and colearning. It is a bleak and violent realization that Black and Brown students' positive schooling experiences are bound up with White educators' willingness and capacity to learn. Indeed, White educators need Black and Brown people's influential presence to catalyze their learning. When reforms are presented as mandates, such as the case with the AP integration, rather than invitations, teachers shut down, resist, and stand aside. "Tell me what you want me to do. How am I supposed to do that?" they ask in frustration. Finding successes from within the school community alleviates such tendencies. But again, who has *this much* time?

Another dilemma is that it was difficult to sustain the inquiry because evidence of progress is not easy to pinpoint. Important indicators of racial learning and progress—conceptual breakthroughs, emotional breakthroughs, and practice breakthroughs—are hard-to-see data points. Looking back, I characterize the academic year between the 2014 data retreat and the 2015 relationship retreat as a period of organizationwide racial reckoning. During that year, none of us described it as a time of immense learning in which breakthroughs were occurring. It was a mirror moment when Black and Brown influential presence crept into the school. White people experienced sustained periods of discomfort. Teacher ambassadors laid the groundwork for a courageously confrontational school culture to take root. People racial self-talked in an effort to make sense of their experiences. All of these racial resources intersected with race-conscious inquiry cycles to bolster the school's capacity for equity change.

6

STUCK IMPROVING—KNOWING THAT
RACISM (WHITE SUPREMACY) IS *AT WORK*

In 2012–13, under the demands of a consent decree, Central Waters High School set out to make its school more racially equitable. Their ultimate goal was to graduate Black and Brown students who were college and career ready. Over the duration of my study, CWHS did many things to achieve this goal. They instituted standards for including student representation on governing bodies by codifying the requirement in high school policies. The school established the Black Student Union, Brothers United Club, Sisters Supporting Sisters Club, Latino Nation Club, and All Student Union. CWHS administrators recruited administrators, teachers, and staff of color. They included students and staff of color on interview and hiring committees. They formed partnerships with community organizations and relationships with community leaders. Students and staff attended International Institute of Restorative Practices (IIRP) training and adopted restorative discipline approaches. CWHS increased the number of eleventh and twelfth graders who enrolled in at least one Advanced Placement course for all students. They overhauled existing courses to be more culturally responsive. They created new courses. CWHS leaders and teachers expected that their efforts would show up in conventional outcomes indicators.

Throughout this book I have attempted to substantiate a few simple claims. First, many White educators' individual and collective racial knowledge and thus capacities are inadequate to improve schools to benefit Black and Brown students. They are incapable of enacting racial equity changes that are meaningful and affirming to students they are not like racially, ethnically, and culturally. Second, White educators' racial knowledge and capacities are not inherently inadequate. Organization-wide racial learning, grounded in doing the complex and context-specific work of pursuing racial equity, increases educators' capacity to enact racial equity change. The problem is that CWHS set about doing work for which they had very little organizational capacity. They needed to do substantial racial learning to establish the conditions for racial equity improvement. At the same time, they needed to respond to the immediate needs of Black and Brown students. In previous chapters, I presented stories and analysis to show what their efforts entailed. In this concluding chapter, I bring the accumulation of this learning to the forefront by amplifying what I call equity breakthroughs and relating them to CWHS's capacity for racial equity change.

Racial breakthroughs change structures, routines, practices, and lines of reasoning to affirm and benefit Black and Brown students. Breakthroughs simultaneously do two things. On one hand, they disrupt racially inequitable patterns of mundane violence. On the other hand, they affirm and benefit Black and Brown students. They are indicators of changing racial interactions. Tragically, racial breakthroughs are often fleeting, dually undermined by our collective inability to see them and white supremacy's insistent and ongoing self-reinvention. First, the myriad practices, policies, organizational conditions, and experiences that affirm Black and Brown students, their racial knowledge, contributions, and experiences are invisiblized. Educators erase breakthroughs that affirm Black and Brown students before people who experience them recognize, honor, and testify of their existence. Thus, breakthroughs are not available for people to learn from or carry forward. Breakthroughs threaten the extant racial order. Second, because racial breakthroughs threaten a white supremacist racial order, they are always subject to racial setbacks. Racial setbacks neutralize racial breakthroughs by resetting people's racial interactions, thinking, and behaviors to prior racial patterns and configurations. Unless a school continually sets itself up—builds its capacity for racial equity change—to accelerate and proliferate racial breakthroughs, erasure and guaranteed racial setbacks will continually stunt its racial equity efforts and erase any successes it may achieve.

INCREASED CAPACITY FOR CHANGE: ORGANIZATIONAL BREAKTHROUGHS

In previous chapters I outlined the collection of racial resources that CWHS educators leveraged to strengthen their capacity for racial equity improvement, which are summarized in table 6.1. As such, this book focused primarily on organizational breakthroughs as evidence of organizational racial resources and school capacity. Although I integrated elements of each resource into each chapter, I presented them separately to reduce the complexity of understanding the organizational capacity for racial equity change. The resources, however, do not exist in isolation. They are related, inextricably bound together, in ways that produce mutual reinforcements and tensions. For example, the cultivation of Black and Brown influential presence reinforces the cultivation of collective awareness of racial emotions and beliefs. When colleagues are confronted with real or imagined racial conflict (e.g., fear about Black colleagues who are not yet even hired or interviewed), it creates an opportunity to openly learn from and through the exploration of emotions and beliefs. Increased Black and Brown influential presence compels White people to critically self-reflect, to become aware of their racial emotions and ideologies. Also, race-conscious inquiry bolsters a courageously confrontational school culture. If a team of educators commit to race-conscious inquiry, the process necessitates courageous confrontation, which spurs the demand for curated white racial discomfort.

Considering all racial equity resources together, a conceptual framework for understanding organizational capacity for racial equity improvement might look something like figure 6.1, which presents racial resources and principles as a constellation of ideas. I use constellations to signal that the groups are related but would look different in every school and that the relationships between the resources change over time. The

TABLE 6.1 Organizational racial equity resources

ORGANIZATIONAL RACIAL EQUITY RESOURCES	RESOURCE IS DORMANT IF ...	RESOURCE IS BEING CULTIVATED IF ...	RESOURCE IS BEING LEVERAGED IF ...
Black and Brown influential presence	Black and Brown students (and adults) are not present in and do not influence decision-making.	Some Black and Brown students (and adults) are present and indirectly influence decision-making.	Many Black and Brown people actively inform decision-making. Teachers and adults actively recruit input and use it to reshape their own practices.
Curated spaces of white discomfort	Leaders and teachers do not routinely engage in planned professional learning about race and racism; display an aversion to discomfort associated with racial learning.	Some leaders and some teachers engage in planned professional learning about race and racism; display a willingness to engage despite potential for discomfort associated with racial learning.	All leaders and teachers routinely engage in planned professional learning about race and racism; display a willingness to engage despite potential for discomfort associated with the risks inherent to racial learning.
Courageously confrontational culture	Congenial culture where confrontations about racially inequitable policies, practices, and consequences are invisible, happenstance, and informal.	Collegial culture where confrontations about racially inequitable policies, practices, and consequences are visible but not routine or formal.	Courageously confrontational culture where confrontations about racially inequitable policies, practices, and consequences are visible, routine, and formal. Lessons learned from confrontations reshape school policies and practices.
Open awareness of racial emotions and beliefs	Members of the school are not aware and do not openly acknowledge the range and prevalence of racial emotions and beliefs that exist in the school or broader community.	Some members of the school are aware of and openly acknowledge the range and prevalence of (competing) racial emotions and beliefs that exist in the school or broader community.	Most members of the school are aware of and openly (i.e., name) acknowledge the range and prevalence of (competing) racial emotions and beliefs that exist in the school or broader community. They are willing to critique emotions and beliefs that marginalize students.
Race-conscious inquiry leadership	Members of the school do not ask questions about race, racism, racial patterns, nor engage cycles as an improvement methodology.	Some members of the school ask questions about race, racism, or racial patterns but do not use cycles as an improvement methodology. Or some members of the school use cycles as an improvement methodology but do not center questions about race, racism, or racial patterns in the process.	Most members of the school integrate racial learning—asking questions about race, racism, and its impacts on their selves and school—with cycles of inquiry as an improvement methodology.

FIGURE 6.1 Constellation of racial equity resources and critical principles

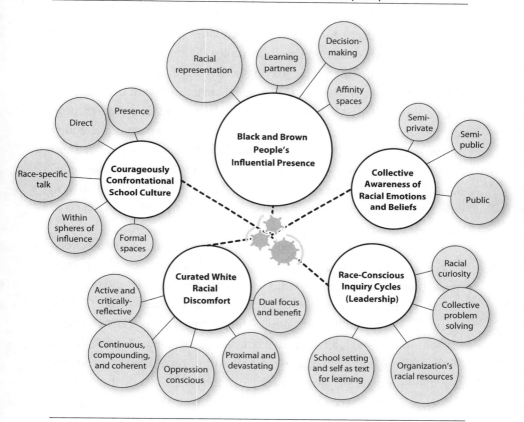

size, which indicates the strength of the capacity, also varies across time and place. Offering guidance on how to diagnose organizational capacity for racial equity resources is beyond the scope of what I intend to accomplish in this book. However, a school's inquiry-driven equity improvement efforts should reasonably involve a continuous process of mapping its collection of racial equity resources and assessing its organizational capacity to enact racial equity improvement. The resources I presented in the book offer one set of concepts for doing so. At minimum, I want readers who finish this book to have a shared frame for seeing the constellation of resources that are important for racial equity improvement, and in particular, a frame that reflects the complexity of the work.

A central lesson I learned in my research collaboration with CWHS is that what is often taken as simple and straightforward usually is not as simple as it seems. Improving white-dominated organizations to benefit Black and Brown students is more complex than conventional rhetoric lets on. I came into the project having internalized sayings such as "We know what needs to be done. White people just don't want to do it. They don't want to change." By the time I withdrew from the research project, my pattern of thinking differed. My thoughts about racial equity improvement evolved into "Some White people know what to do. Their numbers are very few. Most have no idea. And the lack of knowledge stems from different reasons. Some that have an idea of what to do have little clue about how to move forward. Or where to start." My evolved thinking reflected the reality of complex work.

Increasing Black and Brown influential presence offers a school-specific example. Hiring and retaining Black and Brown employees who would bolster influential presence seems simple enough. Find people to recruit. Hire them. Pay them well. And so forth. For schools like CWHS, it's not that easy. But it can be done. The process of hiring and retaining Black employees actually requires concerted, repeated, and substantial effort. Acknowledging that hiring and retention are complex tasks is a first step. It requires White people's racial humility, all people's willingness to challenge deep-seated racial beliefs, and a commitment to expending resources, establishing affirming conditions, and organizationwide racial learning. It demands that people get curious about how to make hiring and retention work. Some aspects of increasing Black and Brown influential presence require technical changes. But the work mostly requires attention to transforming school culture, policy and structural change, and adaptive leadership that is often not accounted for in antiracist leadership literature. Making these sorts of changes requires organizational racial learning. And it can lead to personal breakthroughs.

TRANSFORMED PRACTICE AND BELIEFS: PERSONAL BREAKTHROUGHS

Breakthroughs also happen at the personal and interpersonal level and are evidenced through transformed racial interactions. Because they are small, difficult to see, and too often remain invisible and unrecognized, they seem insignificant. Yet, they cut to the core of the human experience. They show up in smiles. They are revealed when people who are different muster the vulnerability to laugh together or sit in collective discomfort. Breakthroughs manifest in people's life beyond schools— stronger marriages, spiritual awakenings, divorces, renewed relationships with children and siblings. They show up when work is harder but more worthwhile, meaningful, and purposeful. Learning to notice racial breakthroughs offers insights into a school's potential. During my time at CWHS, I observed and listened to countless seemingly small breakthroughs, many of which appear in the chapters of this book. By the end of the project, I was often struck by how differently many CWHS teachers and leaders acted in comparison to when I first met them. A department chair, Patrick, described how the structured professional learning he experienced alongside his colleagues changed his teaching and leadership practice and ultimately his vision and philosophy.

> As a department chair I had more of an active role in some behind-the-scenes work with Dr. Irby, which was a very empowering process that changed the direction of our department-level work. Through that, I saw how the school changed. I saw how our department fit into that process, how all the departments had to work together towards that process to help our lower-end-performing students find more success. What I was doing before wasn't serving the needs of all of my students.
>
> Over the last four years because of the equity work and the district focus on personalized learning, my educational philosophy and practices have greatly changed. I used to be the lecture, worksheet, test-taker teacher just like everybody else. I now incorporate more student voice and choice into the classroom. I don't give tests anymore. Students choose their own kind of assessment pathways, which give students more success because they can get into and dig into and get behind a process versus being told what to do. I'm much more of a facilitator of information versus giving the information. I've built stronger relationships with students because I have more time to be able to devote towards students and their personal learning.

Monday night we had parent conferences, and one of my students showed her parents the project she had just finished. So she chose the 100-point project option, which means she put all of her eggs into one basket. It took her four weeks to complete. When she sat down and invited her parents to take a look at it, she was really proud of the quality of the work. She demonstrated mastery of her skills in fifteen different content standard areas. That was the first time she had ever invited her parents to the conferences because she wanted them to look at something that she had created. That's a common theme that I hear time and time again now that I didn't before. Kids find pride in this creation and display of what they can do. When they get that fever, when they understand that "I can control this" and "I can do whatever I want," they tap into their passions and their strengths and find greater success.

During my lunch hour, a female minority student came in who chose the 100-point option as well. She just wanted to talk with me about her work. We had a twenty-five-minute conversation about what she learned, and I asked her questions where I was trying to connect concepts with her, probing into deeper levels with her. At the end I asked her how she felt about things. She had a huge smile on her face and she said, "This is awesome and I really enjoyed it." Those moments with students make a world of difference. That's what I work toward now.

I feel like I've been able to tap into all of my students now, where I felt before that what I was doing I, to be honest, I felt like I knew that there was going to be a certain number of students in my classrooms that were going to "struggle." But it was because of how it was inherently set up to make them struggle. Some are still there, but I've tried to reduce those barriers within my own classroom.

For me personally, it's created more work for myself. But I enjoy my work so much more. I'm in a better place to help each and every student to find success and setting them up to find success in the classroom, and I think I'm doing a better job as far as trying to help, in particular my minority students, find a greater success because of the way that I've changed my own educational practices and viewpoints. I've been super excited by my own personal evolution, within my own classroom, but I actively enjoyed the grander scale of a vision of having all of our students being successful. A lot of it depends on giving students voice and choice in making decisions about the learning process.

Racial breakthroughs disrupt a preexisting racial pattern of behavior as well as conventional thinking and sense-making. The numerous racial breakthroughs Patrick described are largely invisible when using conventional measures of school success. Conventional indicators of success do not account for lunchtime conversations about science. They fail to appreciate "huge smiles" and the emergence of Black girls' agential learning identities. They ignore that more work, when it is the right kind of work, is enjoyable for students and teachers alike because it grounds student-teacher relationships in mutual learning and reciprocity. Such new racial patterns abounded in CWHS. They were significant sources of information that illuminated the experiences and meanings of schooling and education for both teachers and students. Racial breakthroughs are an experienced phenomenon so they are easy to miss and, when noticed, difficult to make sense of. Hence, they are an untapped site for racial learning.

Throughout this book, I have amplified practices, structures, routines, and the principles that guided CWHS improvement efforts. I have chosen to lead with what people did, how they behaved, and what they said. I have focused on how people reacted to the everyday experiences of leading, teaching, working, and learning in a school rife with racial conflict. I also have focused on how people felt, their opinions, and the actions that likely stemmed from their beliefs. As important as beliefs were, we learned early on that we did not have the time to wait for people to change their beliefs to start the work. Attempting to effect change by appealing to White people's hearts and convincing them to believe anything other than what they already believed would lead us into an abyss of white disbelief. It is not that beliefs are unimportant. They are. But if a school is interested in enacting racial equity reforms, beliefs are not the ideal entry point.

Educators can do things differently—practice, talk, create policies, develop structures—to enact changes that will benefit Black and Brown students without asking anyone to change their beliefs. Patrick was late in welcoming the changes at CWHS. He only began the process of challenging his own beliefs when he started to practice differently. His changed practice stemmed from active learning in collaboration with colleagues. Speeches, readings, and testimonials did not change his practices or beliefs. Countless breakthroughs like Patrick's happened at CWHS. In general, the most consistent means by which people at CWHS challenged their racial beliefs was through the commitment to repeated opportunities to (un)learn through structured sustained practice. The practices disrupted past patterns. It created space for new interactions. Practice when combined with local experience and collective critical reflection deepens and accelerates the accumulation of racial knowledge, which in turn disrupts deeply held racial narratives and beliefs.

The creation and maintenance of conditions and structures sustain practice changes. If you want the practices to change, change the structures and conditions. Work to modify practices before beliefs rather than the other way around. For example, early on we invited the administrative team to listen to teachers. Elizabeth hated it. It was not easy for them to do. But they eventually believed listening needed to be a cornerstone of their leadership practice. They, in turn, started to appreciate teachers more. The same trend followed when teachers began listening to students. Teachers who believed that being tough prepared Black and Brown students for the "real world" eventually understood that being tough, even if equally tough as they would be for White students, upholds racism.

For Black and Brown students, and all students for that matter, *school is the real world* where they learn from their experiences what is and what is not possible, what is unjust and what is fair. White girls who cheat should be given the opportunity to retake tests. Why? Something must be wrong with the teaching. Black girls who fight at school should lose the opportunity to attend senior prom. Why? Something must be wrong with the girls. Starting with white "whys" is less effective than creating opportunities to learn by starting with *why not,* a perennial *Black question.* Ethan adopted why not into his decision-making repertoire: "Does allowing kids to try out without a physical change my core values as an educator or a coach? In my opinion, no it doesn't." In other words, why not let the students try out for the baseball team? For Patrick, why not let students have a say in their learning and the methods they will use to demonstrate what they know? To thrive in a real racist world, Black and Brown students need to have opportunities to voice their opinions, narrate their experiences, and decide their own courses of action about how to navigate such a world or if they so choose to transform it.

It could be standard practice to provide Black and Brown students with curricula and learning opportunities that give them a sense of their own power and possibilities. And make space for a Black Student Union or Latino Student Union. A culturally responsive curriculum and affinity spaces are structures that signal care and concern. Racially affirming structures and routines diminish the need for individual white intervention by providing the learning and social resources and spaces of respite for Black and Brown students to engage in their own dignity-affirming educational work. To be clear, there is not a compelling face-value reason for White people to believe these sorts of equity efforts are worthwhile. So the task for leaders who are concerned with racial equity improvement is to create learning conditions and opportunities that help educators change their own racial beliefs by disrupting typical racial interaction patterns and in doing so making space for new racial patterns—realities—to emerge.

Implementing racially equitable practices before focusing on belief changes is counterintuitive. It asks people to get to work. It creates trouble. For many at CWHS, the experience of trying something different and learning from it drove them away from the school. Ironically, even people who witnessed others' efforts to change did not *believe* the people who were making efforts were changing. They looked into their intent rather than their action. Many people refused to believe that Elizabeth was changing regardless of what she said or did, even in the face of evidence that suggested her and many other people's actions and behaviors were very different. My point is this: some people's feelings or beliefs about a person, people, or practice are unlikely to change in the face of breakthrough indicators. The belief that any person is inherently flawed and thus irredeemable is rooted in racism. It may be the case that many people will not change. But it is also the case that, with the right supports and conditions, many people can and will.

STUCK IMPROVING: RACIAL KNOWLEDGE BREAKTHROUGHS

Stuck improvement is a racial knowledge breakthrough. It emerges when a person or group of people work toward creating a racially equitable school and as a consequence come to understand the deeply entrenched, permanent, and evolutionary character of racism and white supremacy. They understand how it works and that it is always at work. They understand that on the other side of racial breakthroughs there are racial dilemmas that have the potential to set back their efforts. The awareness of stuck improvement signals the presence of collective racial intelligence that enables a school community to see, think, and analyze problems and devise solutions using a race-conscious lens. Being stuck improving makes complex cognitive, emotional, relational, adaptive, and technical demands of attempting school-based racial equity change visible as a learning resource. A school that is stuck improving has a critical mass of educators who work toward racial equity change with a full understanding that racism and white supremacy are continuously *at work* thwarting their efforts to achieve and sustain racial equity. It is experienced as making progress and not making progress. It is accepting that racism is permanent while also committing to making it impermanent. It is the sobering realization that our understandings, visions, and theories of how to achieve racial equity are more developed than our ability to enact the theories we espouse.

Most schools like CWHS are not stuck improving. They are either stuck *or* supposedly improving. Schools that are stuck do not leverage racial resources because they are unaware that organizational racial resources are such a thing. So Black and Brown people are present but not influential. Their experiential knowledge and racial practices are disregarded, dismissed, and disdained by the White people who dominate the organizational culture. Racially and ethnically charged episodes and racism are swept under the rug instead of being used as resources to make authentic racial learning and discomfort possible. People suppress their racial emotions and beliefs because racially charged emotions and racial beliefs are typically viewed in a negative light. People protect themselves by refusing to openly talk about race and racism. Racism thrives unchecked. Schools that are "supposedly" improving share similarities with stuck schools, but they are good at making the numbers look good. They do not leverage racial resources. Indeed, educators in such schools are largely unaware that organizational racial resources are such a thing.

Supposedly improving schools often achieve some outcomes that White educators convince themselves (and others) count as successes—a Black History or Latino Heritage assembly, a narrower but still pronounced achievement gap, fewer racial disparities in suspensions, teachers and staff who share the race of a growing student population, and so forth. Such visible opportunity and outcome indicators are assumed to reflect a supposed commitment to racial equity. In the early years of the project, CWHS accomplished these objectives. The number of recorded suspensions for Black students reached an all-time low. Yet, the early hands-off approach and lack of structure and support did very little to sustain low suspension rates, minimize the racial violence of alienation, or challenge erasure and disdain for Black and Brown students. New systems such as restorative circles can be taken up in form and ritual yet still fail to generate new relational connections that reconstitute the school as an institution. A forced restorative justice or peace circle yields experiences of coercion disguised as good deed and effort. In short, both input and outcome indicators reveal less about Black and Brown students' experiences, meaning-making, and day-to-day interactions than do opportunities, breakthroughs, and outcomes together.

A school that is stuck improving grows attuned to the racial experiences, interactions, and meanings that occupy the space between opportunities and outcomes. It is in this space that breakthroughs happen and in which new interactions occur. If educators can learn to see racial breakthroughs and setbacks, they can use this knowledge as a source for organizational learning and ultimately leverage the knowledge to sustain racial equity change. To clarify the nature of breakthroughs and setbacks, I offer an example to illustrate how a breakthrough can be diminished to the point where it offers less potential to generate powerful organizational learning opportunities.

By the end of the 2014–15 academic year, a hallmark of CWHS's equity efforts was the inclusion of Black and Brown students in problem framing and decision-making spaces. At a professional development session that year, a group of teachers, administrators, and students collaborated to explore ways to increase school connectedness and belonging by expanding Black and Brown students' access and involvement in athletic programs. By most accounts, the interactions represented a breakthrough moment. Administrators, teachers, and students devised strategies to address a large systemic issue together. This established a new precedent. But without knowing it, the process and conversation harmed James, a Black student who was initially enthusiastic to participate. A White teacher, Meredith, who witnessed the harm shared her concerns:

> When we formed a team to address racial discrepancies in extracurricular activities, I was sitting next to an African American male student named James. As our conversation progressed, a White male staff member suggested that we could increase Black and Brown students' participation in extracurricular activities if we provided transportation to and from the low-income neighborhoods. So we started identifying neighborhoods that didn't have access.
>
> I could sense the student's leg shaking. I leaned over and asked James, "Are you okay? Do you need to, like, step out?" During a break he told me:
>
>> *"I just hate this assumption that the only way you're going to be a Black kid playing a sport is to send buses into low-income neighborhoods. I don't live in those neighborhoods. I live in a nice neighborhood right here close to school. The whole group is assuming that if kids are Black, they must be coming from the hood."*

Meredith continued.

> I do believe this particular staff member's heart was in the right place. But, like, what's the deeper assumption? We—White people as

a whole—are we really getting it? "Send more buses into the hood."
I thought it was a good idea too. But I listened to this young boy's
perspective, and I'm like, oh my God . . . how often does he hear these
stereotypes every single day? He came to a setting to address the racism
he and Black students experience and then he experiences racism.

So are we even doing any good, or are we just, like, making this
even worse by, like, presenting a format where kids are going to feel
safe and then are bombarded with stereotypes and generalizations?
Later, I asked him if he wanted me to address it to the group, without
identifying him. He just flatly said, "No. Just let it go."

The episode reveals the complexity of racial equity work. White teachers intended to solve a problem they learned about through their racial problem identification. The problem identification relied on their
analysis of survey data showing disparate participation patterns, student
focus groups, and their own first-hand observations of racial exclusion.
Problems included the suburban culture of league sports play, participation fees, and home responsibilities. Lack of transportation to summer
tryouts and odd practice hours also led to disparities. As became the
routine, teachers and staff invited students of color to participate in their
inquiry process. Meredith rightfully paid as much attention to students
at the table as she did to the data. She cued into James's anxiety. Although
Meredith owned the role she and her White colleagues played in in-
flicting harm by "generalizing" their policies and stereotyping students,
she missed an opportunity to colearn from and through a breakthrough
moment in which strategies were put forward.

Meredith understandably consoled James. It was the right thing to
do. Yet in doing so, she retreated from her initial concern about the many
Black and Brown students who, unlike James, are doubly subjected to
stereotypes and geographic isolation from the school. Her singular focus on James's visible, justifiable anger trumped the invisible harms of
structural geographic isolation. Geographical isolation severely limited
large swaths of Black and Brown students' ability to participate in school
activities. Students stood to benefit from the new bus policy, as did those
already engaged. Their interactions would disrupt their racial isolation.

Latinx students benefited from the expanded bussing options too. Additional efforts such as waiving fees and the shift to A/B schedule also aimed to expand overall extracurricular involvement. Recognizing harm and working to correct it are important aspects of racial equity work. However, it is important to understand disrupting racism's harmful effects on groups and communities is a more ambitious equity goal than attempting to reduce individual instances of hurt. If a school community works to reduce systemic violence and harm, it will reduce the likelihood of individual harm. The converse does not hold.

If Meredith's racial analysis accounted for the fact that James's hurt was bound up with the harm his peers experienced as a result of the geographic and racial marginalization, she could have critically explored this as the source of his discontent. But she didn't. Meredith misunderstood the nature of racial oppression, its structure, and its consequence. She focused on the highly visible and present violence only. Her emerging racial consciousness and action to support James became pity for him, self-doubt for herself, disdain for White people, and eventual resolve to inaction. White supremacy is always at work reasserting itself. The work of recognizing racial harm can be more than offering emotional support. It is deeply intellectual.

After all, white supremacy is an ideology that is tied to the practice of total degradation of people who are not of European descent. It is an attack on the idea that people, if they are not of European descent, are incapable of thinking. The anti-intellectual nature of white supremacy keeps the focus of justice and antiracist work bound primarily to emotions. But racial learning is also intellectual work that benefits from practice in the same way any other learning does. An intellectual understanding that racial harm is inflicted through structural violence is critical. When moved beyond individualization, the exploration of harm can become a matter of intellectual engagement and learning that lends to racial solidarity, at which point an educator might ask a student like James, "Why do you think there is something wrong with the hood?" Black and Brown students benefit from teachers who push them to explore and understand racism, both its immediate and present forms and the way it structures itself as geographic racial isolation. Black and Brown students benefit from teachers who ask them to explore feelings and thoughts. Of course, this is risky for White teachers because it invites racial knowledge that they may not possess into the learning process. Unless White teachers possess the capacity to be discomforted, they do not engage Black and Brown students' minds. Because doing so requires colearning. It creates possibilities that they might learn something they'd rather not know (or openly acknowledge). It invites uncertainty and discomfort.

Meredith and James's dilemma is a final example of why CWHS is stuck improving—making progress and not making progress. At the end of the day, the effort to make progress still hurt James, unbeknownst to the White people who inflicted the harm. They never had the chance to address the harm. And James experienced a moment that confirmed for him that CWHS is filled with racist teachers, including several White teachers who actively worked to expand opportunities for Black and Brown students. Had the teachers not tried, the risk of improving or failing would have not emerged. Did this group of teachers succeed? Did they fail? Can their efforts be lauded given James's experience?

As tempting as it is to conclude that CWHS either succeeded or failed in its effort to improve learning opportunities for Black and Brown students, neither accurately conveys the work itself or the impacts of the work. There was good. There was bad. Central Waters continuously failed and improved and failed and improved. At times, as demonstrated here, they did both at the same time and instance. CWHS became stuck improving. This consciousness is itself an outcome that leaves CHWS in a better place than merely stuck or supposedly improving. During my final interview with administrators, Elizabeth shared a similar statement of bewilderment:

> I feel like we have a foundation and we know what to do. We built some capacity with our team [administrators] and with others. The part that is disheartening is that I don't know that our kids of color are actually doing any better. . . . *How could we have come so far yet had such little effect on students?* I can only justify it in my mind as that we had to get the staff first before we could get to kids. We are at a place now where we can have the conversations and face the challenges. But we've got

a long way to go to be the kind of school we want to be. I take that very personally. It's the good. And it's the bad.

CWHS equity efforts involved learning about what they were doing while doing the work. For example, CWHS did not first figure out what they needed to do to hire and retain Black and Brown administrators, teachers, and staff before attempting to hire them. Instead, they hired people and also figured out how to retain them as one and the same. CWHS benefitted from Black and Brown employees' and research partners' consultation, willingness to colearn, and experiential knowledge. Of course, this required discomfort. It required Black and Brown people to give. And for me, as a Black person, it's discomforting to admit that racial learning requires both within and across race learning. The school, their efforts, and what they learned from their failures and successes, both small and large, provided the opportunities to learn that books, curricula, and trainings can only supplement. The mutually reinforcing practices of action and active learning developed their capacity to enact racial equity changes. And although they are not where they want to be, they also are not where they were.

CWHS moved from being stuck to improving to seeming to move backward again and in doing so became disoriented and unsure whether they were actually getting any better. The CWHS story was/is not a linear sequential one. It was/is also not a singular story. Capacity development for racial equity change is not as simple as "stages" or a linear process. It is cyclical and compounding in nature. Central Waters increased (and at times lost) its capacity to enact its reforms. Many problems of the past often carried forward into subsequent years. But CWHS developed an increased capacity to address the problems. In particular, their effort and capacity to address problems generated new and more complex problems that called for yet more capacity development to address. Tidy conceptions of improvement and progress cannot account for the comings and goings of people and the historical and experiential knowledge that shaped people's ability to narrate the CWHS story (my own included). For example, members who joined the school during the 2016–17 year had no direct point of reference for year two's racial reckoning. People who left during year three had no point of reference for structural changes that would come to full form in 2017–18. Students who experienced the racial violence of a race-neutral curriculum did not see the fruits of their "complaining" to get their teachers to serve their needs.

SUSTAINING EQUITY BREAKTHROUGHS

I still don't know how to dismantle racism. The more I know, the less I know. But I do see differently now. Racism is more visible. It is more present. It requires disrupting and reimagining structures and routines, practices and beliefs, and knowledge. Working on all three areas is critical because they reinforce one another, creating the potential that a school can move its racial equity breakthroughs into sustained racial equity change. As I have argued, the missing link in improving schools to benefit Black and Brown students is often organizational capacity for racial equity change, as depicted in figure 6.2. Racial knowledge and individual practices in changes and beliefs, neither alone nor in combination, can sustain and proliferate change.

FIGURE 6.2   Racial equity breakthroughs

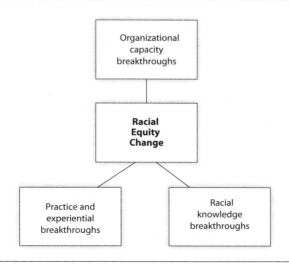

In December 2019, I received an invitation from Elizabeth to present at the second annual social justice teach-in. I agreed. I had not been to the school since its 2018–19 social justice teach-in a year earlier. I walked into a school that felt unfamiliar. We walked through the commons areas where Elizabeth introduced me to a group of Black males who graduated from CWHS. They were teacher's aides and staff working in various capacities in the school. We shook hands and exchanged greetings. As we walked toward Elizabeth's office, she explained that the men I had just met were enrolled in college to gain their teaching credentials with plans of returning to their alma mater, CWHS, as classroom teachers. They were among the first participants in the district's "grow your own teachers" program.

During social justice teach-ins, CWHS supplanted the school curriculum, invited community partners, and asked White teachers to coplan and deliver lessons on topics of race and justice. I cofacilitated two sessions on the role of culture and race in school. It was the same lecture I'd given at the first summer data retreat some six-plus years earlier. This time I presented to students. In the morning to freshmen and sophomores and in the afternoon to juniors and seniors. For a community like CWHS, the social justice teach-in was a breakthrough. But could it become a sustained equity change if CWHS prioritized treating it as more than a once per year opportunity? The day was a proverbial fork in the road of its equity journey. To some, it was an inconvenience. To some, it was a tokenizing event. For some, it was progress. Was it beneficial and meaningful? For whom? *Why not* make the topics part of the school curriculum?

After the day ended, I joined the leadership team and staff at a restaurant for evening dinner. As the dozen or so of us dined, they caught me up on recent school happenings and reflected on the day's events. I updated the leadership team about my life in Chicago, my family, and to a lesser extent my university work and the very slow progress I was making on "the book." As the evening progressed, I noticed James Baldwin, the Black scholar, essayist, and activist peeking from behind the badges, keys, and cards hanging behind associate principal Jose's

CWHS lanyard. Baldwin wouldn't have it any other way but to be with us that evening, listening as we talked about the problem of racism. As the waiter cleared the table and we prepared to leave, I asked José about his shirt: "I don't see Baldwin shirts often. Where did you find that?" He matter-of-factly responded, "Black Student Union made these shirts as part of their fundraising effort last year." I was not expecting that answer. It rolled off his tongue as though it was not a big deal. To me, it was. It felt impressive—an act of everyday resistance. But why not? Of course, Black Student Union made the shirts. Students were going to learn about James Baldwin at some point, in spite of resistance and racial oppression. The school's organizational conditions demanded it.

Central Waters was systematically working toward racial equity improvement. The processes of inquiring into the existing racial order enabled CWHS administrators and teachers to imagine a new racial order. It helped students to do the same. When White people begin to look inward at improving themselves and rethinking the racial implications of their leadership and instructional practice, that is a sign of progress. Early on, many White CWHS teachers did not accept the fact that Black and Brown students and families must be partners in their work, that they cannot improve the school *for* Black and Brown students without their partnership. This realization opened up new possibilities. An imaginative equity vision, combined with active strides to reach for that vision, can produce more racially conscious administrators, teachers, and students who will lay the groundwork for the next, more ambitious, radical iteration of equity reforms.

In this formulation of school improvement, critical moments when school members notice they are stuck improving, imagine ways to get unstuck, and take on the risk of getting unstuck, even if faced with the possibility of being stuck again, are perhaps the most profound indicators that mark a school community as engaged in authentic meaningful racial equity improvement. Not only did my analysis of CWHS help me to see the invisiblized and thus oft-overlooked organizational indicators of school capacity for racial equity improvement, but it also helped me see breakthroughs, including what it means to be stuck improving.

Being stuck improving reveals a distinct quality of organizational life and a school's potential to do better by Black and Brown students. It illuminates some of what is going to happen, at some point, to benefit them, even if in unconventional and uncertain ways. The best chance we have to improve is to realize the promise of being stuck improving and work toward continually getting there. Why not?

APPENDIX

Research Methodology Notes

The research team did some amazing things. It's hard for me to not see them in the book.

—CWHS INSIDER
(member-check focus group)

In summer 2020, my research assistant Shannon Paige Clark and I codesigned focus group and one-on-one sessions to solicit feedback on an early draft of *Stuck Improving*. As part of the process, insiders from CWHS, both people who remained and people who left the school and district, read initial drafts. I wrote the book to tell their story of change. But I learned from them that I managed to write myself and the research team out of the story. Other trusted academics and practitioners who were not associated with CWHS noted the same. Of the numerous people who offered feedback, they unanimously thought I needed to better convey my role and the research procedures that were such an integral part of the project. I attempted to revise the full text to make the research contributions more apparent without disrupting the CWHS story. These methodological notes extend this effort to demonstrate the role that participatory action research can play in disrupting school racism and improving schools to benefit Black and Brown students. I amplify three aspects of the research project itself: the positionalities and roles of research team members, the iterative project design and analysis process, and the ethics of reporting dilemmas I encountered in writing the book.

I never intended to conduct research in a suburban school setting, to self-study and colearn with White people, or to apply principles of participatory research in a school community like CWHS. Prior to working with CWHS, I focused almost exclusively on collaborating with Black populations, trying to use research as a tool for addressing the myriad problems Black people experience as a result of living in a white supremacist world. Coming into the project, I brought a great deal of skepticism, curiosity, and want to learn.

I grew up in South Carolina, and I attended a high school that was very similar to CWHS. I managed to do well socially and a little less so academically. But I graduated and attended a four-year college almost a four-hour drive from my hometown. To say that my going to college was a big deal is an understatement. I was fortunate to have been reared in a working class family, surrounded daily by stubbornly persistent Black women who took my greatness as a given fact of life. My grandmother Esther Irby instilled in me from my earliest recollections that I would be president of the United States. She meant it and believed it for me, even if I didn't believe for myself. When I became senior class president of my high school, she was all the more convinced. After she cast her vote for Barack Obama, she confided in me that the first Black president was supposed to be me, but that "she voted for him anyway." My mother, Janice Irby, forbid me and my sisters Brandy and Joree from talking about what we couldn't do. "Have you *really* tried?" she retorted, whenever she believed I had not exhausted all possibilities before accepting any sort of defeat. She was my first professor. She taught me how to do Black working class cycles of inquiry. I learned how to figure things out, to make a way, to fail, and to learn from failure. I learned to imagine far beyond the visible horizon. My mother's and grandmother's deep sense of spiritual fire, quiet rage, strategy, patience, will to forgive, grace, and power to love are in me. The qualities they pour(ed) into me help me be who I am and undertake research the way I do.

Probably because of their influence in my life, there is little in life I do without the partnership of Black women. They are the people I trust most deeply, the people who teach me the most, and the people I find my humility and courage in relationship with. When I invited Liz Drame, a senior colleague of mine, to partner with me to conduct the research at CWHS, she took on an academia big sister role. She is a mother and partner, daughter of Haitian immigrant parents, and at the time was an associate professor of Exceptional Education. I also had the fortune of working with Cindy Clough, also a mother, who with her partner raised her three children in an almost all-white suburban community that itself was undergoing demographic shifts. Cindy is White. She joined the project because she "just wanted to learn." In 2013, she was a doctoral student who was just beginning to learn about racism and white supremacy, mostly by way of her graduate studies.

Leemay Chang was a master's level graduate student who responded to an ad I posted seeking a graduate student to support the research project. Lee is Hmong and grew up in a very small farm town in a large family where she was one of many siblings. She was a quantitative researcher who joined the project because she wanted to learn about qualitative research. Thor Stolen was the final researcher to join the project during the early years. He was also a student in my advanced qualitative research course, and when the course ended, he expressed wanting to continue to work with me in whatever manner possible. He is a White man who at the time was, like myself, a new father. Thor's mother is of South American descent, and so he grew up speaking Spanish, an asset that proved invaluable to the project given the large number of Spanish-speaking students who attended CWHS. The five of us formed the initial research team that worked with CWHS in the 2013–14 year. Besides Lee, who graduated the next year, different configurations of this core research team facilitated the early years of the project.

I characterize the project's early years, from the 2013–14 academic year to the 2016–17 academic year, as the period of deep collaborative engagement with school administrators, teachers, and staff to carry out a participatory design-based research project that aimed to build the capacity of the school to improve its discipline culture and climate. To do this, the administrators and our research team collected and analyzed data, codesigned professional developments and interventions at multiple scales and with multiple subpopulations. My research team produced and presented reports and research evidence to support the school's equity improvement efforts. We did not offer directives. We fed back what we learned from events to inform and develop iterative stages · of further organizational learning. Our primary method of improvement was generating sense-making opportunities at numerous scales that would improve the community's decision-making by centering racial considerations into their deliberation processes. Over time, the project emphasis on developing the school community's capacity for racial learning focused and expanded.

As a research team, we immersed ourselves in the research process by doing the same research and learning activities CWHS educators did. Whatever we codesigned, we committed to experiencing. In some instances, in particular ones that required our full facilitation, we put ourselves through the activities and learning before CWHS educators did. If we asked people to journal or talk, we did so a week or so before our site visit. In other instances, we chose one person from the team to facilitate and all other members participated right alongside CWHS community members. We did critical self-reflections and racial improvement mini-challenges. We forced ourselves to talk explicitly and often about race and racism and how it showed up within our own interactions as a research team and within the project itself. We mapped our immunities to change. We offered testimonials. We passed rocks. We turned CWHS people toward conflict, and we turned one another toward conflict, both within the research project, our workplaces, and in our everyday lives. Indeed, my deep engagement in the work brought me to the point I realized I wanted and needed to find a new workplace for myself. In 2015, in the third year of the project, I accepted a position at a university a much farther distance from the school. When I disclosed my new job and plans to relocate to the people I worked closest with at CWHS, we shared sadness and joy for the transformation that the work caused in our lives. The distance would make it difficult for me to remain present. It was all very disruptive. The work of trying to fix problems was creating trouble for our personal selves.

We committed to modeling, coexperiencing, and colearning and in doing so breaking down the barrier between the researcher and the researched. Much of this occurred in real time at the school. Just as much took place out of CWHS's view. But the approach allowed us to relate experientially and participate in racial learning. When I asked CWHS educators to trust students or listen to students, I did the same—in my university classes as well as at CWHS, and wherever I encountered young people. We needed to understand what it felt like. Using this approach meant that we began to see the ways racism, white supremacy, and oppression manifested in our own lives, thoughts, and behaviors. It showed us how we oppressed. It also invited us to confront these realities, be they at home, work, or at CWHS. We gained opportunities to confront ourselves and for me personally my masculinity and patriarchal world view. At CWHS, it meant making race-conscious research decisions. We used our influential presence and roles in a racially strategic manner. Thus, our roles varied in terms of what we each did to carry out the research. Whom we worked with, what we studied in a given time period, and *why* shifted as we learned and strategized to deepen and proliferate learning in consideration of the CWHS context.

We made decisions about which research team members would do what based largely on our continued inquiry into the context, with consideration of what would help us learn in different ways. For example, by year four, we intentionally chose Thor and Rebecca Fine (a White female graduate student who joined the project for a year as part of her graduate studies) to conduct interviews with White people who had not yet participated in voluntary aspects of the project. We did this because we anticipated they may be more willing to be truthful with White people than with me or Liz or even Cindy. Moreover, we had formed clearly visible relationships with administrators. We wanted and needed people to talk candidly. Otherwise, we would not be likely to codesign learning opportunities that would meet their racial learning needs. On the other hand, we realized it was important for CWHS educators to see Black people as intellectuals capable of teaching and helping them as a matter of disrupting patterns that suggested otherwise. So we were continually mindful of who should speak. It meant that Liz and I talked a lot, representing ideas and conveying complex information, knowing that both who we are and what we said mattered for disrupting white supremacy.

We used multiple methods of data collection. We conducted participant observations and reconstructed events post-observation. We audio-recorded almost everything that we could—one-on-one interviews and focus groups, administrative and team meetings, planning sessions, debrief conversations and phone calls, assemblies, and professional development sessions down to individual tables during breakout sessions. We did this by assigning audio recorders to small groups and placing them at tables. If we planned twelve breakout sessions, we prepared with twelve audio recorders and assigned them by number to groups. As part of the protocols, we integrated consent and permissions to record. The insiders managed the recordings and positioned them. As a team, we studied our own process. We conducted individual and group reflections, which we also audio-recorded. Because the project was so collaborative, we shared access to our research study drive, and CWHS shared access to the many drives that contained relevant information for what we wanted to learn about CWHS's efforts to improve. We amassed hundreds of hours of audio recordings, many of which captured different audio angles of the same event.

After four years of active participation, I withdrew myself from the field to monitor and study Central Waters' change, what I call the "late years" of the project. Throughout the late years (2017–18 to 2019–20), I wanted to reduce my research team's influential presence. I hoped to see that CWHS's capacity to carry on the work without the intellectual and emotional support of my research team was indeed present. I remained updated via emails and a shared project e-drive. I spent months, almost a full year, not looking at any past data because I wanted to gain intellectual and emotional distance from the experience and relationships that had so profoundly shaped me over a five-year period. My goal was to see the research project anew and in particular to see the flaws and shortcomings of the project, myself, and the people I'd grown to appreciate as learning partners and colleagues. I wanted to see the good. I also wanted to see the bad.

Two people helped me achieve distance throughout the late years. Shannon Paige Clark is a Black woman and doctoral student at my university, who joined the project in 2017–18. She and I conducted phone interviews with teachers and staff to study the project impacts on individuals, their practices, and beliefs. Shannon's presence played an important role in my distancing process because she had no relationships with CWHS administrators or staff. So she asked critical questions that were easy for me to take for granted. She asked for evidence. How do you know that? Ahreum Han, a Korean woman and doctoral student at my university, worked with a CWHS school data specialist to collect localized district and school data, such as enrollment patterns, teacher and staff hiring trends by race and ethnicity, new course creations, discipline records, Advanced Placement course enrollments, postsecondary enrollment data, and much more. Ahreum's work forced me to look at the numbers and to account for structural trends and patterns that both reflected and contradicted the narrative that emerged from my analysis of qualitative data. For example, I was forced to grapple with the fact that CWHS changed its methods of data collection and reporting over the years, thus complicating my ability to make claims about trends. Both asked me questions that I would otherwise take for granted, Shannon as a critical scholar and Ahreum as a person raised outside the US culture of racism and white supremacy.

As I began to gain distance, I started systematically rereading transcribed field notes, meetings, and interviews. I organized and analyzed data, combed through years of artifacts, and spent months listening to audio-recorded data to jog my memory about the emotional underpinnings of key moments. When necessary, I member-checked to clarify issues and fill in gaps in my understanding of what happened at Central Waters. As I started writing the book, I sought feedback from CWHS insiders. I continually asked them to hold me to capturing their collective experience of change. It was during the writing stage that I encountered reporting choices and dilemmas of writing up critical qualitative research for an outsider audience. I laser-focused on the school. But of course schools do not exist in vacuums. My school-centric focus downplayed how district-level personnel and decisions supported and did not support the high school's work. Indeed, CWHS benefitted from stable leadership over the duration of the project, a supportive superintendent, and ample resources. Several district initiatives, districtwide and school trainings, and consultants supported the work described in the book. These included the hiring of a district equity director, the adoption of a district equity framework, the implementation of a districtwide continuous improvement model, as well as the work of a district behavioral and emotional support team, to name a few.

Related, I also did not convey many of the broader societal events that shaped the work. I met Ethan and Suzanne in July 2013, the same month vigilante George Zimmerman was acquitted by a Florida jury for his 2012 shooting and killing of seventeen-year-old unarmed African American high school student Trayvon Martin. A full seven years later, the disregard for Black and Brown lives remained. I wrote the majority of this book during 2020 against a backdrop of global antiracism protests, the 2020 US presidential election, and the COVID-19 pandemic that pulled back the curtain on any suggestion that we live in a post-racial or racially just world and society. These events and trends are critically important and provide insights into why the efforts at racial equity improvement continued to be viewed as vitally important. In other words, school data and White people's desires to improve alone did not spur or sustain the urgency to do better.

Making decisions about what stories and people to include at the school level also proved difficult. The dilemma I faced is that it's not possible to tell a full-fledged complete story without leaving out what I and insiders consider important information and insights and also minimizing important people's presence. Throughout the book, although I did not fully present each person who contributed, they are present in composite character form. In other words, I couldn't write every teacher ambassador in the book. The group evolved and changed over time. Instead, I attempted to convey them as a team. I combined multiple ambassadors' personalities and actions into fewer people, who in the book represent the range of ideas, behaviors, and personalities of the whole of ambassadors. I did this by creating composites of multiple individuals. Ms. Jenkins, for example, is a composite of several teachers and staff. Associate Principal Owk, a continued presence over the duration of the project and Asian male, is underrepresented in the book. However, my goal was to have him show up in the behaviors and actions of people such as Ms. Moore and Branden. For me, these were not ideal choices and decisions, but ones that I needed to make. I do wish I could honor the learning that each person experienced coming to terms with and understanding concepts like white supremacy, racial equity, racial consciousness, and race evasiveness. But there are books and articles that do this.

I wanted my unique contribution to school improvement and antiracism scholarship to be conveying racial equity leadership as a collective activity that requires multiple perspectives and actions that no one person can do alone. I aimed to disrupt the common portrayal of heroic leaders by writing about teams and groups of people working together, colearning, costrategizing and planning, confronting one another's thinking and practices. I wrote to show multiple people leading with a focus on collective leadership activity. The myth of the charismatic racial equity leader is a lie. So I hope no one emerges in the story as a hero. Indeed, Elizabeth, as a single leader, was unable to promote transformational change. I was and am not a scholar who could fix the problems of white supremacy or racism. Instead, I hoped to show the many unexpected ways that people can work toward racial equity change. In CWHS, the work proliferated when the school achieved "critical masses" of participation, structure, and active learning routines. This happened a full four to five years into the project. Earlier, about year three, a critical mass of people decided to try—evidenced in leadership surveys and evidence of practice. The mass indicated enough people to have "coverage" across departments, teams, and in meetings, especially professional development sessions—this was the case for restorative approaches and many other powerful school training models.

The critical feedback that insiders offered during member-checking called my attention to four important research practices that characterized the project. One, we developed local indicators of progress that were credible and relevant to CWHS. For example, students collaborated with teachers to determine school climate and culture indicators and look-fors such as "respect." Two, we modeled practices and behaviors that needed to proliferate in order to achieve racial equity improvement, such as being transparent about constantly sharing learning and explicitly talking about race and racism. Third, we believed that people, with the right encouragement and supports, could be the change they wanted to see. "You've got what it takes." We said this often, even if and when we didn't believe it. Because they needed to hear it to keep pressing forward in their work. Fourth and finally, CWHS insiders felt that all members of the research team brought distinct strengths. The recognition of strengths in our differences was not different than how I thought and think of the many insider coresearchers at CWHS, and in particular those who dug into the work in the early years. My wish is that folks at CWHS see themselves as practitioner-researchers who are carrying the work forward. And that the many people—colleagues and students—who contributed to the study design, data collection, and analysis continue to use research for the purposes of effecting change to increase and expand Black and Brown students' learning opportunities.

NOTES

INTRODUCTION

1. See R. L'Heureux Lewis-McCoy, *Inequality in the Promised Land: Race, Resources, and Suburban Schooling* (Redwood City, CA: Stanford University Press, 2014); Amanda E. Lewis and John B. Diamond, *Despite the Best Intentions: How Racial Inequality Thrives in Good Schools* (Oxford, England: Oxford University Press, 2015); and Jessica T. Shiller, *The New Reality for Suburban Schools: How Suburban Schools Are Struggling with Low Income Students and Students of Color in Their Schools* (New York, NY: Peter Lang, 2016).

CHAPTER 1

1. See Daniel J. Losen, ed., *Closing the School Discipline Gap: Equitable Remedies for Excessive Exclusion* (New York, NY: Teachers College Press, 2014).
2. See Sara Estrapala, Ashley Rila, and Allison Leigh Bruhn, "A Systematic Review of Tier 1 PBIS Implementation in High Schools," *Journal of Positive Behavior Interventions* (June 2020): 1–15, doi: 10.1177/1098300720929684; Joshua Bornstein, "If They're on Tier I, There Are Really No Concerns That We Can See: PBIS Medicalizes Compliant Behavior," *Journal of Ethnographic & Qualitative Research* 9, no. 4 (2015): 247–67; Jack Schneider, "Privilege, Equity, and the Advanced Placement Program: Tug of War," *Journal of Curriculum Studies* 41, no. 6 (2009): 813–31; and Elavie Ndura, Michael Robinson, and George Ochs, "Minority Students in High School Advanced Placement Courses: Opportunity and Equity Denied," *American Secondary Education* 32, no. 1 (2003): 21–38.
3. See Amanda L. Sullivan, "Disproportionality in Special Education Identification and Placement of English Language Learners," *Exceptional Children* 77, no. 3 (2011): 317–34; Roey Ahram, Edward Fergus, and Pedro Noguera, "Addressing Racial/Ethnic Disproportionality in Special Education: Case Studies of Suburban School Districts," *Teachers College Record* 113, no. 10 (2011): 2233–66; and Russell Skiba, Ada Simmons, Shana Ritter, Kristin Kohler, Michelle Henderson, and Tony Wu, "The Context of Minority Disproportionality: Practitioner Perspectives on Special Education Referral," *Teachers College Record* 108, no. 7 (2006): 1424–59.

4. See Hilton Kelly, "Racial Tokenism in the School Workplace: An Exploratory Study of Black Teachers in Overwhelmingly White Schools," *Educational Studies* 41, no. 3 (2007): 230–54.

CHAPTER 2

1. See Ibram X. Kendi, *Stamped from the Beginning: The Definitive History of Racist Ideas in America* (New York, NY: Random House, 2017).
2. A consulting firm that supported schools and districts.
3. This issue is discussed in more detail in chapter 4.
4. They defined access as a student's ability to secure a place, have a voice, and participate fully in the school community. Participants described lack of access as having a profound effect on the behavior and attitudes of students of color about school, sense of belonging, and academic success. Participants almost unanimously agreed that increasing access to school-based opportunities was within the school's sphere of influence.
5. Relational resources refer to positive relationships, a sense of being cared for, and having adult advocates and supports within the school community. Structures referred to within school—academic curriculum, schedules, extracurricular activities—and broader societal structures of residential segregation, plus unequal distribution of social resources and economic opportunities.
6. Poor communication was multidirectional within the school. It was a cultural norm manifested in people not listening to one another, withholding information, not paying attention to information, and performing other pervasive behaviors that deteriorated its climate.
7. See Robert Kegan and Lisa Laskow Lahey, *How the Way We Talk Can Change the Way We Work: Seven Languages of Transformation* (Hoboken, NJ: John Wiley & Sons, 2001).

CHAPTER 3

1. For explanations and examples of mundane violence, see Lauren Berlant, "Slow Death (Sovereignty, Obesity, Lateral Agency)," *Critical Inquiry* 33, no. 4 (2007): 754–80; Cynthia Enloe, "The Mundane Matters," *International Political Sociology* 5, no. 4 (2011): 447–50; Elizabeth Lee and Geraldine Pratt, "The Spectacular and the Mundane: Racialised State Violence, Filipino Migrant Workers, and Their Families," *Environment and Planning A* 44, no. 4 (2012): 889–904; and James A. Tyner, *Space, Place, and Violence: Violence and the Embodied Geographies of Race, Sex and Gender* (New York, NY: Routledge, 2012).
2. For practices of courageous conversations, see Glenn E. Singleton, *Courageous Conversations About Race: A Field Guide for Achieving Equity in Schools*, 2nd ed. (Los Angeles: Corwin, a Sage Company, 2014).
3. See Tamara Holmlund Nelson, Angie Deuel, David Slavit, and Anne Kennedy, "Leading Deep Conversations in Collaborative Inquiry Groups," *The Clearing House: A Journal of Educational Strategies, Issues and Ideas* 83, no. 5 (2010): 175–79; Mark Selkrig and Kim Keamy, "Promoting a Willingness to Wonder: Moving

from Congenial to Collegial Conversations That Encourage Deep and Critical Reflection for Teacher Educators," *Teachers and Teaching* 21, no. 4 (2015): 421–36.

4. See Andy Hargreaves, "Contrived Collegiality: The Micropolitics of Teacher Collaboration," in *Sociology of Education: Major Themes*, ed. Stephen J. Ball (London: Routledge, 2000), 1480–1503.

5. I learned the practice as a child while growing up in South Carolina. I have been a part of multiple communities and experiences where I used the practice of passing rocks, including summer camps, schools, and my neighborhood, where we would pass "friendship rocks." I am not sure where it originates, but I am thankful for being introduced to the process.

6. Decoteau J. Irby and Shannon P. Clark, "Talk It (Racism) Out: Race Talk and Organizational Learning," *Journal of Educational Administration* 56, no. 5 (2018): 504–18.

7. See Jules Boykoff and Ben Carrington, "Sporting Dissent: Colin Kaepernick, NFL Activism, and Media Framing Contests," *International Review for the Sociology of Sport* 55, no. 7 (2020): 829–49; Steve Marston, "The Revival of Athlete Activism(s): Divergent Black Politics in the 2016 Presidential Election Engagements of LeBron James and Colin Kaepernick," *FairPlay, Revista de Filosofía, Ética y Derecho del Deporte* 10 (2017): 45–68.

8. See Ashley W. Doane and Eduardo Bonilla-Silva, eds. *White Out: The Continuing Significance of Racism* (New York: Routledge, 2003).

CHAPTER 4

1. For different yet critically important books about talk and racism, see Mica Pollock, *Colormute: Race Talk Dilemmas in an American School* (Princeton, NJ: Princeton University Press, 2009); Eduardo Bonilla-Silva, *Racism Without Racists: Color-blind Racism and the Persistence of Racial Inequality in the United States* (New York, NY: Rowman & Littlefield Publishers, 2006).

2. See Marcos Pizarro and Rita Kohli, "'I Stopped Sleeping': Teachers of Color and the Impact of Racial Battle Fatigue," *Urban Education* 55, no. 7 (2020): 967–91; William A. Smith, Man Hung, and Jeremy D. Franklin, "Between Hope and Racial Battle Fatigue: African American Men and Race-Related Stress," *Journal of Black Masculinity* 2, no. 1 (2012): 35–58.

3. Journaling is useful. However, it often filters out "in the moment" emotions and ideas. It's the reason that we relied so heavily on rapid turn-and-talk activities, constrained the time allotments for people to respond to prompts, and so forth (i.e., "you have two minutes to share"). We processed after the thoughts were out (e.g., "take one minute to think about what you heard or said"). Although our research design didn't aim to capture these specific differences, I suspect a journal entry that a person writes after they said, heard, and thought through a racial self-talk would differ from a journal where they wrote first. Rapidly getting ideas out into public view enabled more powerful learning because it reduced people's ability to filter their internal racial dialogues into more acceptable racial self-talk.

4. See Eduardo Gonzalez, "Stereotypical Depictions of Latino Criminality: US Latinos in the Media During the MAGA Campaign," *Democratic Communiqué* 28, no. 1 (2019): 46–62; Dara Z. Strolovitch, Janelle S. Wong, and Andrew Proctor, "A Possessive Investment in White Heteropatriarchy? The 2016 Election and the Politics of Race, Gender, and Sexuality," *Politics, Groups, and Identities* 5, no. 2 (2017): 353–63.

5. Cristina C. Santamaría Graff, "'Build That Wall!': Manufacturing the Enemy, yet Again," *International Journal of Qualitative Studies in Education* 30, no. 10 (2017): 999–1005.

CHAPTER 5

1. For research that influenced my analysis of design-based inquiry leadership for continuous improvement, see Anthony S. Bryk, Alicia Grunow, and Paul G. LeMahieu, *Learning to Improve: How America's Schools Can Get Better at Getting Better* (Cambridge, MA: Harvard Education Press, 2015); Eleanor Drago-Severson, *Leading Adult Learning: Supporting Adult Development in Our Schools* (Thousand Oaks, CA: Corwin Press, 2009); Robert Evans, *The Human Side of School Change: Reform, Resistance, and the Real-Life Problems of Innovation. The Jossey-Bass Education Series* (San Francisco, CA: Jossey-Bass Inc., 1996); Robert Kegan and Lisa Laskow Lahey, *Immunity to Change: How to Overcome It and Unlock Potential in Yourself and Your Organization* (Cambridge, MA: Harvard Business Press, 2009); Rachel E. Curtis and Elizabeth A. City, *Strategy in Action: How School Systems Can Support Powerful Learning and Teaching* (Cambridge, MA: Harvard Education Press, 2009); Mary A. Hooper and Victoria L. Bernhardt, *Creating Capacity for Learning and Equity in Schools: Instructional, Adaptive, and Transformational Leadership* (New York, NY: Routledge, 2016).

2. For research that influenced my analysis of antiracist and social justice leadership practices, see Colleen A. Capper, "The 20th-Year Anniversary of Critical Race Theory in Education: Implications for Leading to Eliminate Racism," *Educational Administration Quarterly* 51, no. 5 (2015): 791–833; Michael E. Dantley and Linda C. Tillman, "Social Justice and Moral Transformative Leadership," in *Leadership for Social Justice: Making Revolutions in Education*, eds. Catherine Marshall and Maricela Oliva (Boston, MA: Pearson, 2006), 16–30; Sonya D. Horsford, "When Race Enters the Room: Improving Leadership and Learning Through Racial Literacy," *Theory Into Practice* 53, no. 2 (2014): 123–30; Muhammad Khalifa, *Culturally Responsive School Leadership* (Cambridge, MA: Harvard Education Press, 2018); George Theoharis, "Social Justice Educational Leaders and Resistance: Toward a Theory of Social Justice Leadership," *Educational Administration Quarterly* 43, no. 2 (2007): 221–58; George Theoharis, "Disrupting Injustice: Principals Narrate the Strategies They Use to Improve Their Schools and Advance Social Justice," *Teachers College Record* 112, no. 1 (2010): 331–73.

3. See Michael A. Copland, "Leadership of Inquiry: Building and Sustaining Capacity for School Improvement," *Educational Evaluation and Policy Analysis* 25, no. 4 (2003): 375–95, https://doi.org/10.3102/01623737025004375; Mary

Koutselini, "Participatory Teacher Development at Schools: Processes and Issues," *Action Research* 6, no. 1 (2008): 29–48, https://doi.org/10.1177/1476750307083718; Mark A. Smylie, *Continuous School Improvement* (Thousand Oaks, CA: Corwin Press, 2009).

4. See Decoteau J. Irby, "Revealing Racial Purity Ideology: Fear of Black–White Intimacy as a Framework for Understanding School Discipline in Post-Brown Schools," *Educational Administration Quarterly* 50, no. 5 (2014): 783–95; Victor Ray, "A Theory of Racialized Organizations," *American Sociological Review* 84, no. 1 (2019): 26–53.

5. Decoteau J. Irby and Shannon P. Clark, "Talk It (Racism) Out: Race Talk and Organizational Learning," *Journal of Educational Administration* 56, no. 5 (2018): 504–18.

6. They defined access as students' ability to secure a place, have a voice, and participate fully in the school community. Participants described lack of access as having a profound effect on the behavior and attitudes of students of color about school, their sense of belonging, and academic success. Participants almost unanimously agreed that increasing access to school-based opportunities was within the school's sphere of influence and that *the root of unequal access to school-based opportunities was institutional racism.*

7. Relational resources refer to positive relationships, a sense of being cared for, and having adult advocates and supports within the school community. Structures refer to within school—academic curriculum, schedules, extracurricular activities—and broader societal structures of residential segregation, unequal distribution of social resources, and economic opportunities.

8. Even if it was incomplete, if it was shared, that was sufficient to move forward because we expected people to round out their understanding through an incremental process of continual learning and practice.

9. See Cynthia E. Coburn, "Rethinking Scale: Moving Beyond Numbers to Deep and Lasting Change," *Educational Researcher* 32, no. 6 (2003): 3–12.

10. See Carolyn M. Shields, "Is Transformative Leadership Practical or Possible? Learning from Superintendents About Social Justice," *International Studies in Educational Administration (Commonwealth Council for Educational Administration & Management [CCEAM])* 45, no. 2 (2017): 3–20.

ACKNOWLEDGMENTS

I am grateful for the village that supported me throughout the research and writing that culminated in this book. I'm especially thankful to Central Waters district and high school administrators, educators, and students (I wish I could list your names). Without your openness and willingness to let me all up in your school's business, the learning that is reflected in the book would not have been possible. Thank you to Jayne Fargnoli at Harvard Education Press and Rich Milner for believing in the project. Thank you to members of the project research team—Liz Drame, Cindy Clough, Thor Stolen, Shannon Paige Clark, Ahreum Han, Leemay Chang, and Rebecca Fine—for your support through the multiple stages of research and writing. Thank you to my community of scholar-friends who were alongside me at various stages of the writing process: Lynnette Mawhinney, Branden McLeod, P. Zitlali Morales, Danny Morales-Doyle, David Stovall, Jason Salisbury, Elizabeth Todd-Breland, and Chezare Warren. Your showing up for me helped me show up for myself.

Thank you to my colleagues and supporters Pallavi Abraham, Lionel Allen, Terrance Green, Ann Ishimaru, Ananda Mirilli, Emery Petchauer, Brad Rossi, Jason Salisbury, Martin Scanlan, Chezare Warren, and Anjale Welton for graciously reading and giving me feedback on my initial book proposals, chapter drafts, and even the entire book. Your critiques and critical questions sharpened my ability to convey the book's most essential ideas. I wrote this book with the tremendous support of two of the best and most talented graduate research assistants I could ever want for. Shannon Paige Clark and Ahreum Han, thank you for keeping me on task, giving feedback, creating tables and figures, and for continually telling me "it's good" and "let it go." I am thankful for my Derute Cooperative comrades: Cindy Clough, Liz Drame, Dominique Duval-Diop, Katie Elliot, Emery Petchauer, Laura Krystal Porterfield, Latish Reed, Jackie Robinson-Hunsicker, and Jeff Roman for ongoing encouragement and opportunities for personal and professional growth. Thank you to Matthew Birkhold, Muhammad Khalifa, Timothy Lensmire, Latish Reed, and Derrick Rogers for the many conversations that have influenced my writing.

Finally, I thank my immediate and extended family. I want to acknowledge my elders—Grandmother Esther Irby, Grandfather Jimmy Aiken, and Aunt Essie Crockett—for your love and encouragement. Thank you to Janice Irby for guiding and shaping me into who I am. Thank you to Brandy Pearson and Lauren Pitts for always having my back. Thank you to my South Carolina and Philadelphia family and friends who are too numerous to name here. Thank you to Kayla and Miles for bringing wonder and amazement into my life. Finally, thank you to Shemeka Irby, the mother of Kayla and Miles and the boss who holds me together. You helped find the time and energy to write this book despite the very real ways that 2020 upended our sense of normalcy. You were loving, patient, and gracious throughout in more ways than I have room to express. Thank you, thank you, thank you.

ABOUT THE AUTHOR

Decoteau J. Irby is an associate professor in the Department of Educational Policy Studies at the University of Illinois at Chicago, where he teaches and advises in the College's Urban Education Leadership program. His academic research explores how equity-focused school leadership improves Black children's and youth's educational experiences and outcomes and appears in journals such as *Urban Education, International Journal of Multicultural Education, Studies in Educational Evaluation, Educational Administration Quarterly, Equity & Excellence in Education, Journal of Cases in Educational Leadership, Urban Review,* and *Journal of Education for Students Placed at Risk.* Outside of his academic life, he enjoys spending time with his children and partner, playing guitar, traveling, and writing songs and short stories.

INDEX